A Thousand More Amens

A Thousand More Amens

—A One Year Prayer Journey—

by
JEFF VOTH

RESOURCE *Publications* • Eugene, Oregon

A THOUSAND MORE AMENS
A One Year Prayer Journey

Resource Publications
An Imprint of Wipf and Stock Publishers
199 W. 8th Ave., Suite 3
Eugene, OR 97401

www.wipfandstock.com

PAPERBACK ISBN: 978-1-6667-3114-9
HARDCOVER ISBN: 978-1-6667-2331-1
EBOOK ISBN: 978-1-6667-2332-8

10/11/21

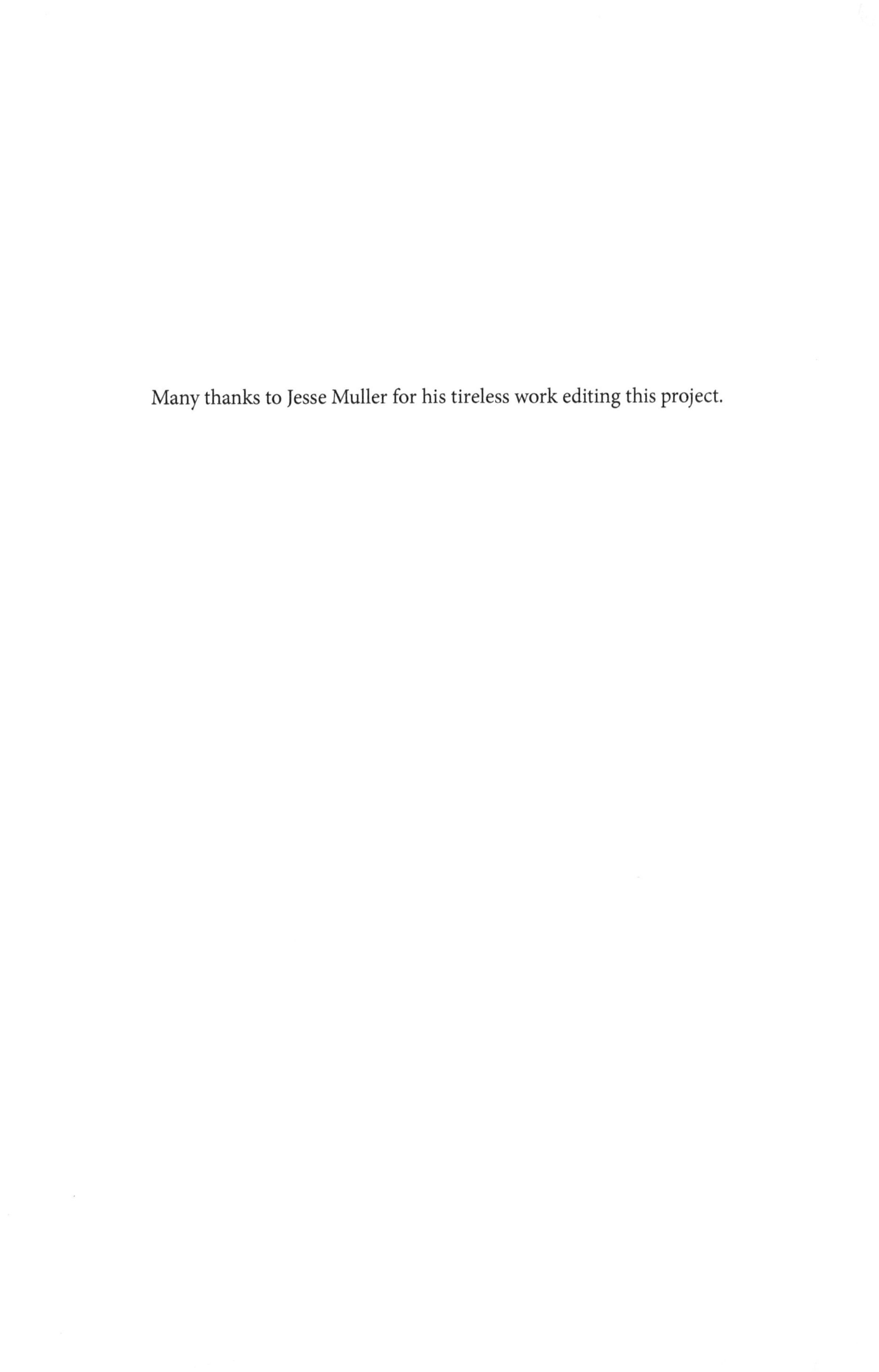

Many thanks to Jesse Muller for his tireless work editing this project.

Introduction

A Buzzword

"AMEN". A RELIGIOUS BUZZ word that is uttered both silently and loudly, billions upon billions of times each day in billions upon billions of contexts . . . but to what end? Is it a period . . . a transition . . . or a statement of something more? It seems that it's simply an afterthought to most people. Something tacked on to the end of a sentence to let everyone, including God Himself, know that you have finished a particular spiritual exercise and are ready to move on to the next thing? I remember when I was officially introduced to the term, amen. It was the doxology that did it. That famous church song that signaled the end of the service, but also instigated a domino effect. One that ended with the last domino crashing down in a hearty and mostly harmonious, "AHHHHHH MMMMMMENNNNNNN".

The first domino of the effect began as our pastor would conclude his sermon with prayer, then make his way to the back of the sanctuary to shake hands with the congregation as they filed out. The next domino was the organist slipping off her shoes in order to feel the old foot keys, on the ancient organ that sat on the stage. The third domino was the robed choir director nodding his head. Domino four was the choir standing to their feet as one. The people followed suit. The flurry of dominoes falling would then somehow queue the old men who were asleep before the Lord to begin to rouse from their spiritual slumber. Bass notes vibrating through the creaky wooden floor, were domino five, then six, we all began to sing, "Praise God from whom all blessings flow, praise Him all creatures here below, praise Him above ye heavenly host. Praise Father, Son and Holy Ghost . . ." And then, in beautiful, harmonious (sometimes not so harmonious) tones, domino number seven . . .

"AAAHHHHH MENNNNNNN"

It was finished. Then like the "Ready, BREAK!!!!" before a football play, we broke. People lined up to shake the pastor's hand. The choir headed back to the room behind the stage to get out of their robes. Kids started running around. But for that brief moment . . . the amen was a pause and a breath between the service and real life. I loved the "AAAAHHHHHHH MENNNNN". And while I wasn't quite ready to dive into the depths of the amen and consider it any deeper than wondering if we were going to eat on the way home at the Bonanza Steakhouse, Burger King, or perhaps if today was the 5th Sunday First Baptist church potluck. The amen had signaled all of these good things. Service was finished, fellowship was ensuing, food was to be eaten and perhaps the Broncos would win this afternoon. And while all of these things were comforting and somehow signaled that spiritual life was now ending and real life was to be engaged in once again . . . as I have grown older I have found that the Amen was and is intended to signal so much more than merely that pause between a service or a prayer and the beginning of real life. In fact, it was much, much more.

Where did it come from?

Amen is ancient and appears first in the Old Testament in the Book of Numbers (5:22) and ultimately used hundreds of times in both testaments. It is what is known as a transliteration. That means that it is taken into other languages untranslated, as it is. It is amen in Hebrew, Greek, English and any other language in which it appears. Amen, is amen. Some of the more prevalent places it is seen in the Bible are:

- It is the last word in the last verse of the Bible (Rev. 22:21)
- It is the last word of the first three books of the Psalms (41:13, 72:19, 89:52)
- It is the word spoken in the Old Testament by the community after a prophecy or proclamation was made (Nehemiah 5:13, 8:6)
- It is the word used by Paul as an ending to many of his books. He also used "Amen" seven times in the Book of Romans (1:25, 9:5, 11:36, 15:33, 16:20, 24, 27)
- It is the word used by Jesus at the end of His teaching on prayer (Matthew 6:13).
- Ultimately, He would use it over fifty times, not only at the end of a statement, but at the beginning, to introduce powerful truths (Matt. 5:18).

Authoritative and Prophetic

While all of the instances outlined above certainly make amen a unique word, the prophet Isaiah takes it to another level of importance. He asserts that the amen is both authoritative and prophetic, in a messianic sense. In Isaiah 22:23 he states that the Messiah would be nailed in a "sure", "firm" or essentially, an "amen" place. And in that place, He (the Messiah, Jesus) would be in a place of honor.[1] The one who would be nailed to the cross would be the final word and ultimately honored forever. AMEN and AMEN!!!

> Isaiah 22: [23] I will drive him like a peg into a firm place; he will become a seat of honor for the house of his father. [24] All the glory of his family will hang on him: its offspring and offshoots—

In the deepest and most holistic sense, the Amen is an affirmation and a blessing of the finished work of God.

Paul and the Amen

The Apostle Paul affirmed repeatedly the power of the Amen in many of his books, but especially in 2 Corinthians 1:20:

> [20] For no matter how many promises God has made, they are "Yes" in Christ. And so through him the "Amen" is spoken by us to the glory of God.

In this text he cuts to the meat of the understanding of the Amen. Jesus is in fact the Amen. The final Word on all that is the focus of the Kingdom community. For Paul, the Amen was an assertion pointing towards the focal point of his gospel . . . Jesus, Jesus, Jesus.

1. Psalm 119 Ministries, *The Hebrew root a amen*

Jesus and the Amen

In fact, Jesus Himself actually gets the final word on the Amen in the Book of the Revelation as He refers to Himself as ". . . the Amen, the faithful and true witness, the Ruler of God's creation." (Rev. 3:14). John describes the reverberating effects brought on by beholding the Amen as the hosts of Heaven and earth as they behold Him in His glory:

> [13] Then I heard every creature in heaven and on earth and under the earth and on the sea, and all that is in them, saying: "To him who sits on the throne and to the Lamb be praise and honor and glory and power, for ever and ever!" [14] The four living creatures said, "Amen," and the elders fell down and worshiped.

Kisses Between Lovers?

So what do kisses and the Amen have to do with one another? Quite a bit actually. In his book, *The Four Loves*, C.S. Lewis aptly stated that, "Kisses between lovers are not always lovers kisses"[2]. What does this have to do with the Amen? Lewis obviously understood the difference between a deep, romantic kiss and the obligatory peck on the cheek. My wife helped me to learn this not too long ago as I gave her the obligatory peck on the cheek on the way out of the house. I had done it thousands of times before, but this time it was different. She grabbed me, pulled me in, cupped my face with her hands and said, "Let's linger a bit." So, we lingered. A shiver summarily went down my spine and I was much more awake than only a few moments before. Leaving for work was different that day. I left more alive than usual and more expectant about coming home. All because of a lingering kiss instead of a peck.

That is what the Amen should be for us. The beautiful, expectant and lingering effects after our prayers, our activities and our lives. A pronouncement of our love for our Lord Jesus; in the context of an understanding that as we live our lives, there is a lingering, loving and beautiful expectation. May we not engage Him like two familiar lovers merely pecking one another on the cheek. Let's linger.

Something Different?

A few years ago, as I began to grow in my understanding of the depth and power of the Amen, I sensed in me a desire to change the blasé and lifeless rhythm of the religious peck on the lips that I felt when I said amen. All of us know that to change something that has become rote and lifeless, something would need to be put in its place. What would that be? I couldn't make up my own word, that could be heretical and heresies are frowned upon. So, I begin to find myself wanting to say, "Amen and a lot more amens." That didn't flow very well. There were a couple more phrases that didn't work either. Then, almost as if dropped from heaven at the end of a passionate prayer one day, I felt leap from my lips, "Amen and A THOUSAND MORE AMENS!!!" It felt really good. And while I know that the Amen is infinitely more than that, a thousand is quite a few and it would take a while to say them. So, I started to say "Amen and a thousand more amens" in my personal devotions. It felt very good. I like how it caused me to linger a bit

2. C.S. Lewis, *The Four Loves*, 46.

and to think about the Amen and what I had said before it. If Jesus is found in the Amen and is remembered when it is said, that is always a good thing. A very good thing.

Ultimately, I began to say "A thousand more amens" after preaching sermons on Sundays, after lectures and speaking engagements. It began to catch on at our church and with many of the students at the university where I teach. It also spurred quite a few conversations regarding the Amen, which ultimately would lead back to Jesus and His ultimate authority and position. He is the reason that our prayers have any power, authority and lingering effect. He is the lover's kiss of the Kingdom that we send towards the Father every time we pray in His name. Amen and a thousand more amens.

How to use this book

This book is meant to be a guide. A tool to help you live in and apply the power of the One who is the Amen to your life.

1. There are 366 Daily entries, one for each day of the year, plus an extra day for Leap Year. You can start anywhere and on any day of the year. Some are prayers. Some are proclamations and exhortations meant to speak to you and keep on speaking. That is why all of them end in "Amen and a thousand more amens . . .". I encourage you to read the words and allow them to stimulate in you a desire to speak even more words directed towards your Lord Jesus.
2. No proclamation or prayer is worth the paper upon which it is written, regardless of who proclaimed it, unless it lines up with God's word in the Bible. Therefore, a specific text has been chosen from the Bible for you to consider in agreement with the words I have written.
3. An exercise is provided for you to take a few minutes, linger and ask the Holy Spirit to apply the truth contained in these proclamations and Bible verses to your life. Remember, no pecks on the cheek here.

A Thousand More Amens

There are two types of prayers within this book: Personal (P) and Exhortation (Ex). Personal (P) prayers are for you to speak over yourself in personal reflection and interaction with God. Exhortation (Ex) prayers are to be read as if another person (the author) is praying over you. Furthermore, you could also share and pray these prayers over others.

January 1

How God Sees You (Ex)

I PRAY THAT GOD gives you a glimpse of what you mean to Him. You need to know that He doesn't just love you because He has to, He is really enamored with you. He loves you and He likes you. HE loves you and HE likes you and He is proud of you. He loves you and He likes you and He is proud of you and He wants to be with you. May you truly understand this amazing fact and believe it today. God is not angry with you or annoyed. He wants you to run to Him again. Receive this beautiful love today in the name of Jesus. Amen and a thousand more amens.

Verse: Romans 8:38–39

> For I am convinced that neither death nor life, neither angels nor demons, neither the present nor the future, nor any powers, neither height nor depth, nor anything else in all creation, will be able to separate us from the love of God that is in Christ Jesus our Lord.

Exercise: Journaling and Prayer

What do you believe God thinks of you? Write these thoughts down on a piece of paper. Afterwards, read the verses for today and ask the Father, "What do you think of me?" Write these statements down (example: I am _______. My Father feels ________ for me.)

JANUARY 2

God's Will First (P)

JESUS, I KNOW THAT you are my sustenance. Please forgive me for seeking anyone or anything else above you. I pray that you will help me to look to and think of You first. You are the Lord of the universe. Please help me to continually submit to you as Lord of my life. Please lead me, guide me, speak to me, cover me, protect me and help me to stay in the middle of Your will for me this day. Show me what You would have me do and reveal Yourself in greater ways so that I may learn to love you more. Thank you for living in me and giving me purpose. Amen and a thousand more amens.

Verse: Matthew 6:33

> But seek first his kingdom and his righteousness, and all these things will be given to you as well.

Exercise: Worship and Meditation

Sometimes, we get so caught up in life that we forget our commitment to Christ as Lord. He is our Redeemer, Love, and Life, but we cannot forget that He is the Most High, the One we submit all things to. Take several minutes to get into a posture of surrender again. If you are able, a physical posture such as being on your knees or laying prostrate can help. When here, in the quiet, take time to put Jesus back on the throne of your life. Begin by giving Him your life in full once again, and then proceed to more specific circumstances and situations in which He has not been the center of. Know that your life has been bought and that He deserves it all.

January 3

Time in the Day (P)

Father, I ask to have Your order in my day. There are many things that can and should be done in these 24 hours. I know that You created time. Please enter mine and order it. Jesus, please be Lord of my time and make it Yours. Multiply, order, make use of and redeem every second of this day. Show me the fights that are mine today and the actions that can wait. You never rush and Your will is never late. Show me to live with peace and purpose in my schedule so that my life may honor you. Amen and a thousand more amens.

Verse: Ecclesiastes 3:1

There is a time for everything, and a season for every activity under the heavens.

Exercise: Prayer

Responsibilities in a day can try to distract you in your time with God. There are things to do and places to go, but do not neglect the place of rest in the time of prayer and Scripture reading. In response, take a portion of your devotional time to pray over your schedule. Begin by submitting the schedule to the Holy Spirit so that He can show you what is necessary and what can be adjusted. Ask God for His perspective on certain events, such as meetings, assignments, and other responsibilities. In this, God will be honored through your schedule instead of you trying to fit Him in pockets of time or offering a quick prayer alone in the business of the day.

January 4

Reach Out to Others (Ex)

As Jesus reached out to those in dire need, may you do so to someone today. When He said "Thy Kingdom come, thy will be done", He meant for it to happen through you and me. So on behalf of the Kingdom, start touching. On behalf of the Kingdom, bring the power and influence of Heaven to this planet one act of love at a time. May the Holy Spirit open your eyes to the world around you and empower you to love others with the love of Christ. Be the Good News in your world today. I pray this in the mighty name of Jesus, the name above all other names. Amen and a thousand more amens.

Verse: Philippians 2:3–4

> Do nothing out of selfish ambition or vain conceit. Rather, in humility value others above yourselves, not looking to your own interests but each of you to the interests of the others.

Exercise: Service

Ask the Father to direct your steps today and surrender your time to Him. Enter today deciding that interruptions in your schedule are allowed. This will not be completed in your devotional time, but throughout the day. Intentionally listen for the Spirit's guidance to show someone the love of Christ. This could be a word of encouragement, a gift, or a kind action. Record the results at night to reflect on the event and to pray for those you interact with.

January 5

Freedom and New Creation (P)

Father, may I know your freedom today. Free to speak to You like never before. Free to be who I am in Christ. Free to live a real life in Him. Free to be healed. Free to think like Jesus. Free to act like Jesus. Free to see His Kingdom come and His will be done in my life and in my home as it is in Heaven. May the Holy Spirit do His liberating work in me. I am no longer bound by the mistakes or wounds of the past. There is no condemnation and I am new. Thank you God for this life I do not deserve. Amen and a thousand more amens.

Verse: Psalm 34:5 John 8:36 2 Corinthians 5:17

> Those who look to him are radiant; their faces are never covered with shame. Psalm 34:5; So if the Son sets you free, you will be free indeed. John 8:36; Therefore, if anyone is in Christ, the new creation has come: The old has gone, the new is here! 2 Corinthians 5:17

Exercise: Reading and Journaling

Read over today's verses out loud, slowly. Pause after reading each verse for 30 seconds, meditating on their truth and how it applies in your life. Do this three times and record what you believe God is speaking to you.

January 6

Direction from heaven (P)

I PRAY THAT TODAY You give me a direct and specific word from heaven. I am dependent on your direction and rely on Your guidance, concerning both needs I see and those that I do not. You have not forgotten me and you will not leave me stranded. Your word declares that I am important to you, and I will rest in this truth. May Your Kingdom come and Your will be done in my life. Teach me to hear Your voice again today so that I may know your will. Amen and a thousand more amens.

Verse: Romans 12:2

> Do not conform to the pattern of this world, but be transformed by the renewing of your mind. Then you will be able to test and approve what God's will is—his good, pleasing and perfect will.

Exercise: Journaling and Prayer

Write down an area or situation that you would like direction in. During your devotional time, have a Bible and a piece of paper in front of you. If any verses or ideas come to mind that you believe could be from God, write these down. God will confirm His messages in several ways. These include corresponding Bible passages, circumstances that support His answer, and the council of other believers. For example, there once was a college student who was deciding if he should move back to his home state after graduation or pursue a different path in a Graduate program. In the course of several months, he was offered a job that would coincide with a Masters program, was reminded of a verse about places he had never been before (Joshua 3:3–4), and was advised by more mature believers to make this decision. The situation you are asking about may receive an answer immediately or it may take months or even years. But be listening and do not take for granted messages that could be in front of you in the mundane.

January 7

Condemn the lies from the enemy (Ex)

May any lies from the enemy be exposed, dealt with and rendered powerless, in the name of Jesus. Yes, you will not be held down anymore. Shackles, chains, bondage, enslavement die this day. End of story. You are free, now go and live like a free person. Those voices of the past have no power over you anymore. You have been cleaned and redeemed. You are called. You are chosen. You are loved. You are new. You are His. May the Holy Spirit open your eyes to this so that you may believe this beautiful reality. Amen and a thousand more amens.

Verse: John 10:10

> The thief comes only to steal and kill and destroy; I have come that they may have life, and have it to the full.

Exercise: Prayer and Journaling

Very often we believe things about ourselves that are not true. The enemy often uses these beliefs to keep us imprisoned in our own doubts and fears, but Christ came so that we might have life to the full. These lies cannot stay in His presence. Ask the Father to reveal to you lies you have placed on yourself or that others have placed on you. After writing these down, ask God to show you how He feels for you in response.

January 8

Peaceful Mind (Ex)

I AM PRAYING FOR your mind today. May He who made your mind quiet it. Yes, may all of the noise of our loud and often senseless culture be stilled. And in that stillness, may you hear the one and only word that will give everything else context, meaning, order and sense; may you hear JESUS . . . JESUS . . . JESUS. And when you hear it, may you say it. And when you say it, may you feel it. And when you feel it, may you live it. And when you live it, may you spread it. And when you spread it, may the senseless craziness that was once all around you be brought into order, peace and purpose because of that word . . . JESUS. Amen and a thousand more amens.

Verse: 1 Kings 19:9–18

> There he went into a cave and spent the night. And the word of the Lord came to him: "What are you doing here, Elijah?" He replied, "I have been very zealous for the Lord God Almighty. The Israelites have rejected your covenant, torn down your altars, and put your prophets to death with the sword. I am the only one left, and now they are trying to kill me too." The Lord said, "Go out and stand on the mountain in the presence of the Lord, for the Lord is about to pass by." Then a great and powerful wind tore the mountains apart and shattered the rocks before the Lord, but the Lord was not in the wind. After the wind there was an earthquake, but the Lord was not in the earthquake. After the earthquake came a fire, but the Lord was not in the fire. And after the fire came a gentle whisper. When Elijah heard it, he pulled his cloak over his face and went out and stood at the mouth of the cave. Then a voice said to him, "What are you doing here, Elijah?" He replied, "I have been very zealous for the Lord God Almighty. The Israelites have rejected your covenant, torn down your altars, and put your prophets to death with the sword. I am the only one left, and now they are trying to kill me too." The Lord said to him, "Go back the way you came, and go to the Desert of Damascus. When you get there, anoint Hazael king over Aram. Also, anoint Jehu son of Nimshi king over Israel, and anoint Elisha son of Shaphat from Abel Meholah to succeed you as prophet. Jehu will put to death any who escape the sword of Hazael, and Elisha will put to death any who escape the sword of Jehu. Yet I reserve seven thousand in Israel—all whose knees have not bowed down to Baal and whose mouths have not kissed him."

Exercise: Reading

Read the story of Elijah hearing God's voice in the midst of chaos. God met him in a place of despair and frustration. He wants to do the same with you. Read the passage and ask God how He wants to move in your life in the midst of chaos.

January 9

Peaceful Mind (Ex)

As Jesus said "Quiet! Be Still!" to the wind and the waves in Mark 4, may His words reverberate to the wind and the waves that endeavor to intimidate you today. May the Shalom of Heaven Himself be your calming presence. He is Lord of ALL. ALL elements, forces, persons and circumstances must bow and behave as the wind and the waves did on that day. They were quiet and they were still. Receive this same peace in the name of Jesus. Amen and a thousand more amens.

Verse: Mark 4:35–39

> That day when evening came, he said to his disciples, "Let us go over to the other side." Leaving the crowd behind, they took him along, just as he was, in the boat. There were also other boats with him. A furious squall came up, and the waves broke over the boat, so that it was nearly swamped. Jesus was in the stern, sleeping on a cushion. The disciples woke him and said to him, "Teacher, don't you care if we drown?" He got up, rebuked the wind and said to the waves, "Quiet! Be still!" Then the wind died down and it was completely calm.

Exercise: Reading and Meditation

Read the story of Jesus calming the storm. Now imagine your mind being the storm. Allow Christ to speak peace into your chaos today and bring His rest into your thoughts. Imagine Jesus proclaiming "Peace, be still" over you today and focus on His voice. What do you feel? How does He sound? Take a breath and receive all He has for you.

January 10

Pride (P)

Jesus Christ, Son of God, please save me from myself. This is my prayer today. Save me from thinking that I am the center of the world. May You ever be the reason that I live and move and have my being. Your word states that Jesus is the one who "holds all things together." May I remember that I am here for Your glory. I am your servant. I reject pride and selfish pursuits today. May my life be about You as I take up my cross daily. Amen and a thousand more amens.

Verse: Luke 9:23–25

> Then he said to them all: "Whoever wants to be my disciple must deny themselves and take up their cross daily and follow me. For whoever wants to save their life will lose it, but whoever loses their life for me will save it. What good is it for someone to gain the whole world, and yet lose or forfeit their very self?"

Exercise: Journaling and Meditation

Who is Jesus to you? On a piece of paper, write down how you see Christ. Think back to when you first accepted His life. Write down why you gave your life to Him. Do not rush, but remind yourself of who God is, how wonderful His love for you is, and the fact that we exist entirely for His pleasure and glory, not our own. He is Lord and we have no claim to glory except for that which we give to God and see in His holiness.

January 11

Grace (P)

Jesus Christ, giver of Grace, You have saved me from myself and given me more grace than I can make mistakes. I know that I have the capability to make many mistakes in a day, but grace has more time than minutes in the day. I have the capability to be insensitive and "me" focused, but grace has the presence to wait me out, see me convicted and broken and then rush in and wash over the pieces. Thank You that I am not, nor ever will be, too far gone. May I not take this for granted. Amen and a thousand more amens.

Verse: Ephesians 2:8–9

> For it is by grace you have been saved, through faith—and this is not from yourselves, it is the gift of God— not by works, so that no one can boast.

Exercise: Prayer

Grace is receiving what we do not deserve, namely, God's forgiveness and love. When we say yes to Jesus, His blood covers over all of our sins, past, present, and future. Nothing can separate us from His love. Today, let the Father show you His love again. Write out your prayer to God. Ask for forgiveness in any area of your life that you have not submitted to Him and thank Him again for His unfailing grace.

January 12

Speech (P)

JESUS, PLEASE HELP ME have a change of mind to go along with the change that You have brought in my heart. I want to think like You, react like You and then speak like You. Please forgive me for my hurtful words and redeem relationships that have been damaged due to my thoughtless words. Your kingdom come and your will be done in my speech. I submit my words to You. Amen and a thousand more amens.

Verse: James 3:3–12

> When we put bits into the mouths of horses to make them obey us, we can turn the whole animal. Or take ships as an example. Although they are so large and are driven by strong winds, they are steered by a very small rudder wherever the pilot wants to go. Likewise, the tongue is a small part of the body, but it makes great boasts. Consider what a great forest is set on fire by a small spark. The tongue also is a fire, a world of evil among the parts of the body. It corrupts the whole body, sets the whole course of one's life on fire, and is itself set on fire by hell. All kinds of animals, birds, reptiles and sea creatures are being tamed and have been tamed by mankind, but no human being can tame the tongue. It is a restless evil, full of deadly poison. With the tongue we praise our Lord and Father, and with it we curse human beings, who have been made in God's likeness. Out of the same mouth comes praise and cursing. My brothers and sisters, this should not be. Can both fresh water and salt water flow from the same spring? My brothers and sisters, can a fig tree bear olives, or a grapevine bear figs? Neither can a salt spring produce fresh water.

Exercise: Reading and Prayer

Read today's passage and reflect on how you use your words. Are there situations in which you spoke too hastily or callously? Have you caused harm or discouragement? Surrender your words to God once more, ask for His forgiveness, and, if possible, seek to heal and build up those whom your words hurt. Furthermore, if there are situations in which you were silent when you should have spoken, go through the same process as if you had spoken negatively.

January 13

Identity in Christ (P)

Father, today I pray that You will help me act like what I am. I am saved. I am redeemed. I am born again. I am a new creation. I am included in a royal priesthood. I am seated at the right hand of the Father. I am a friend of God. I am in Him. I am filled with the Holy Ghost. I am made in the image of God. I am whole. I exist to enjoy Your presence and bring You glory. May I believe these truths and teach others the joy in them, as well. Amen and a thousand more amens.

Verse: Romans 8:29–30

> For those God foreknew he also predestined to be conformed to the image of his Son, that he might be the firstborn among many brothers and sisters. And those he predestined, he also called; those he called, he also justified; those he justified, he also glorified.

Exercise: Reading and Meditation

The Most High has chosen you. This is not something to take lightly. It is easy to allow ourselves to get used to this beautiful fact. Today, read the prayer out loud to yourself, slowly. Take your time. Pause after reading it, thinking about what it means for you. After a minute, read it again and do the same as before. Read the prayer three times, each time followed by the minute of reflection. Do not write anything down until after the last reading. Take a breath and just be with the Father.

January 14

Time Management (Ex)

May you who seem to be running out of time be blessed by He who is outside of it. May the crazy pace and the impending deadlines come under the Lordship of Jesus Christ, the One who never ever worried about how He would get it all done. May an obvious sense of Shalom come blowing through your lives today as His Kingdom comes and His will is done in and through you. Know what burdens are yours to take up today and what can be left alone. May God's peace and direction go before you today. Amen and a thousand more amens.

Verse: Acts 10:37–38

> You know what has happened throughout the province of Judea, beginning in Galilee after the baptism that John preached— how God anointed Jesus of Nazareth with the Holy Spirit and power, and how he went around doing good and healing all who were under the power of the devil, because God was with him.

Exercise: Silence and Journaling

Christ came into the world on the greatest mission there ever was: the redemption of creation. These verses state that He was anointed with the Holy Spirit to do good works and bring freedom to those under Satan's power. There were many things Jesus could have been doing, many good opportunities, but the Holy Spirit showed Him what work was His to do. The Spirit will do the same with you when you take time to listen. God sees you where you are at and knows the burdens. Commit to listening for God's leading to know what your priorities should be today. Record how your responsibilities went at the end of the day and continue to practice hearing His voice.

January 15

Christ's Rescue (Ex)

May you know today that He has rescued you. You had been taken captive by sin and shame and all the wrong thinking that goes with them and Jesus led the rescue effort. He has forcibly taken you back because of your great value to the Kingdom. Yes, you are valuable, worthwhile, precious and very expensive. You could never be replaced. Jesus took you back! May the Holy Spirit reveal to you how much the Father treasures you. Amen and a thousand more amens.

Verse: 1 Peter 1:18–20

> For you know that it was not with perishable things such as silver or gold that you were redeemed from the empty way of life handed down to you from your ancestors, but with the precious blood of Christ, a lamb without blemish or defect. He was chosen before the creation of the world, but was revealed in these last times for your sake.

Exercise: Meditation

Read these verses to yourself. Find a mirror, look in your own eyes, and say these statements over yourself from the passage:

"You have been bought with the precious blood of Christ. Jesus came for your sake."

Memorize the two statements and speak them to yourself in the mirror ten times (or as long as you'd like.)

January 16

Spiritual Warfare (P)

Today, I will assault the enemy in Jesus' name. Yes, I will do everything in my power to perpetuate and forward His cause. I am His slave, He is my Master. Holy Spirit, teach me to be relentless for You that I may have no compromise with darkness in my life. Any past habits of sin, die. I turn away from any agreements I have made with the enemy. I will speak and live the truth of the Gospel today through the power of my Risen Savior. Amen and a thousand more amens.

Verse: Psalm 118:6–12

> The Lord is with me; I will not be afraid. What can mere mortals do to me? The Lord is with me; he is my helper. I look in triumph on my enemies. It is better to take refuge in the Lord than to trust in humans. It is better to take refuge in the Lord than to trust in princes. All the nations surrounded me, but in the name of the LordI cut them down. They surrounded me on every side, but in the name of the LordI cut them down. They swarmed around me like bees, but they were consumed as quickly as burning thorns; in the name of the Lord I cut them down.

Exercise: Prayer

In prayer, speak against any and every attack of the enemy today. Write down the areas that you have been attacked in frequently (temptations, emotions, etc.) and pray over these. Do not only ask the Father to relieve you of these pressures, but proclaim boldly God's will in your life. On the cross and at the outpouring of the Holy Spirit we were given the same power as Christ. You are not at the mercy of any darkness. You are a child of the Most High. Be reminded of this and proclaim how the Father sees you to any other voice that is trying to influence you today.

January 17

Time Management (P)

Father, I give my schedule to You today. May You miraculously multiply my time. You who caused the sun to stand still and time to come to a halt, do the same today in some form or fashion. May my efforts be miraculously multiplied and may my work be effective beyond what I ever imagined. Your Kingdom come and Your will be done through me today exponentially. Amen and a thousand more amens.

Verse: Joshua 10:13b-14

> The sun stopped in the middle of the sky and delayed going down for about a full day. There has never been a day like it before or since, a day when the Lord listened to a human being. Surely the Lord was fighting for Israel!

Exercise: Reading and Prayer

Read the story of Joshua and the sun standing still (Joshua 10:5–14). Note how this answer to prayer pointed back to God, giving Him glory and allowing Joshua to complete God's commands. In the same way, our prayers should not be for our betterment or convenience alone, but to give glory to God. When submitting your schedule to God today, remember that ultimately we are here for God's pleasure, yet He loves us enough to listen to our requests and care for our concerns. Pray today's prayer once more, giving both your desires and results to Him.

January 18

When There is No Progress (Ex)

I pray for those situations in your life in which you believe you are doing exactly what God told you to do, but struggling and making no progress. May Jesus come to you this day in the middle of your struggle and speak to the things that are impeding your progress. He is Lord of ALL creation and has the power to move obstacles and bring you peace. May you know that you are not alone and that He is Lord over your situation.

Verse: 1 Corinthians 15:58

> Therefore, my dear brothers and sisters, stand firm. Let nothing move you. Always give yourselves fully to the work of the Lord, because you know that your labor in the Lord is not in vain.

Exercise: Journaling and Silence

Write an honest prayer to God, expressing any frustrations or doubts about a situation in your life, including those you have stopped praying or hoping for. These could include personal challenges, difficulties in the lives of loved ones, or unrest in the world. After you have finished, take several minutes to be quiet and listen for the Father's response. Record what you hear. Know that your worth or success is not found in results, but in obedience. All that you do for Christ is not in vain, but will produce fruit both in the world and in your own self.

January 19

Healing for Emotional Wounds (Ex)

May God heal the deep hurts that you have received at the hands of your family and closest friends. May He be a balm to help you move on and come to a place of releasing all bitterness. May His Spirit be like warm and soothing oil to you each time that you have an opportunity to become angry or bitter. And may you soon walk out of the place in which you are, and have been, stuck. Amen and a thousand more amens.

Verse: Matthew 6:14–15

> For if you forgive other people when they sin against you, your heavenly Father will also forgive you. But if you do not forgive others their sins, your Father will not forgive your sins.

Exercise: Prayer

Both forgiving and being forgiven require the work of the Holy Spirit. We can only stand before God as righteous because of what Jesus did on the cross and through His resurrection. In the same way, we can truly forgive others when the Holy Spirit works through us to reveal the same grace shown through the cross. Think of someone or a situation that has hurt you. Bring this to God, release the pain to Him, and ask Him to walk with you through the process of healing.

January 20

Against Fear (Ex)

I am praying for fear to lose its grip on you in the Name of the One who knows no fear. Fear can't grip Him, neither can it grip those who are His. So, may you walk, rest, reside and live in the powerful, fearless place that is Jesus. Amen and a thousand more amens.

Verse: 2 Timothy 1:7

> For the Spirit God gave us does not make us timid, but gives us power, love and self-discipline.

Exercise: Meditation

Spend this time not thinking about the things that have brought you fear, but on the One who drives out fear. Ask the Father to allow you to see clearly who He is, how He is all powerful and all good. These just begin to describe His nature, but these two alone are enough to drive out our worries and doubts. Spend 5 minutes meditating on God's character and record any thoughts from the exercise.

January 21

Protection and Peace (Ex)

In this day of terror and fear, I pray a prayer of covering and peace over you and your people. May no outside situation or circumstance take away your peace. In the name of Jesus, I speak Hope, Light and Life to you all. Amen and a thousand more amens.

Verse: John 16:33

> I have told you these things, so that in me you may have peace. In this world you will have trouble. But take heart! I have overcome the world.

Exercise: Prayer

Today is a prayer of covering over your life and those in your life. Read the day's prayer over your family, your friends, and directly to any tragic or difficult situation in society. Bathe in prayer the people and responsibilities God has given to you.

January 22

One's Speech (Ex)

Today, may God order your words. May you be cognizant of the words that you speak and the power that they have to assault the Kingdom of darkness and bring about hope and light and life in those with whom you speak. Remember that you are speaking on behalf of Jesus, so do so with clarity and love and truth. The Holy Spirit goes before you and works through you to speak things beyond yourself. Speak prophetically. Speak encouragement. Advance His Kingdom with your speech on behalf of our Risen Savior. Amen and a thousand more amens.

Verse: Colossians 4:6

> Let your speech always be gracious, seasoned with salt, so that you may know how you ought to answer each person.

Exercise: Prayer and Community

Think about those you will encounter today (or tomorrow if you are completing this in the evening). Ask God to give you a word for someone you will interact with. This could be a verse, an idea, or a message you believe is from God. If you receive something while praying, write it down. If not, continue to listen throughout your day and continue to ask the Father to speak through you in your responsibilities.

January 23

Stand Strong (P)

Holy Spirit, help me to stand strong today. In the name of the Lord Jesus, may I have the strength to stand, even when it seems too difficult or unbearable. And as I stand, may I be filled with the power of the Holy Spirit to draw others to stand with me. In the face of temptation, I will stand. When challenges arise, I will stand. For your glory alone, I will stand. Today, I stand for you, my God. Amen and a thousand more amens.

Verse: Ephesians 6:10–17

> Finally, be strong in the Lord and in his mighty power. Put on the full armor of God, so that you can take your stand against the devil's schemes. For our struggle is not against flesh and blood, but against the rulers, against the authorities, against the powers of this dark world and against the spiritual forces of evil in the heavenly realms. Therefore put on the full armor of God, so that when the day of evil comes, you may be able to stand your ground, and after you have done everything, to stand. Stand firm then, with the belt of truth buckled around your waist, with the breastplate of righteousness in place, and with your feet fitted with the readiness that comes from the gospel of peace. In addition to all this, take up the shield of faith, with which you can extinguish all the flaming arrows of the evil one. Take the helmet of salvation and the sword of the Spirit, which is the word of God.

Exercise: Prayer and Journaling

While reading this prayer, recognize what situations come to mind that you will need the strength to stand in. Pray this prayer again over these areas. In the middle of your day, pray this prayer again. At the end of the day, write down the areas in which you experienced victory. What did you do well? How were you obedient? Also, write down moments in which you were not fully obedient, in which you could have done better. Thank God for the victories and surrender the moments of weakness as you ask for His grace to grow you more in those areas.

January 24

Difficult Relationships (Ex)

I am asking the Lord to help you navigate the difficult relational situations in your life today. May you know when and how to speak to whom you should speak. May you have the grace to forgive and maybe even forget. And may you be able to see those who have caused you pain through Jesus' eyes of love. He is the God of healing and redemption. May He be so in your life today. Amen and a thousand more amens.

Verse: Romans 12:17–21

> Do not repay anyone evil for evil. Be careful to do what is right in the eyes of everyone. If it is possible, as far as it depends on you, live at peace with everyone. Do not take revenge, my dear friends, but leave room for God's wrath, for it is written: "It is mine to avenge; I will repay," says the Lord. On the contrary: "If your enemy is hungry, feed him; if he is thirsty, give him something to drink. In doing this, you will heap burning coals on his head." Do not be overcome by evil, but overcome evil with good.

Exercise: Journaling and Prayer

There will be people in our lives who we do not get along with or who have hurt us. Emotions that we feel for others may or may not have valid reasons, but our responsibilities as followers of Christ are not to determine whether we have the right or not to be annoyed, hurt, or callous towards others. Our call is to love as Christ loved. Today, write down the names of those in your life who are difficult to get along with or who have hurt you in the past. Regardless of how you feel as you pray, I challenge you to pray a blessing over them and that you would have God's heart for them. This does not mean we will be the best of friends with everyone, as some people should not have a place of influence in our lives. But God will give us the grace to forgive, to love, and to move on through His healing presence and process.

January 25

Hearing God's Voice (P)

I choose to hear the voice of God today. Through a word, a thought, a picture, a friend, a song, a verse or whatever mode You choose; but may I undoubtedly, unequivocally hear You this day. May You speak directly to me and to that issue that has been plaguing me. Speak ,Lord, for your servant is listening. Amen and a thousand more amens.

Verse: 1 Samuel 3:8–10

> A third time the Lord called, "Samuel!" And Samuel got up and went to Eli and said, "Here I am; you called me." Then Eli realized that the Lord was calling the boy. So Eli told Samuel, "Go and lie down, and if he calls you, say, 'Speak, Lord, for your servant is listening.'" So Samuel went and lay down in his place. The Lord came and stood there, calling as at the other times, "Samuel! Samuel!" Then Samuel said, "Speak, for your servant is listening."

Exercise: Silence and Meditation

Today is all about listening. So often we fill our prayer time with our own words that we neglect what the Father is saying. Set aside an amount of time to sit quietly before God (this could be 5 minutes, 10 minutes, etc.) and just listen. No music or agenda. Simply ask your Heavenly Father what He wants to say to you and write it down.

January 26

Salvations (Ex)

My prayer for you today is that the Holy Spirit would give you precise strategies to see people come to salvation in your spheres of influence. May you get intriguing ideas and thoughts that will turn into plans and works and ministries that will bring about salvation in the lives of the people with whom you do life this day and this week. May salvation surround you this day, where you live and work and learn and play. Amen and a thousand more amens.

Verse: Matthew 9:35–38

> Jesus went through all the towns and villages, teaching in their synagogues, proclaiming the good news of the kingdom and healing every disease and sickness. When he saw the crowds, he had compassion on them, because they were harassed and helpless, like sheep without a shepherd. Then he said to his disciples, "The harvest is plentiful but the workers are few. Ask the Lord of the harvest, therefore, to send out workers into his harvest field."

Exercise: Prayer

Ask the Holy Spirit to show you what individuals you should pray for, that they may receive salvation. After you have written down their names, pray for each person to see Jesus as He truly is. End with committing to be a willing vessel for the Gospel in their lives. Contact each of them this week, either giving them a call or sending a message via text or email. These communications are more about showing love and connection, so you do not need to expressly describe the Gospel to them unless you believe they are in a place to receive it.

January 27

Identity in Christ (P)

Today, I will not be defined either by people's opinions nor by a fear of failure. In Christ, I cannot fail. Jesus, I will abide in You today and rest in the identity You have given me. I will follow You and I will not seek validation from others. I am a success because of how You see me and not how others perceive my progress. I do not have to be afraid of not being enough. Thank you for setting me free from others' opinions. Amen and a thousand more amens.

Verse: Proverbs 29:25

The fear of man lays a snare, but whoever trusts in the Lord is safe.

Exercise: Journaling

Write down the different positions and titles you have. Some examples include Parent, Worker, Student, Son/ Daughter, Adult, etc. among these, in what areas do you look for approval in order to feel validated? Do you not feel fulfilled until you receive recognition in some area? Or are you paralyzed by the opinions of others? Ask the Father why this is and surrender these insecurities to Him again. You are defined by God alone. Whatever was said about you, or that you think others think about you, is not meant to hold you captive. You are a child of the Most High. Act like what you are.

January 28

Peace (Ex)

I AM PRAYING THAT peace would descend upon you and be with you all day. May confusion depart from you and may you feel the calm presence of His Holy Spirit in your mind, body and spirit. Peace in your relationships. Peace in your home. Peace in your car. Peace at work. Peace as you speak. Peace as you listen. Peace as you give and peace as you receive. In the name of the Prince of Peace, our Lord Jesus. Amen and a thousand more amens.

Verse: John 14:27

> Peace I leave with you; my peace I give you. I do not give to you as the world gives. Do not let your hearts be troubled and do not be afraid.

Exercise: Silence and Worship

Take a deep breath. Slow down. Whether life has been crazy or not, we are still dependent on Jesus. We constantly need Him and are drained whenever we seek peace anywhere else. In your mind, lock eyes with Jesus. No pen or paper today. Just be with Him. You can turn on a song that speaks to you, instrumental music, or sit in silence. Read the verse for today and imagine Jesus saying this to you. You are the one He knows completely, with complete love and acceptance. Take a deep breath.

January 29

Clarity (Ex)

May God bring clarity where there has been confusion. The enemy has endeavored to steal your time, your relationships and your money through confusing situations and interactions, but God Himself is moving to make the path straight and the way obvious. Doubt, fear and hesitation will dissipate today like fog in sunlight as our Lord brings you revelation from Heaven. His Kingdom come and His will be done in your life. Amen and a thousand more amens.

Verse: Proverbs 3:5–6

> Trust in the Lord with all your heart and lean not on your own understanding; in all your ways submit to him, and he will make your paths straight.

Exercise: Journaling and Prayer

Today, write down any and every area that is causing confusion and distraction in your life. Give each of these to God. He is above all and not surprised by any situation. You belong to Him. As a child of the Most High, you have no need to worry, fear, or doubt because He is with you. Even if you do not feel confidence or optimistic about these situations, say to the Father, "I give you ______ and I thank you that You will be with me through it all. Guide me through the confusion." He is faithful and will not leave or forsake you.

January 30

Healing in Relationships (Ex)

Today I am praying for relational breakthrough in your lives. Where progress has seemed impossible, may the Holy Spirit of God melt the ice from cold hearts and calloused minds. Jesus died for these types of things and either He is Lord of our relationships or He is not. May He exert Himself as the healing, melting, warming, blessing, peace-bringing and love infusing Savior that He is. Amen and a thousand more amens.

Verse: 2 Corinthians 5:16–21

> So from now on we regard no one from a worldly point of view. Though we once regarded Christ in this way, we do so no longer. Therefore, if anyone is in Christ, the new creation has come: The old has gone, the new is here! All this is from God, who reconciled us to himself through Christ and gave us the ministry of reconciliation: that God was reconciling the world to himself in Christ, not counting people's sins against them. And he has committed to us the message of reconciliation. We are therefore Christ's ambassadors, as though God were making his appeal through us. We implore you on Christ's behalf: Be reconciled to God. God made him who had no sin to be sin for us, so that in him we might become the righteousness of God.

Exercise: Prayer

The Father heals relationships. It is one of the main results of the life, death, and resurrection of Christ: we are brought back into a relationship with God. He has called and equipped you to do the same work through His Holy Spirit. Today, and however long you would like after this, find a small stone, coin, or similar item that can easily fit in your pocket. Every time you feel or see that item today, pray for broken or hurting relationships in or around your life.

JANUARY 31

Forgiveness (P)

FATHER, TODAY TEACH ME to know and act rightly in my relationships. Give me the strength to make the first move towards those who have done me wrong. May the Spirit of Jesus infuse me with His supernatural power of forgiveness to override my fleshly desire for revenge and retribution. I cannot grow in God and have ill feelings towards my brothers and sisters. Help me Jesus. Show me how to love like You love. Amen and a thousand more amens.

Verse: 1 Corinthians 4:12–13

> We work hard with our own hands. When we are cursed, we bless; when we are persecuted, we endure it; when we are slandered, we answer kindly. We have become the scum of the earth, the garbage of the world—right up to this moment.

Exercise: Journaling and Prayer

In this passage, the Apostle Paul is speaking of the difficulties he has faced in spreading the Gospel and how he and his coworkers have responded. Ask the Father to give you this same selfless love, humility, and heavenly perspective. Even when you feel mistreated or taken advantage of, God honors your choice to forgive and is honored through your Christ-like conduct. Write out a prayer to God concerning those you need to forgive or whom you could love better.

February 1

Step of Faith (Ex)

My prayer for you today is that you will be able to do that thing that you know you must do, but haven't had the strength to. Jesus, please help us to ask for forgiveness, extend forgiveness, reach out, pray, establish boundaries, say no, say yes or whatever else it is that we must do in order to live like you would. Not our will but Yours is our prayer. Please help us to mean it and then do it. Amen and a thousand more amens.

Verse: Philippians 2:12–13

> Therefore, my dear friends, as you have always obeyed—not only in my presence, but now much more in my absence—continue to work out your salvation with fear and trembling, for it is God who works in you to will and to act in order to fulfill his good purpose.

Exercise: Journaling and Silence

Upon first reading this prayer, what was the first thing that came to your mind? A person that you should share the Gospel with that you haven't yet? A sinful habit that you can't seem to get away from? A step of faith that you are afraid to take? Whatever this first thought was, write it down. Ask God what He says about it. If you already know the answer but haven't had the courage or confidence to follow through yet, surrender the challenge to Him. If you do not know what you should do, ask Him. Spend 5 minutes listening and record what you believe the Holy Spirit is saying to you. Then, plan one step you can take today to walk in obedience and the power of God. Share your problem with someone else. Approach that person with an intentional conversation. Do something to walk in obedience today.

February 2

Remain (Ex)

He has put us in a good place: Himself. Right there in the middle of whatever is going on in your lives, He is your safe-place. Regardless of your circumstance, He is your harbor in the storm. He is the calm in the middle of the raging sea. He is the point of life, the fulcrum, the reason, the tipping point and critical mass. May the truth of this word envelope and bless and keep you today. Amen and a thousand more amens.

Verse: John 15:4

> Remain in me, as I also remain in you. No branch can bear fruit by itself; it must remain in the vine. Neither can you bear fruit unless you remain in me.

Exercise: Silence and Meditation

Christ has called you to remain in Him. Slow down. Ask Jesus to be with you today. Make that the cry from your heart: "I want to be with You, Jesus. Nothing else." Remind yourself of His love for you. What has He brought you through? How many difficult situations have you faced in the past that overwhelmed you and kept you up at night? The Holy Spirit helped you through those. What reason do you have to be afraid? Be at peace, my friends.

February 3

Fear and Doubt (Ex)

Be released from all fear, intimidation and doubt. May the perfect love of Jesus surround you and fill you with a peace and confidence that overwhelms every doubt, hesitation and other voices that lie to you incessantly. May the indwelling power of His Holy Spirit propel you through this day and sling you into the next with such force that doubt can neither find nor attach itself to you any more. Amen and a thousand more amens.

Verse: Psalm 27:1

> The Lord is my light and my salvation— whom shall I fear? The Lord is the stronghold of my life— of whom shall I be afraid?

Exercise: Reading and Meditation

Read the entirety of Psalm 27. Read it again. Today, do this to remind yourself of the power of Scripture. It is empowered by the Holy Spirit to affect change in your life and the world around you. Allow the power of God's Word to drive out all fear and doubt today. Read it a third time. Pray these truths over your life and over the lives of those who are in a place of fear or doubt today.

FEBRUARY 4

Reminded of Christ's Living in Us (P)

GOD, REMIND ME OF who I am in Christ. Not just conceptually, but in reality. I want to know and feel Jesus. To see Him and smell Him and be close enough to hear His heartbeat. I often hear of and even speak of Jesus living in me, but show me the weight and beauty of this truth. I know that I can't live for nor be sustained by my feelings, but today would you allow me to feel my Savior's nearness and life. Thank you for choosing me. Amen and a thousand more amens.

Verse: Galatians 2:20

> I have been crucified with Christ and I no longer live, but Christ lives in me. The life I now live in the body, I live by faith in the Son of God, who loved me and gave himself for me.

Exercise: Prayer and Meditation

Christ's life enters your life at the very moment you say "yes" to Him. No outside power can change that. We have been given the greatest gift possible: God Himself. We exist for His honor and glory, yet He loves us enough to lavish us with His love and presence. Your faith should not be founded on emotions, because feelings come and go. But God still meets us where we are at. God often uses an intimate encounter with His presence to encourage and bring us out of dark places. Today, ask for this kind of encounter with God if you are in need of encouragement or direction. Also, if someone in your life needs a personal encounter with Jesus, pray for that as well.

February 5

Praying Peace for Others (P)

Lord, make me an instrument of Your peace. Help me to seek Your peace in every aspect of my existence. Peace in my home. Peace in the schools. Peace at work. Peace in my city. Peace in this world. Jesus, only You are true peace. Help us to seek You. Jesus, You are the Prince of Peace. May You rule and reign over all things in and around my life. Amen and a thousand more amens.

Verse:1 Timothy 2:1–4

> I urge, then, first of all, that petitions, prayers, intercession and thanksgiving be made for all people— for kings and all those in authority, that we may live peaceful and quiet lives in all godliness and holiness. This is good, and pleases God our Savior, who wants all people to be saved and to come to a knowledge of the truth."

Exercise: Prayer and Journaling

One of the greatest ways we as believers can impact the world for God's Kingdom, is through consistent prayer. Today, speak peace into the world around you in each of the areas listed above: your home, the schools, your place of work, your city, and the world. For each topic, write down a person or a group to pray for. Write out these prayers, focusing on the peace of Christ to rest in each of these places so that He may be glorified and that more people may come to Him.

February 6

Salvations (P)

Today, I am praying that salvation would come to those I have been praying for. Lord, release messengers of every kind to encourage, convict, and draw them close to You through the power of Your amazing Holy Spirit. I also pray that the efforts of the enemy to thwart salvation coming to these people would be rendered ineffective and harmless. Salvation has come. Salvation will come! Amen and a thousand more amens.

Verse: John 6:44

> No one can come to me unless the Father who sent me draws them, and I will raise them up at the last day.

Exercise: Prayer

We are drawn to salvation by the grace of God alone working in our hearts and through other people and circumstances around us. The pressure is not on you alone for the salvation of those you love. Jesus wants to see them in His family more than you do. His love is so great beyond our comprehension that sometimes we forget that He is the one drawing people to Himself. Bring those people before God in prayer again today and rejoice that God is already at work in their hearts. Ask that He would draw them to Him in the ways that best reach each individual.

February 7

Faith (Ex)

May the faith of Jesus Christ rise up in you today. Faith for healing. Faith for life. Faith for finances. Faith to get started. Faith to stand. Faith to ask for help. Faith to show up. Faith to go on another day. Faith to get out of bed. Faith to start running. Faith to stop running. Faith that He will show up. Faith to give. Faith to love. Faith to smile. Faith to laugh hard. Faith to have faith. Help us Jesus. Amen and a thousand more amens.

Verse: 1 John 5:3–4

> In fact, this is love for God: to keep his commands. And his commands are not burdensome, for everyone born of God overcomes the world. This is the victory that has overcome the world, even our faith.

Exercise: Journaling

"Faith" in the Bible can stand for both belief and faithfulness. As you ask for greater faith today, realize that often one of these meanings comes before the other. Either our belief increases and we walk out the new conviction through our actions, or we step out through our conduct and our mind follows after as we live in faithfulness to the call of Christ. Write down 2–3 areas in which you want greater faith and how you can live in faithfulness in these areas even if the feeling or desire does not manifest immediately.

FEBRUARY 8

God's Intentions (Ex)

MAY YOU BE FULLY aware of God's intentions towards you. They are good and Life-giving. They are well intentioned. They are Holy Spirit induced. They are living. They are productive. They are full. They are Kingdom building. They are uplifting. They are grace focused. They are redemptive. They are loving. They are fruitful. They are hopeful. They are eternal. They are Jesus. Amen and a thousand more amens.

Verse: John 3:16–17

> For God so loved the world that he gave his one and only Son, that whoever believes in him shall not perish but have eternal life. For God did not send his Son into the world to condemn the world, but to save the world through him.

Exercise: Reading and Meditation

God reveals in this famous passage the reason for Jesus: not to condemn, but to save. Salvation is not only receiving eternal life, but receiving God Himself and experiencing His power and true life in every facet of our existence. Read today's prayer towards yourself twice to remind yourself of how God sees you and of His future intentions for you.

February 9

Empowerment (Ex)

May the Lord Himself empower you today to go preach, be, live, speak, act, do, pray, engage, talk, walk, knock, stand, kneel, reach, teach, sing, point, help, laugh, give, write and move in an all out effort to see His Kingdom come and His will be done right there where you live as it is in Heaven. Live today in passionate, relentless, and audacious fashion by the power of the Holy Spirit! Amen and a thousand more amens.

Verse: Matthew 5:14–16

> You are the light of the world. A town built on a hill cannot be hidden. Neither do people light a lamp and put it under a bowl. Instead they put it on its stand, and it gives light to everyone in the house. In the same way, let your light shine before others, that they may see your good deeds and glorify your Father in heaven.

Exercise: Meditation and Prayer

You have been chosen and empowered by the God of the Universe. Do not think less of yourself. God can and will do amazing things through you to help others and to bring glory to His name. Write down today's passage of Scripture and put it in your pocket or on your phone. Throughout the day, read the passage over yourself and listen to how God wants to work through you in your world for His kingdom.

February 10

Healing (Ex)

I am believing that God will heal you. Whatever it is that is ailing you, I am asking that you will be touched by the hand of the Almighty. I pray that your spirit will be calmed. I pray that your body will work perfectly. May your mind be renewed. May your sleep be deep and restful. May anything that is causing you pain be dealt with in the name of Jesus and may you feel it when it happens. Healing to you all! Amen and a thousand more amens.

Verse: James 5:14–15

> Is anyone among you sick? Let them call the elders of the church to pray over them and anoint them with oil in the name of the Lord. And the prayer offered in faith will make the sick person well; the Lord will raise them up If they have sinned, they will be forgiven.

Exercise: Community and Prayer

Although today's prayer is addressed to you, you can pray this over another person as well. At salvation, we not only enter into a relationship with God, but also other believers. We are a part of the Church and are not meant to live in isolation. As you pray for healing, either for yourself or for another, reach out to 2–3 other believers to join you in prayer through email, a call, or in-person interaction.

February 11

Shame (Ex)

I am praying today for the intimidating force of shame and guilt to be gone from your life. May the cloud of your past be an ineffective tool in the hands of the enemy. You are a "new creation" and old things have "passed away". May the dead things of your past trouble you no more in the name of Jesus Christ. Amen and a thousand more amens.

Verse: 2 Corinthians 5:17

> Therefore, if anyone is in Christ, the new creation has come: The old has gone, the new is here!

Exercise: Meditation and Worship

If possible, listen to a song that speaks to the shame of your past (examples could be "Tremble" or "No Longer Slaves") and speak death to what used to hold you down. Sing in victory over the attacks of the enemy that have failed. If you do not have access to music, speak out a prayer against those things and command them to stay dead as you worship the Father for giving you true life.

February 12

Direction (Ex)

I AM PRAYING THAT God will give you specific and pointed direction in your life. May confusion be eradicated from your mind and clarity come in like a flood. Yes, may a mighty flood of clarity overwhelm you with ideas and thoughts and plans where before there was only a fog. And as the fog lifts, may you know that you are smack dab in the middle of His will. Amen and a thousand more amens.

Verse: Psalms 37:3–4

> Trust in the Lord and do good; dwell in the land and enjoy safe pasture. Take delight in the Lord, and he will give you the desires of your heart.

Exercise: Meditation and Prayer

As you listen for the next step today, do not forget to be faithful with what you do know. Yes, ask for direction, but also commit to wait with excellence. As today's verse states, "do good." Often God will reveal His plans for us as we pursue Him in the areas we do know. In your work, with your family, with your own health, and any other facet of life you have right now, be faithful and listen. This may seem counterintuitive, but focus on today. Do not spend your time wishing you were somewhere else. Spend the next 5 minutes thanking God for where He has you and giving each of your responsibilities back to Him. As you run after Him, He will show you your next steps.

February 13

Selfishness (P)

Please deliver me today from manipulative thoughts and actions. Free me from using people for my own gain. May I value them as the immeasurably precious treasures that they are. They possess Your image and likeness. How could I ever merely use them? I commit to honor, value, perpetuate, lift up, caress and protect Your image in the people with whom I do life this day. Help me Jesus. Amen and a thousand more amens.

Verse: Mark 9:35

> Sitting down, Jesus called the Twelve and said, "Anyone who wants to be first must be the very last, and the servant of all."

Exercise: Service

One of the greatest ways to be delivered from a self-centered approach to life is to focus on the needs and dreams of others. In the verse prior to Mark 9:35, the Twelve Disciples had been arguing about which of them was the greatest. In response, Christ called them to lives of servitude and submission. In your devotional time, pray for the needs and dreams of others. These could be family or friends, but also those you do not get along with as well. Choose two or three people to pray for. Find a small rock or trinket that will fit in your pocket or somewhere on your person (this could also be a ring or necklace). Every time you touch or see this object today, pray for those people. Also, take these moments to intentionally look at the people around you if you are around others. Get outside of yourself and focus on others today. Ask God how you can bless them and then go.

February 14

Thinking Like Christ (P)

Jesus Christ, Son of God, please rule over my thoughts and mind this day. I want to think like You do about others. Help me to see them through Your eyes. I want to think like You do about the world. Help me work to see Your kingdom come and Your will be done wherever I am. I want to think like You do about my enemies. Help me to pray for them, because it is not natural for me to do so. I want to think like You do about my family and friends. Help me to get outside of my comfort zone to show them more of You. I ask You to show me to not think about myself so much. Through Your Holy Spirit I will look more and more like You, Jesus. Amen and a thousand more amens.

Verse: Philippians 4:8–9

> Finally, brothers and sisters, whatever is true, whatever is noble, whatever is right, whatever is pure, whatever is lovely, whatever is admirable—if anything is excellent or praiseworthy—think about such things. Whatever you have learned or received or heard from me, or seen in me—put it into practice. And the God of peace will be with you.

Exercise: Reading and Meditation

One of the greatest ways in which we begin to think like Jesus, is to remain in the Bible. Through meditation on His Word, we gain a heavenly perspective and increasing revelation. Today, take the next 10 minutes (or more if you'd like) to read the Bible. If you are already reading through a book or other reading plan, you can read in those sections. If you do not have a current place you are reading in Scripture, start at the beginning of Philippians. Over the 10 minutes, read one chapter. Read it once quickly to understand overarching themes. Then, ask God to direct you and speak to you as you read. Read the chapter a second time, this time slower and out loud. Repeat your prayer and ask God to highlight one verse or section in the chapter. Read this portion several more times and record what you believe God is saying to you.

February 15

Salvation for Family and Friends (Ex)

Today, I pray for my family and friends who don't know You yet, Jesus. May You show Yourself to them in powerful fashion, soon. And when You do, may the power contained in the prayers that have been offered on their behalf, that has been stored up for years, flood their lives. Salvation to my house, to their houses. May the party in Heaven be prepared for and may my loved one's name be on the welcome home banner. Amen and a thousand more amens.

Verse: Like 15:7

> I tell you that in the same way there will be more rejoicing in heaven over one sinner who repents than over ninety-nine righteous persons who do not need to repent.

Exercise: Prayer and Community

Write down the names of family and friends who do not know Jesus yet. There may be some who you have lost hope for or can't imagine what they would be like in the Kingdom. Bring their names before the Father again. Keep their names in your prayers. Ask other believers to join with you. Make this a family effort in the body of Christ to get those people into the family. Finally, thank God for their salvation and rejoice in the unbelievable hope you have in Christ, the Risen King of kings.

February 16

Guidance (Ex)

I am praying today that our Lord would subvert any attack that the enemy has planned for you. May the Holy Spirit be active and speak to you about with whom, where and what you should be about today. May the Blood of Jesus cover you and may you sense His presence guiding you. If you don't feel peace, don't do it. Plain and simple. Let the peace that passes understanding rule in your heart and mind in Jesus. Amen and a thousand more amens.

Verse: Exodus 33:15–17

> Then Moses said to him, "If your Presence does not go with us, do not send us up from here. How will anyone know that you are pleased with me and with your people unless you go with us? What else will distinguish me and your people from all the other people on the face of the earth?" And the Lord said to Moses, "I will do the very thing you have asked, because I am pleased with you and I know you by name.

Exercise: Prayer

Approach the responsibilities and opportunities of today with the same conviction as Moses: if the Lord does not go with you, you will not move. Welcome God into each area of your life. Into your family, work, desires, hopes, fears, and dreams. Just as the pillar of cloud and the pillar of fire went before the Israelites, ask the Holy Spirit to go before you today. Take time in the morning (during breakfast, in your car, or during a run) to present your day to God. Ask Him to go before you and take your time in just being with Him before your day gets going.

February 17

Thwarting the enemy (Ex)

May your discernment be on high alert. Just as the Father has plans for you to prosper and to be in health, the enemy comes to steal, kill and destroy. I am praying that you see his efforts to do so before they are set in motion and do what is necessary to thwart them. And I mean thwart them. Thwart them through prayer, good deeds and doing everything within your power to advance the Kingdom of Heaven. Be empowered through the Most High today. Amen and a thousand more amens.

Verse: Isaiah 54:17

> "No weapon forged against you will prevail, and you will refute every tongue that accuses you. This is the heritage of the servants of the LORD, and this is their vindication from me," declares the LORD.

Exercise: Journaling, Prayer, and Community.

Take 5 minutes to listen with a pen and paper in hand. In what areas have you experienced attacks of the enemy? Where have you stumbled spiritually before? Write these down. Next, identify how you can resist these attacks. We fight not against flesh and blood, but we are called to fight with every ounce of our flesh and blood and soul and spirit, being empowered by the Holy Spirit to live in His victory. If you experience stress or conflict at work, memorize a scripture about God's peace. If you struggle with doubt or fear, contact a fellow believer whom you trust so they may pray with you and continue to be with you. If you struggle with a sinful habit or temptation, make a plan before you are tempted. Stay away from those who would want you to join them in sin. Turn off your phone at night. Have someone you are accountable to who you can call when struggling. We overcome by the blood of the Lamb and the word of our testimony. Fight with God. Fight alongside your brothers and sisters. Today is a new day.

February 18

Pure Heart and Motives (P)

"Create in me a clean heart oh God" (Psalm 51:10) This is my prayer today. God, I am asking You to purify my motives and plans and strategies. That You would cause me to be a transparent, honest and open person. A person who desires to be a real witness and example of the real person of Jesus Christ. No fake religious platitudes, rhetoric and jargon. Create in me a clean heart and mind.Holy Spirit, have Your way. Amen and a thousand more amens.

Verse: Psalm 51:1–2

> Have mercy on me, O God, according to your unfailing love; according to your great compassion blot out my transgressions. Wash away all my iniquity and cleanse me from my sin.

Exercise: Reading and Prayer

Read Psalm 51 in its entirety. Ask the Father to show you where you have missed the mark. Where you are not living in the fullness of his life. Ask Him to cleanse you of self-righteousness, pride, and a need for your own comfort. Not only that you would feel different, but that you can live out His pure love. Ask for opportunities to reveal God's heart to the world for His glory alone, not yours.

FEBRUARY 19

Pure Heart and Motives Pt. 2 (P)

"CREATE IN ME A pure heart, O God, and renew a steadfast spirit within me" (Ps. 51:10). I say yes to this today, Lord. Please straighten my crooked motives and understandings. Please bring a spirit of humility into my relationships, so that I might admit and see my wrongdoings. Please help me to say that I am sorry (and mean it) to You and to all whom I have wronged. Deliver me from myself O God. Amen and a thousand more amens.

Verse: Psalm 51:10

Create in me a pure heart, O God, and renew a steadfast spirit within me.

Exercise: Service and Journaling

The moment you said yes to Christ you received the fullness of His life. He did not hold back any of Himself. Instead, we gradually learn more things about Jesus and grow closer to Him through walking with Him and seeing more of who He has always been. You are clean in Jesus name. You are new. And God can and will work through you. If possible, intentionally bless someone else today because you have been chosen to reflect the Most High. Already. It is who you are. Go out. Talk with a stranger. Let a homeless person know that you see them. Leave an extra big tip at the restaurant with a note. Help those who can give you nothing in return and you will see God's heart and motives right before your eyes. Write about your experience afterwards.

February 20

To Know Him

Today I pray that you would get a revelation as to why you exist. You exist for the purpose of loving God and enjoying Him forever. May your love for Him be kindled today and go beyond a mere feeling. And may your desire for His presence be insatiable. We love You, O God, and our hearts beat to be with You. Glory to Your name. Amen and a thousand more amens.

Verse: John 17:3

> "Now this is eternal life: that they know you, the only true God, and Jesus Christ, whom you have sent."

Exercise: Worship and Silence

Our greatest purpose is to be with God. To know Him and love Him while being known and loved by Him. Today, take at least 15 minutes by yourself to just be with Him and worship Him. Turn on some worship music if available. No other agenda but to be with Him for this time, for that is your highest calling.

February 21

Direction for the Future (Ex)

I am praying that God would give to you the strategic steps that you need to take to see your visions and dreams come to life. May those steps be clear, decisive and obvious. Don't give up, as these revelations are on their way and will be real epiphanies to you. I am believing that this day you will receive assistance from heaven and this assistance will bolster your faith and propel you forward in Jesus' name. Amen and a thousand more amens.

Verse: Proverbs 29:18

> Where there is no revelation, people cast off restraint; but blessed is the one who heeds wisdom's instruction.

Exercise: Prayer and Silence

Many times, the visions and dreams that we have are greater than ourselves. They could include our family, work, church, nation, or world. Dreams from God never find the end result in ourselves alone. Today, pray for those future plans and dreams, but specifically pray for those whom it affects beyond yourself. Pray for your current leaders, for the groups you hope to help someday, or for the next generations of your family. While praying, listen for any words from the Holy Spirit concerning them. It is when we are busy doing our Father's work that we will see where He wants to lead us. If you can't think of any "big" plans or dreams, what has God entrusted you with in this season? Pray for current coworkers, unsaved family or friends, or for your local church. If we keep our eyes focused on Christ, we will get where we need to be, especially if we need to be exactly where we are. Next steps will come, but remember to be faithful in this season so you are prepared for the next.

February 22

Healing Relationships (Ex)

I pray that Jesus would heal relationships that you thought were irreparably marred and dead. He healed lepers, the blind, and raised the physically dead, He can also raise the relationally dead. You must pray, believe and be willing to take the first small step, then He will do the healing. You step, He heals. Don't fret if the stepping is slow, things that were once dead can forget how to walk. Just keep stepping and the Holy Spirit can and will breathe new life into the past. I pray this over you in the name above all other names, Jesus Christ. Amen and a thousand more amens.

Verse: Ephesians 4:2–3

> Be completely humble and gentle; be patient, bearing with one another in love. Make every effort to keep the unity of the Spirit through the bond of peace.

Exercise: Service and Community

Relationships often suffer from the presence of negative experiences, or the absence of good ones. For your devotional time today, seek to rectify either of these. For those of your relationships that have been places of hurt, pursue forgiveness and healing. Or if you have those in your life that you have not spoken kindly or encouragingly to in an intentional way, do so today. Take your devotional time to write a letter (or text or email) or plan a time to meet with the person you want to have a healthier relationship with. There is a time to pray and a time to act. Today is the day to take those first steps.

February 23

Prayer over Your Dwelling (P)

I pray today for protection over my dwelling place. May the Blood of Jesus cover it. May the Holy Spirit of God enliven it. May angelic hosts bring good news to it. May happiness permeate it. May healing be throughout it. May laughter's music be a sweet noise in it. May life be good in it. May the presence of God be unmistakable in every inch of it. Praise be to the omnipresent One. Thank you for being with me, Lord. Amen and a thousand more amens.

Verse: Isaiah 32:18

> My people will live in peaceful dwelling places, in secure homes, in undisturbed places of rest.

Exercise: Prayer

Read this prayer as you walk through your dwelling place.. Think of the people who live there, of its maintenance, and of its security. Pray this blessing over your home today and repeat it each day this week.

February 24

Who God is (Ex)

God is faithful, no doubt about it. He is ever-present. He is ever-loving. He is ever-knowing. He is incomparable. He is unfathomable. He is boundless. He is our covering. He is our wisdom. He is our peace. He is our defender. He is our joy. He is our laughter. He is our provider. He is our strategy. He is our answer. He is our life-source. He is our healer. He is our deliverer. He is our hope. May He show you more of Himself today. Amen and a thousand more amens.

Verse: Jeremiah 29:13

> You will seek me and find me when you seek me with all your heart.

Exercise: Meditation

The prayer for today contains a list of God's attributes. Although this is not an all-inclusive list, grasping these attributes will lead to greater freedom and appreciation for God's beauty. Read the list slowly. Choose three that stick out to you. Meditate on them one at a time. Say one repeatedly, either out loud or in your mind. Ask the Father, "what does this mean? Can You show me more of You through this?" Don't rush the process. Hold onto those three aspects of God and keep meditating on them throughout the day.

February 25

Interrupt My Schedule (P)

Lord, please help me to mean it when I say that I live to serve You and not that I live to serve you "if": If it is convenient, or if it is fun, or if it makes me immediately happy, or if it is profitable, or if it is easy, or if it is popular, or if it is pleasurable, or if it fits into my schedule, or if it. . .deliver me from myself Jesus. Amen and a thousand more amens.

Verse: Luke 10:29

> But he wanted to justify himself, so he asked Jesus, "And who is my neighbor?"

Exercise: Reading and Meditation

Read the story of the Good Samaritan (Luke 10:25–37). You may know this by heart and have heard it a thousand times. Do not assume you know what you are going to learn. The Word is alive and active. Ask the Father to speak to you in this time. Read it once. Pause. Read it again, slowly. Pause and listen. Read it once more, slowly. Slowly. Slowly. Pause, listen, and write down what you receive from the passage.

February 26

A Prayer of Blessing for Friends (Ex)

I pray today for all of those who have blessed me so richly through the gift of friendship. May You touch them and bless them today, Father. Anoint them with health and peace and prosperity and joy. May the projects to which they put their hands be successful and may they reap some amazing benefits. May they be fully alive for You today and may You smile upon them. Thank you for my friends and for showing more of Yourself through them. Amen and a thousand more amens.

Verse: Proverbs 17:17

A friend loves at all times, and a brother is born for a time of adversity.

Exercise: Prayer

Think of those individuals in your life that have added joy and growth because of their friendship. They are a gift from God, as it is through the unity we have in Christ that we can have such deep friendships. Choose two or three people who have filled this role as friend in your life (whether you still interact with them or not) and pray today's blessing over their lives.

February 27

Who Christ Is (P)

Jesus, You are not a concept. You are not a philosophy. You are not a baby born in a manger any more. You are not a mere prophet. You are not my servant, whose name I tack on to the end of my prayers for good luck. You are Lord. God. Creator of the Universe. The One who holds the keys of death and the grave. You are the controversial figure who died for the sins of humanity, resurrected and will come again. Glory to Your name! Holy, Holy, Holy! Receive the honor that is due to Your name from this heart. Amen and a thousand more amens.

Verse: Revelation 4:8b,11

> "Holy, holy, holy is the Lord God Almighty, who was, and is, and is to come."
>
> "You are worthy, our Lord and God, to receive glory and honor and power, for you created all things, and by your will they were created and have their being."

Exercise: Worship and Meditation

Read the entirety of Revelation 4. This is the level of worship that God receives. These beings exist in His presence, yet cannot help but fall prostrate before Him, crying out His praises. Jesus has this same level of holiness, of majesty, and glory as He is one with the Father. After reading the chapter, imagine you are in the throne room beside the Apostle John who recorded this experience. See the throne and all the beings worshiping God. His holiness permeates the atmosphere, the air vibrating with His glory. Who are we to stand in such a place? If possible, take a posture of worship such as kneeling or laying prostrate. Repeat the worship of the heavenly beings (Revelation 4:8b and verse 11 as stated above). Continue to repeat these offerings of worship and join with the heavens in bringing honor to His name.

February 28

Time Management (P)

Lord Jesus, will you please organize my thoughts? So much to do and as I try to make a plan, the clock continues to tick and makes me concerned that I don't have a plan yet. You are not bound by time and are Lord over it, so will you please help me as I live my life in it. Will you redeem my time? Will you anoint my time? Will you multiply my time? Will you order my time? I love you, O timeless Savior. May Your will be done today. Amen and a thousand more amens.

Verse: Psalm 90:17

> May the favor of the Lord our God rest on us; establish the work of our hands for us-- yes, establish the work of our hands.

Exercise: Journaling and Prayer

Write down everything that is on your mind right now: your responsibilities, worries, and schedule. Then, pray over them one by one. Give them back to God. If you have accepted Christ as Lord, then everything you are is His, including your schedule. Listen for any response over the areas and receive His peace.

February 29

(Leap Year) Peace in Every Area (Ex)

I am praying that the Holy Spirit would descend upon your dwellings and bring the peace of God into every aspect of your lives. May your marriages, your children, your work-places, your schools, and your travels today be places where the shalom of Heaven is present and prevalent. May the "peace of God, which transcends all understanding" guard your hearts and minds in Christ Jesus.

Verse: Philippians 4:7

> And the peace of God, which transcends all understanding, will guard your hearts and your minds in Christ Jesus.

Exercise: Prayer

Pray Philippians 4:7 over each area listed in today's prayer: family, work, school, and travels. If you have other areas in need of Christ's peace, speak this verse over them as well. Then, commit this verse to memory. Keep a small rock or similar item on your person all week. Every time you feel or see the object, repeat this verse and pray for Christ's peace to rest on you and flow through you to the world around you.

March 1

Against Fear (Ex)

In Jesus' name, may God eradicate the fears that have been stealing life from you. The fear of people (they have no real authority). The fear of disease (Jesus is Lord over every one of them). The fear of losing your money (It's His anyway). The fear of not being enough (you are more than a conqueror through Him who loves you). The fear of success (To Him be the glory). The fear of the devil (He is defeated). You are a child of the Most High God. You have no reason to allow fear to remain in your life. Receive the Father's peace of mind and covering once again in the name of Jesus Christ. Amen and a thousand more amens.

Verse: 2 Timothy 2:7

> For the Spirit God gave us does not make us timid, but gives us power, love and self-discipline.

Exercise: Memorization and Meditation

Read today's verse out loud. Repeat it until you have committed it to memory. Select a small rock or similar trinket that you can keep on your person (possibly in a pocket). Every time you see or feel this object this week, repeat the verse in your mind or out loud. Recite this truth over your life and into the lives of others who have fear. Allow the power of God's Word to transform your mind.

March 2

His Direction in All Things (P)

Lord, please fill me up with Your Spirit and guide my every moment. That I may be led where You want me to go. That I may look at what You want me to see. That I may say what You want me to say. That I may hear what You want me to hear. That I may rest when You want me to rest. That I may pray when You want me to pray. Yes Lord, direct my day. Amen and a thousand more amens.

Verse: Romans 14:7–8

> For none of us lives for ourselves alone, and none of us dies for ourselves alone. If we live, we live for the Lord; and if we die, we die for the Lord. So, whether we live or die, we belong to the Lord.

Exercise: Silence and Meditation

The Apostle Paul wrote these verses to address a division in the church over correct diets and celebrations. He is stating that whatever we do, we do it for the glory of Christ. Read this verse and keep it in front of you. For 5 to 10 minutes, sit in silence. Allow God to speak to your priorities and schedule for the day. Does He want to show you something new? Does He want to reveal where you have not put Him first? Does He want to remind you of your first love? Listen today, my friends.

March 3

Reflecting on God's Grace (P)

Lord, I am not worthy of Your grace. You favor me just because. Help me to never act as if it is an entitlement, because it is not. I am entitled to nothing. Your grace is incomprehensible. It makes no sense. You, the infinite and perfect, receive me, the finite and very flawed. It is senseless. Please help me to receive this senseless gift carefully, yet extend it liberally. Jesus, You are God's grace to me. Amen and a thousand more amens.

Verse: Titus 2:11–14

> For the grace of God has appeared that offers salvation to all people. It teaches us to say "No" to ungodliness and worldly passions, and to live self-controlled, upright and godly lives in this present age, while we wait for the blessed hope—the appearing of the glory of our great God and Savior, Jesus Christ, who gave himself for us to redeem us from all wickedness and to purify for himself a people that are his very own, eager to do what is good.

Exercise: Worship and Service

We are saved by the grace of God alone, and nothing we do can earn that gift He has given freely. However, as we increasingly grasp the gift we have been given, our lifestyle will change to reflect the life we have received. We don't stop trying when we accept forgiveness in Christ, but now we try for different reasons. No longer for salvation, but simply because we are His. Take your devotional time to reflect on the prayer. Honor God for who He is and sit in awe of His presence. See Him in a new light. Then, commit to live today permeated in God's grace as you go about your responsibilities and interact with others.

March 4

Fulfillment from God Alone (P)

Lord, help me to get to a place where the only affirmation that is truly necessary for my happiness and sustenance is that which comes from You. You are my source. You are my life. You are my happiness.You are my affirmation. Amen and a thousand more amens.

Verse: Psalm 16:2

> I say to the Lord, "You are my Lord; apart from you I have no good thing."

Exercise: Fasting

Read the entirety of Psalm 16 and reflect on its meaning in your life. After your devotional time, choose one thing to fast from today. If possible, include food in this practice as it weakens the body as we seek to strengthen our spirit. This could be a meal or certain types of food. Whenever your time for fasting comes, reflect on the Psalm today and ask the Father to help you find fulfillment in Him alone.

March 5

Peace (Ex)

May the peace that passes understanding rule in your life today. And stop trying to figure things out; that's what "passes understanding means". And get out of the way, that's what letting it "rule" means. Peace to your intimidating thoughts. Peace to your scrambled mind. Peace to your rattled relationships. Peace to your messed up life. Peace as you sleep. Peace as you awaken. Jesus to you. He is your Prince of Peace, so may He make His peace known in every area of your life. Amen and a thousand more amens.

Verse: Philippians 4:6–7

> Do not be anxious about anything, but in every situation, by prayer and petition, with thanksgiving, present your requests to God. And the peace of God, which transcends all understanding, will guard your hearts and your minds in Christ Jesus.

Exercise: Prayer and Worship

The Apostle Paul instructs us to bring our worries to God through prayer. Take the next few minutes and have a conversation with the Father. Be honest about how you are feeling and what is weighing you down. These could be things in your life or in the lives of those you care about. After this, enter into a time of simply praising God for who He is and what He will do in those situations. We come before His throne with both prayer and thanksgiving. He gives the peace.

March 6

Refuge in the Lord (Ex)

May the Lord establish Himself as your shelter from the storm. May you know beyond the shadow of a doubt that He is your protector, defender, counselor, healer and coverer. Yes, He is a refuge and a place where you can run and not be afraid. May He be your refuge this day. Run to Him. Hide there. Rest in Him. Amen and a thousand more amens.

Verse: Proverbs 30:5

Every word of God is flawless; he is a shield to those who take refuge in him.

Exercise: Memorization and Meditation

Write down Proverbs 30:5. Commit it to memory and keep it on your person all day. Over every challenge in your life and in the lives of others, repeat this verse. At random times, repeat it in your mind. Meditate on the Word and its truth will increasingly become your reality.

March 7

Salvation for Loved Ones (Ex)

I AM PRAYING FOR my loved ones who aren't serving Jesus, yet. They are marked men and women. They are on God's radar screen. Prophetic words and people are on their way into their lives, right now. Angelic hosts have been dispatched to pay them a visit and demonic ones are rendered powerless, bound and helpless because of the blood. I see a mansion in Heaven with their name on the mailbox. Salvation to them in the name of Jesus. Amen and a thousand more amens.

Verse: John 6:44

> No one can come to me unless the Father who sent me draws them, and I will raise them up at the last day.

Exercise: Prayer

If you have already written the names of those who needed salvation in your journal, take a look at that list now (if you have not, write down a list of people in your life who do not know Jesus yet). Have any accepted Him? Have there been any changes since the last time you prayed for them? Continue to bring them before the Father in prayer. Ask to see them like He sees them, and for the Holy Spirit to continue to draw them. He is the faithful one. Remain diligent in prayer and record on the same list how God is moving in their lives.

March 8

In Defense of Others (Ex)

Be a protective WALL of faith for those whom you know who are being attacked by the enemy. Stand for them, so that they might be safe. Stand for them, so that they might be healed. Stand for them, so that they might be able to catch their breath. Stand for them, so that they might know that God still cares. Stand for them, so that they might hear the voice of God again. Stand for them, because if you don't, no one will. Stand, stand, stand in Jesus' name and keep standing. Amen and a thousand more amens.

Verse: Isaiah 58:6–8

> Isn't this the fast that I have chosen: to break the chains of wickedness, to untie the cords of the yoke, to set the oppressed free and tear off every yoke? Isn't it to share your bread with the hungry, to bring the poor and homeless into your home, to clothe the naked when you see him, and not to turn away from your own flesh and blood? Then your light will break forth like the dawn, and your healing will come quickly. Your righteousness will go before you, and the glory of the LORD will be your rear guard.

Exercise: Fasting, Prayer, and Service

The Christian life is one of spiritual warfare. We have an enemy who is constantly trying to separate humanity from God, but the Holy Spirit has empowered us to take part in His heavenly rescue plan. Today, lean into this fight. It is not about you, your comfort, or your prosperity. Deny yourself today so that you may live out the call of Isaiah in today's passage. If possible, fast today for either the day or for a meal. Take this time to intercede for others who are being oppressed by the enemy. Speak life to them in encouragement, pray for victory over darkness and freedom in the light. You have been given the authority to bring heaven to earth. Do not leave that weapon hidden. Stand today and keep standing.

March 9

Protection (Ex)

May you feel a sense of security and affirmation today, deep in your spirit, because God is a wall for you. He is a hedge of protection, a city of refuge, a wall of fire to lead you, a wall to ward off enemy attacks, a wall upon which you can stand to see your way, a wall of unconditional love through which no lie about you can penetrate and a wall to stand against the shifting winds of our culture. That wall is our Rock, Jesus. Amen and a thousand more amens.

Verse: Psalm 91:1–2

Whoever dwells in the shelter of the Most High will rest in the shadow of the Almighty.
I will say of the Lord, "He is my refuge and my fortress, my God, in whom I trust."

Exercise: Meditation and Prayer

Read the entirety of Psalm 91 at a normal pace, then read it again. This time, pray each verse over your life. This can either be reading the verse itself or altering it into a prayer (example for verses 1 and 2: "I choose to dwell in Your shelter today, Lord. Thank you that You are my refuge and my fortress. I trust You with all of me.") Pray through the entire passage and meditate on the meaning of each verse as you pray.

March 10

Being Used By God (Ex)

God is going to use you today. Be ready. Listen for that still small voice to direct you. Notice that need staring at you. Be waiting for that leper to cross your path, so don't go to the other side of the street. Look for Him to move, then stop, because He wants you to take over. Be aware of your surroundings as He is going to use you to change them. Jesus meant it when He said, "His Kingdom come and His will be done on earth as it is in Heaven." He meant the earth. Right there where you live. May the Holy Spirit speak clearly and move powerfully through you today. Amen and a thousand more amens.

Verse: Luke 10:37b

Jesus told him, "Go and do likewise."

Exercise: Meditation and Service

Read Luke 10:25–37. Commit to love in the same way as the Samaritan did in Jesus' parable. Yes, listen for the direction of the Holy Spirit today, but also realize that God has already called you to love others. If you see a need or a hurt today, approach it knowing that God has equipped you to make a difference. Be the love of Christ in your world today.

March 11

New in Christ (Ex)

Jesus is alive in you, right now. You are new, right now. The shameful, depressed and sin laden state in which you found yourself last night is gone and has no effect upon you because His mercies are new every morning. Every morning my friends. That means this morning! You are new in Jesus. Old shame be gone and give way to new hope. Old depression be gone and give way to fresh joy. May your entire person be flooded with that new life from Jesus, right now. Amen and a thousand more amens.

Verse: Lamentations 3:22–24

> Because of the Lord's great love we are not consumed, for his compassions never fail. They are new every morning; great is your faithfulness. I say to myself, "The Lord is my portion; therefore I will wait for him."

Exercise: Worship

The book of Lamentations was written in a time of great loss and suffering in the land of Israel. Yet, the author still clings to the faithfulness of God. In the same way, regardless of how good or challenging your life is at this moment, celebrate God's faithfulness. If you know joy today, worship. If you struggle with negative thoughts or burdened by worries, worship. If the world seems to be falling apart, worship. Intentionally change your perspective to focus on the faithfulness of Christ. Read today's prayer again and thank God for who He is and what He will do.

March 12

Provision (Ex)

I am praying for miraculous provision. May you be surprised by the crazy miraculous ways that God will provide for you. May He bring bona fide miracles into your house. Salvation to a loved one. Healing to your body. Food in the pantry. That job for which you have been praying. Restoration to a long lost relationship. You are seen by the Most High. May He act on your behalf today. Amen and a thousand more amens.

Verse: Matthew 6:33

> But seek first his kingdom and his righteousness, and all these things will be given to you as well. Therefore do not worry about tomorrow, for tomorrow will worry about itself. Each day has enough trouble of its own.

Exercise: Journaling

Write down the areas in which you need a miracle. Mark where this list is kept. Throughout today, this week, month, or however long it takes for the answer to come to pass, wait for the answer. When a resolution comes, write it down next to the need. This is both for your encouragement and for others. This list can and should include the needs of others as well. As God shows up, share how He has been faithful with others to remind them and yourself of His goodness.

March 13

Advice of the Holy Spirit (Ex)

I am praying this morning that you would listen intently for the advice of the Holy Spirit. May your decisions be clear and blessed by Him. May you be protected from the unhealthy manipulations of the people and the forces around you who would use you for their own gain. You have the mind of Christ and I am asking that He would be thinking through you, because you have labored intensely over some issues in your life lately and it is time to rest. Rest. Peace. Clarity and a sound mind to you. Amen and a thousand more amens.

Verse: Psalm 27:14

Wait for the Lord; be strong and take heart and wait for the Lord.

Exercise: Memorization and Prayer

Read the entirety of Psalm 27 once at a normal pace in order to understand the Psalm as a whole. Then, pray each passage over your life. As you interact with the text. Choose one verse or portion to memorize. Keep a small rock or trinket in your pocket or on your person today. Whenever you feel or see this item, repeat the memorized Scripture and meditate on what God is speaking to you. Allow the Holy Spirit to impart His presence and direction in your life throughout the day.

March 14
Worship (P)

Worship Him now! Glorify His name. Worship Him now! Give Him glory, praise, honor and fame. Worship Him now! He is Christ our Lord. Living, moving, confirming His word! Worship Him now! He's still healing the lame. Worship Him now! Today and forever, always the same. Worship Him now, put the devil to chase. Worship Him now, He conquers all evil in every dark place. Worship Him now, worship Him now, together we stand. It's Jesus, He's moving, He will smile on our land! Amen and a thousand more amens!

Verse: Psalm 95:1–2

Come, let us sing for joy to the Lord; let us shout aloud to the Rock of our salvation.
Let us come before him with thanksgiving and extol him with music and song.

Exercise: Worship

Intentionally set aside 15 to 30 minutes today to worship Jesus. This time is yours to come before Him in your own way. This could be in a quiet adoration, loud singing, or joining with fellow believers simply to adore and praise His name. Step away from the business of life and lift up His name!

March 15

Allegiance to Christ (P)

Jesus, if You are my Lord, then that is what You must be. May You have nothing less than my undivided attention. I exist to focus upon You. You are "THE" way, "THE" truth and "THE" life, not one of the many ways. I will follow You only. Forgive me for putting other things above You. You are Lord of all. You are the Lord of my life. May You have all of my allegiance. Amen and a thousand more amens

Verse: John 14:6

> Jesus answered, "I am the way and the truth and the life. No one comes to the Father except through me."

Exercise: Prayer

Reflect on how you view Jesus today. Is He at the center of your life? Does He have Lordship over every area in your life? Ask the Father to reveal the areas that you have kept back from Him. Then, ask for forgiveness and repent of having a divided loyalty. All submission to Christ. Once again, make Him THE way, THE truth, and THE life in your heart.

March 16

Jesus, Lord of your Life (Ex)

May Jesus rule and reign in your life. This means that as "ruler", He doesn't just make it into the top five on your priority list, but that He is in fact sitting on the seat of authority, the very throne of your life. He is the boss. He is the king. He "reigns" means that He is actively making decisions and taking measures to advance His Kingdom through you. You are one of His subjects. His slave. He is your Lord and He is directing you where and how He wants for you to go. Jesus, our Christ, use us this day according to your will. Do whatever you want whenever you want. Amen and a thousand more amens.

Verse: Philippians 2:8–11

> And being found in appearance as a man, he humbled himself by becoming obedient to death— even death on a cross! Therefore God exalted him to the highest place and gave him the name that is above every name, that at the name of Jesus every knee should bow, in heaven and on earth and under the earth, and every tongue acknowledge that Jesus Christ is Lord, to the glory of God the Father.

Exercise: Prayer and Meditation

How often do you look up? How often do you see if what you are doing aligns with God's will? Take a small rock or trinket wherever you go today. Keep it in a pocket or other accessible place. Every time you touch or see it, ask yourself, "Is Jesus Lord over what I am doing at this moment?" Meditate on His sovereignty and commit all things to Him today.

March 17

Discernment (P)

I AM PRAYING TODAY that the Holy Spirit would give me an increased sense of discernment. May the things that are grey to me now become very black and white. May those things that are confusing me become brutally obvious. May any sense of panic and anxiety that has been weighing on me turn into shalom, the peace of Heaven. Jesus, meet me and show me how You are able to give me rest, real rest. Thank you for going before me today. May Your will be done and Your kingdom come through my life today. Amen and a thousand more amens.

Verse: John 14:26

> But the Advocate, the Holy Spirit, whom the Father will send in my name, will teach you all things and will remind you of everything I have said to you.

Exercise: Journaling

Are there areas of confusion in which you need direction today? Pray today's prayer over yourself and others in need. Write down your prayer and listen for direction from heaven. Expect the Holy Spirit to guide you and speak. He is still active and is with you. May discernment and power be yours today for His glory.

March 18

God is Smiling (Ex)

Please know that God is smiling at you. I know that you might not feel it, but He is. He has good thoughts towards you and is not mad. He is not keeping track of your mistakes, nor does He revel in punishing you for every little sin that you commit. He is not a cosmic cop waiting to give you a ticket for every offense. He is a redeemer, a reconciler, a gatherer and a healer. In fact, His ultimate and biggest smile at you is Jesus. He smiles at you through the resurrected Christ. Yes, He smiles at you because Jesus is alive and redeeming and reconciling and gathering and healing. When you accept Christ, the Father sees you through His Son. Live in His acceptance and love today. Amen and a thousand more amens.

Verse: 1 John 4:15–19

> If anyone acknowledges that Jesus is the Son of God, God lives in them and they in God. And so we know and rely on the love God has for us. God is love. Whoever lives in love lives in God, and God in them. This is how love is made complete among us so that we will have confidence on the day of judgment: In this world we are like Jesus. There is no fear in love. But perfect love drives out fear, because fear has to do with punishment. The one who fears is not made perfect in love. We love because he first loved us.

Exercise: Silence and Meditation

It is easy at times to misplace our need for achievement into our relationship with God. In this mindset, we may feel like we aren't enough, that God is frustrated with us, or that we are a disappointment. Yes, we are called to obedience and submission, but our identity is found in what Christ has done for us. Take 10 to 15 minutes to sit in silence before the Father. Ask Him what He thinks of you. Read today's passage as many times as you need and allow God to reveal His love for you once again.

March 19

Living In Eternity Now (P)

Father, please show me today that because of Jesus, I am living eternally right now. Eternal life is already mine. The eternal and miraculous are pulsating through my life. That which seems impossible does not rule any more. You have brought me into the realm of hope and faith. Every day has the potential for Jesus to show up and create the miraculous. Even if I don't see or feel it, I know You are working out everything for my good and Your glory. Jesus, Jesus, precious Jesus, O for grace to trust Him more. I choose to focus on You and the magnificent life You have placed inside of me. Thank you my Lord and my God. Amen and a thousand more amens.

Verse: John 5:24

> Very truly I tell you, whoever hears my word and believes him who sent me has eternal life and will not be judged but has crossed over from death to life.

Exercise: Meditation and Journaling

Jesus tells us that we have eternal life, not that "we will" have eternal life. When we accept Christ, we have that life. Take out a piece of paper or your journal and write down what you think it means to have eternal life right now. Ask the Holy Spirit to teach you what this means. Often we glance over amazing truths in Scripture because we are used to the vocabulary. Reflect on the gift you have received from Your heavenly Father.

March 20

Hope for Others (Ex)

Today, I pray for those who have not had much hope as of late. Holy Spirit, send Your Hope to them right now. The despair that has resided in their minds and any heaviness cannot remain any longer. I do not pray for a distraction from despair or for any worldly peace from people or things. No, I pray for the Hope that has a name: Jesus. Jesus, clean out, renew, and rearrange the order of their minds and bring life to their parched and weary hearts. Draw out the darkness and replace it with Your light. Amen and a thousand more amens.

Verse: 1 Peter 1:3

> Praise be to the God and Father of our Lord Jesus Christ! In his great mercy he has given us new birth into a living hope through the resurrection of Jesus Christ from the dead.

Exercise: Prayer

Think of those in your life who have been struggling with their thoughts lately. Those that do not have joy or peace or excitement for the future. Speak today's verse over their situations. Pray specifically for the challenges each person faces. Pray for a renewed hope in each of their lives. One that is founded on Christ.

March 21

New Life to Your Relationship with God (Ex)

I AM PRAYING TODAY that your faith in Jesus would increase dramatically, exponentially. May your sense of His presence there with you right now be palpable. May your reluctance to have a conversation with Him be replaced with an insatiable desire to have a cup of coffee with Him and express your deepest and most secret thoughts and dreams. May a powerful sense of His ability to forgive and forget sins release you to forgive and forget them as well. And may the insane nature of true grace wash over you and pull you away from the depressive nature of sin, judgement and religious bondage, like a rip-tide pulling you out into the sea. Draw close to Him once again. May your eyes behold His beauty through the beautiful work of the Holy Spirit. Amen and a thousand more amens.

Verse: Psalm 63:1

> You, God, are my God, earnestly I seek you; I thirst for you, my whole being longs for you, in a dry and parched land where there is no water.

Exercise: Meditation and Bible Reading

Intentionally spend time with the Father today. Set aside 30 minutes if possible just to be with Him. Make a cup of coffee (or your drink of choice) and read Psalm 63. Reflect on your desire to be with God. How has your pursuit of His presence been lately? Allow His presence to draw you in again and meditate on Psalm 63. Record any thoughts or prayers you have during this time.

March 22

Protection for Loved Ones (P)

Father, would you please cover all of my people in the blood of Jesus, the blood that protects and cleanses. I thank you that you will keep the enemy of their bodies from harming them. I thank you that you will keep the enemy of their minds from tormenting them. And I thank you that you will keep the enemy of their spirits from haunting them. Thank you that you are the true WALL in their lives and that you will use me to help them know that this is true. You are our WALL, O God, and I praise you for that fact. You are our WALL through Christ Jesus, and may your kingdom come and your will be done through Him and in us this day. Amen and a thousand more amens.

Verse: Psalm 5:11

> But let all who take refuge in you be glad; let them ever sing for joy. Spread your protection over them, that those who love your name may rejoice in you.

Exercise: Prayer

Read today's prayer and think of those God has put in your life. Ask Him if there are any you should pray for specifically. Once you have these people in mind, change your surroundings. If you usually have your devotionals in a specific room, go to a different room. Sit outside. Go for a walk. Change the routine for the day. Pray God's covering over your people today as you remain with the Father.

March 23

Song of Victory (Ex)

I AM PRAYING TODAY that you would be set free from the issues that are plaguing, dogging and mocking you. There is no place for plagues where the mind of Christ is in operation. So, may the hope, light and life that is Jesus invade your mind and take up the space that was previously occupied by plague. There is also no place for demonic dogs and devilish mockers where Jesus dwells. Therefore, may those incessantly barking demonic dogs that rattle around in your mind be chased back to the abyss by the Great Hound of Heaven whose bark is that of a roaring lion. And may the mockers be stifled and quieted by the noise of your shouting voice and the tapping and shuffling of your dancing feet. Dance and shout, my friends. Dance and shout with Jesus as He does His resurrection dance that rids you of the plague and chases away foolish mockers and barking dogs. Dance feverishly, pray loudly, praise fervently, love passionately and speak the Word boldly in the direction of any barking, mocking or plaguing and watch those things run away howling. Amen and a thousand more amens.

Verse: Joshua 6:20–21

> When the trumpets sounded, the army shouted, and at the sound of the trumpet, when the men gave a loud shout, the wall collapsed; so everyone charged straight in, and they took the city. They devoted the city to the Lord and destroyed with the sword every living thing in it—men and women, young and old, cattle, sheep and donkeys.

Exercise: Worship

Just as Joshua's victory over Jericho was preceded by shouts and music, so too can we experience God's victory in our lives. Christ already has won the war. We already have reason to celebrate. Take time today to shout and sing because of the victory our God has won. Turn on some music. Dance without overthinking what you're doing. Smile. Laugh. Don't be afraid to enjoy the freedom Jesus has brought you!

March 24

Re-surrendering Me (P)

LORD, PLEASE HELP ME to stay wholeheartedly committed to You. May I never be totally satisfied with the status of our relationship, lest I become complacent and neglectful, taking You for granted. The disciples who walked with you dozed off, fled, and denied knowing you, so who am I to think that I would do any different? Please save me from myself, O God. Please help me to remember that although I want to be like Peter, John, James and Paul, I possess in my DNA the potential to be Judas and not even know that it is happening. O God, may that never ever happen, so please save me from myself and that Iscariot potential in me this very instant. When I pray "Your Kingdom come and Your will be done", may nothing remain unsurrendered to You. Take total possession of me. Take every bit of the real estate of my heart, soul, mind, and strength. You are King, Magistrate, Ruler, and Lord of me and may that always be so. Jesus the Just, Glory to His name and its power in me and over me now and forevermore. Amen and a thousand more amens.

Verse: Romans 12:1

> Therefore, I urge you, brothers and sisters, in view of God's mercy, to offer your bodies as a living sacrifice, holy and pleasing to God—this is your true and proper worship.

Exercise: Fasting

Today, deny yourself through fasting. This may mean no food throughout the day or fasting a meal if possible. Intentionally reflect on where you are in your relationship with Jesus. Have you become complacent? Have you taken Him for granted? Ask Him to open your eyes and to help you turn back to Him today.

March 25

Awareness of Christ (Ex)

I pray today for you to get a revelation about the Resurrection of Jesus that is deeper and more profound than you have ever had before. May you be keenly aware that He is alive. May you sense Him in you, around you, behind you, in front of you, driving with you, eating with you, at school with you, at work with you, and at play with you. Jesus Christ, Son of God, Savior, in you. Amazing. Amen and a thousand more amens.

Verse: Colossians 1:16–17

> For in him all things were created: things in heaven and on earth, visible and invisible, whether thrones or powers or rulers or authorities; all things have been created through him and for him. He is before all things, and in him all things hold together.

Exercise: Meditation and Prayer

Slow down and intentionally notice the little things today. Look for the hand of God at work around you and in you as you pursue Jesus. During your devotional time, pay attention to your surroundings. Listen and watch. If you have a view of nature, look for God's characteristics in the midst of it all. If you are alone in a room, quiet your senses to hear Him. Read the verses again and ask Jesus to open your eyes to Him again. Continue to look for Him today and write down any other ways you see Jesus.

March 26

Healing in Your Mind (Ex)

My prayer for you today is that you would be healed deep in your mind. I am not sure what you need healing for, but I am asking Jesus to touch you. I mean to touch you in a way that you cannot mistake it for the touch of anyone else. May He reach through the years of emotional pain this morning and do what even the most brilliant therapist could not do and that is to create something new in you. This is what He does, my friends. It is His specialty. He is the Creator of new things that did not previously exist. He does not mimic nor does He copy. He specializes in making things brand new. A new hope. A new thought. A new relationship. A new vision. A new marriage. A new dream. A new day. He gave Lazarus' corpse a new heartbeat. He gave a leper new skin. He gave a dirty woman at the well a new reputation. He gave a man a new hand. And now it is you who are next in line. New things to you this day. Amen and a thousand more amens.

Verse: Isaiah 55:10–11

> As the rain and the snow come down from heaven, and do not return to it without watering the earth and making it bud and flourish, so that it yields seed for the sower and bread for the eater, so is my word that goes out from my mouth: It will not return to me empty, but will accomplish what I desire and achieve the purpose for which I sent it.

Exercise: Journaling

The earth produces life when it rains. It cannot help but do so. It is the same when we allow ourselves to be covered in the Word and Presence of God. New life can't help but be formed. Take out your journal or something else to write on. What life does God want to create in you today? What wounds does He want to address? Sometimes these hurts come to mind immediately. Other times we aren't aware of their existence. Ask God to reveal to you if there are any emotional wounds you have that He wants to address. Write these down and process when they were caused, why they are there, and what God says about them. If nothing comes to mind, pray for someone else's wounds. Though, do not rush to this second option. Take time sitting before the Father and let Him speak to you today.

March 27

Thought Life (Ex)

I am praying that Jesus would be Lord of our thoughts today. Jesus, please help us to think cleanly, purely and righteously. May the lusts of the flesh be executed and die a quick death in our minds, before they become reality. And may those nasty thoughts be replaced by your thoughts. Please help us to think about people like You think about them. Meaning that our new thoughts will lead us towards actions that will bless, not how we might use individuals for our own purposes, pleasures or gain. Please deliver us from judging anyone based upon their outward appearance, by giving us a case of blurred vision. Blind us. We are asking to be delivered of that inherent mechanism in our minds that categorizes people because of their physical appearance. Please help us and deliver us from those thoughts that are not like You, the ones that we don't even know that we are thinking. We have thought them so many times that they have become part of us. Deliver us from ourselves. Save us from ourselves. Think Your thoughts through us, Jesus. Give us Your mind. Amen and a thousand more amens.

Verse: Romans 12:2

> Do not conform to the pattern of this world, but be transformed by the renewing of your mind. Then you will be able to test and approve what God's will is--his good, pleasing and perfect will.

Exercise: Scripture Memorization

Read today's prayer out loud and think of any ways this applies to you. Ask the Father to transform your mind so that any ideas that are not of Him would disappear. Commit today's verse to memory. Place a small rock or similar trinket on your person. Any time you see or feel this object, repeat the verse and ask God to make your thoughts like His.

March 28

The Reality of the Cross and Resurrection (Ex)

I am praying that you would be keenly aware of the sacrifice of our Lord Jesus. The body of Christ broken for you and the blood of Christ shed for you. His passion compelled Him to show up and do what needed to be done to save our souls. How do we even begin to say thank you? It sounds so trite, "Thank you Jesus". If you really want to thank Him, you are going to need to die too. May He lead you in His footsteps both today and the days to come. Amen and a thousand more amens.

Verse: Matthew 16:24–25

> Then Jesus said to his disciples, "Whoever wants to be my disciple must deny themselves and take up their cross and follow me. For whoever wants to save their life f will lose it, but whoever loses their life for me will find it."

Exercise: Fasting and Meditation

After reading the day's prayer and passage of Scripture, spend time reading it again. Matthew 16:24–25. Ask the Holy Spirit to make these verses real to you.. Then, choose to either fast for the day or for a meal if possible. Use this time to reflect more on this concept of dying to self and ask Jesus to reveal any ways that you have not been putting Him first.

March 29

Awareness of the enemy's attacks (Ex)

My prayer today is that you would get a sense for what the enemy of your soul is trying to steal from you, and how the power of Jesus will arrest him. The enemy wants to steal your joy, but Jesus will put a smile on your face that is contagious. The enemy wants to pervert your thoughts, but you have the mind of Jesus at work in you and Jesus cannot conceive of anything perverted. The enemy wants to bring darkness to your doorstep, but Jesus is that light shining in darkness that can never be dimmed. The enemy wants to cause you to fail, but Christ in you will always win. The enemy wants to depress you, but Jesus cannot be held down or depressed because He has all the life of God in Him. When that much life is present, it cannot help but dance and praise and yell and scream of eternal life, here, now, today, in your life, on your life, saving your life. Thank you Jesus for saving my life. Yes, you are Lord of my life and Lord of all of me! Amen and a thousand more amens.

Verse: 1 Peter 5:8

> Be alert and of sober mind. Your enemy the devil prowls around like a roaring lion looking for someone to devour.

Exercise: Journaling

What has the enemy been trying to steal from you? Your integrity? Your joy? Your purity? Your authority? How has he been doing this? In what areas have you experienced these pressures? Record the responses you have to these questions as you recognize the strategy of the enemy. Then, submit each of these to Christ, proclaim His victory over them, and think of ideas to counteract these attacks. Bring other believers into the process as well, including any mentors or close friends. Christ has placed you in His body for this mutual support.

March 30

Lies From Your Past (Ex)

I AM PRAYING TODAY that you would be free. Free from past definitions of who you are. Definitions that say that you don't measure up, can't measure up and never will. These definitions have plagued you with the remembrance of past defeats and they suggest that you will most assuredly lose, fail or not measure up in the future. They assure you that it is a done deal, you will fail. Well, I want you to know that it is not a done deal, in fact, it is a new one. It is a deal based on the definition of who Jesus says that you are and how He defines you. He says that you are FREE because He paid a very expensive price. You are indescribably valuable and are now free of what has held you back and formerly defined you incorrectly. May the Holy Spirit reveal this to you anew today. Amen and a thousand more amens.

Verse: Genesis 50:20

> You intended to harm me, but God intended it for good to accomplish what is now being done, the saving of many lives.

Exercise: Journaling and Reading

Read the account of Joseph and his dreams in Genesis 37:1–11. Have you been discouraged by others in a similar way because of who you are or what you believe God has called you to do? Record any events like this from your past and ask the Father to show you any wounds you may have from these. Write down any thoughts or prayers that come to mind and ask Him to show you how He sees you.

March 31

New in His Resurrection (Ex)

Jesus' face was shamed through beatings, spit, a crown of thorns and the kisses of a traitor so that you and I might have shame wiped from our faces. May the shameful things that we have done and the accompanying memories that haunt us be wiped away by the cleansing power of our amazing Lord. "Those who look to Him are radiant, their faces are never covered with shame" (Psalm 34:5). Thank you, Jesus! Amen and a thousand more amens!

Verse: Isaiah 53:4–5

> Surely he took up our pain and bore our suffering, yet we considered him punished by God, stricken by him, and afflicted. But he was pierced for our transgressions, he was crushed for our iniquities; the punishment that brought us peace was on him, and by his wounds we are healed.

Exercise: Reading and Meditation

Take this time to think about Jesus' death: the punishment and the cross. Read one of the accounts in the Gospels and picture the scenes in your mind. Jesus, the Son of God, endured this so you could be free. His death and resurrection defeated all sin: past, present, and future. Yes, we have been called to a holy life, but the price Jesus paid covers all of the sins we will ever commit. Ask the Holy Spirit to help you realize and believe that God treasures you and wants you to run to Him, not hide in shame. Ask to be set free from your sins and the weight they are upon you..

April 1

Loving Others (P)

Jesus Christ, son of God, would you please love people through me today. May I realize that, like You, I exist for the sake of others. Help me to serve them, touch them, hear them and love them well. Please help me to be transparent and life giving as I interact with them and may I stop using them for my own gain as if they were some object created for my pleasure. I really need your help to truly, deeply and wholeheartedly forgive those who have wronged me, as I realize that I cannot walk in the forgiveness that You want to give me unless I have released their offenses towards me. Please eradicate all unforgiving thoughts, actions and words from my being right now and stop me dead in my tracks if I come back to them. May I love others as I love myself and learn Your selflessness. Jesus, please free me from myself so I am free to love and live for You. Amen and a thousand more amens.

Verse: Leviticus 19:18

> Do not seek revenge or bear a grudge against anyone among your people, but love your neighbor as yourself. I am the Lord.

Exercise: Prayer

Are there people in your life that have hurt you, annoyed you, or you simply do not get along with? Take your devotional time to pray for them, to have God's heart for them, to see them as He sees them, and that they would be blessed with an understanding of who God is. We are called to be like our Lord, who forgave the very men who crucified Him and loved the unlovable. However we treat the least of these, shows our love Jesus.

April 2

Hope (Ex)

I am praying today that you will have an undeniable assurance deep in your heart that everything will be alright. It may not look like it right now, but the One who is outside of time will undoubtedly show up, just in the nick of it. And He will show Himself faithful to you this day, very soon. May you be astounded and even a bit confounded as He blesses, covers and provides for you in manners that seem impossible and improbable. May our improbable, faithful, timely, powerful, able and unflappable God prove to you this day (once again) that He is involved, interested and engaged in the events of your life. You have reason to hope. Our God is alive and in His prime. Amen and a thousand more amens.

Verse: Romans 15:13

> May the God of hope fill you with all joy and peace as you trust in him, so that you may overflow with hope by the power of the Holy Spirit.

Exercise: Journaling

List situations, people, and worries that are weighing on your mind today. Remind yourself that God is in control and ask Him to enter each of these situations once again. He will work all things for His glory. Begin today with a renewed expectation for the Holy Spirit to be at work in your life. It may not look how you thought it would, but remind yourself: God is good, He is love, and His ways are higher than yours. Trust Him.

April 3

Renewed Passion for His Kingdom (Ex)

May God ignite a passion in you today that will jerk you out of that complacent place where you have been living. Let a fire be kindled in you like a lightning strike from Heaven, that it might burn away the heaviness that lays upon you like dead wood. Burning away habits, attitudes, sorrows and regrets, to free you for a Kingdom-focused life that you were intended to have. You are to be free today in Jesus name. You are to be full of Kingdom force and focus. A tornado of life, a consuming fire: forces that blow away the demonic and burn the effects of sin into oblivion. Passionate life to you this day, my friends, in the name of life itself, Jesus the Christ. Yeshua. The Risen One. Amen and a thousand more amens.

Verse: Philippians 3:12–14

> Not that I have already obtained all this, or have already arrived at my goal, but I press on to take hold of that for which Christ Jesus took hold of me. Brothers and sisters, I do not consider myself yet to have taken hold of it. But one thing I do: Forgetting what is behind and straining toward what is ahead, I press on toward the goal to win the prize for which God has called me heavenward in Christ Jesus.

Exercise: Memorization and Meditation

Choose a portion of today's passage (or the entirety) to memorize. Our goal is to be united with Christ without the hindrance of sin or the broken world we live in. We have been given Christ already, but will one day experience Him fully. That is the reason we believe and follow Him. Repeat your chosen passage to yourself this week to remind yourself of why you are a Christian, to remind you of Christ in your life. Utilize a small rock or similar token on your person so that every time you feel or see the object you repeat and meditate on your passage.

April 4

Christ Formed in You (Ex)

My prayer today is that Christ would be formed in you. That you would begin to act like Him and confront judgmental and pious religious systems. That you would begin to feel like Him and be moved to tears as you enter the plight of hurting people. That you would begin to walk like He did, being on the side of the street to which lepers had been banished and upon bodies of water and regions where natural men feared to tread. That you would laugh like He did when an overlooked tax-collector like Zachaeus became alive on the inside, giving back 4 times the amount that he had stolen. And may you dance like Jesus did when He rose from the dead and showed up in the devil's own house, with an army of Patriarch's and Saints who had been waiting on Him. He is alive in you. He is being formed in you. Let Him confront and cry and walk and laugh and dance through you this day. Amen and a thousand more amens.

Verse: 1 John 4:17

> This is how love is made complete among us so that we will have confidence on the day of judgment: In this world we are like Jesus.

Exercise: Fast and Prayer

Choose a meal to fast today if possible. Take this time (or a different time set aside if you are physically unable to fast) to ask the Father how much you look like the Son. During this time, you could go on a walk, sit in your car, or do whatever works best for you. In what ways does God want to transform your life, so you can look more like Jesus? In what ways have you been missing the mark? Have you sought your own glory instead of His? Take time today to listen and respond.

April 5

Resurrected Life (Ex)

I am asking God today for your hopes to be resurrected. Your thoughts to be resurrected. Your faith to be resurrected. Your plans to be resurrected. Your health to be resurrected. Your potential to be resurrected. Your visions to be resurrected. Your dreams to be resurrected. Your relationships to be resurrected. Your desire to be resurrected. May the Resurrected One resurrect these things. Amen and a thousand more amens.

Verse: 1 Peter 1:3–4a

> Praise be to the God and Father of our Lord Jesus Christ! In his great mercy he has given us new birth into a living hope through the resurrection of Jesus Christ from the dead, and into an inheritance that can never perish, spoil or fade.

Exercise: Prayer

Just as Christ resurrected so that we too may live again, spend this time praying this prayer over those in your life who are not living in Jesus' resurrection life. These people may not know Jesus yet or have lost sight of His authority and need to be renewed. Read the prayer and passage from 1 Peter over their lives and the specific areas that have been dead.

April 6

Being Aware of our Words and Actions (Ex)

Today I am asking for God to speak the truth to you about your blind spots, so that you will stop offending unknowingly. There are things about you of which you are unaware, that are offensive and don't allow for people to fully appreciate the life of God in you. Be prepared however, for Him to speak such truth through someone who rubs you the wrong way and therein lies your first blind spot. God help us. Deliver us from ourselves. Amen and a thousand more amens.

Verse: 1 Corinthians 9:19

> Though I am free and belong to no one, I have made myself a slave to everyone, to win as many as possible.

Exercise: Silence and Journaling

The Gospel is not about us. It is not about our comfort, our desires, or our reputations. It is about Christ. Since we carry the Gospel, we are called to share the good news with all people, including those who differ from us in their opinions. Take 5 to 10 minutes in silence to listen for God's voice. Have you valued being right over showing love and humility? Have others been hurt because of your opinion? Yes, we should stand for what is right, but we must do so with wisdom and grace so that we do not bring any slander to the name of Christ. Listen and record your thoughts from this time.

April 7

Strength (Ex)

I am praying that strength would come your way, and that it would affect your mind, body and spirit. Yes, strength to every part of you in the name of Jesus. His strength in you, to you, through you. Receive His strength that you will need for today. Amen and a thousand more amens.

Verse: Psalm 121:1–2

> I lift up my eyes to the mountains— where does my help come from? My help comes from the Lord, the Maker of heaven and earth.

Exercise: Worship

Take 10 to 15 minutes to focus on the Father. Turn on worship music or have your Bible in front of you. Praise Him for His strength and His sovereignty. We are saved because of what He did, not because of anything we have done.. Remind yourself of this and worship Christ for His great strength. Through this, you will be reminded that you are sustained by the infinite strength of the Most High.

April 8

Desires of Your Heart (Ex)

I am asking God to give you the desires of your heart today. The ones that line up with His. May yours and His be the same. May He be your greatest desire today and may He show you the good things He has for you. Amen and a thousand more amens.

Verse: Psalm 37:3–4

> Trust in the Lord and do good; dwell in the land and enjoy safe pasture. Take delight in the Lord, and he will give you the desires of your heart.

Exercise: Prayer and Journaling

God created us to be happy and fulfilled, yet we cannot be so apart from Him. Ask God about His desires for your life. These desires may lead to temporary discomfort, discipline, or pain; but it is often in the difficult seasons that you will get a better understanding of the Father and His love. Pray and listen. Write down what you believe His desires for you are and talk to a friend or mentor about them.

April 9

Resurrection Power (Ex)

I AM ASKING GOD to call those things that have died in you back to life in honor of Jesus' Resurrection. May the hopes, dreams, and relationships that have died in you be brought back to life in miraculous fashion. I know that you thought they were dead, but rebirths and resurrections are His specialties. So, when that thing that was once dead begins to twitch with life, set another place at the table. Amen and a thousand more amens.

Verse: John 11:41–43

> So they took away the stone. Then Jesus looked up and said, "Father, I thank you that you have heard me. I knew that you always hear me, but I said this for the benefit of the people standing here, that they may believe that you sent me." When he had said this, Jesus called in a loud voice, "Lazarus, come out!"

Exercise: Prayer

What were the first things that came to mind after reading today's prayer? Pray over these specifically, proclaiming the life of Christ over and in them. Look for them to start breathing again today. Christ is at work, so join in His resurrection power. Take 10 to 15 minutes to pray over the people and situations in your life that you desire to see come back to life.

April 10

Responding to Resurrection (Ex)

Be ready to respond to those hopes, dreams, and relationships that have come back to life and are now sitting with you at your table. Take the grave clothes off. Don't just sit there and act shocked by the whole situation, move into the newness that you prayed for. Now that there is life, you must respond with life. Speak life, think life, feed life, and do not touch those stinky grave clothes again by the power of the Holy Spirit. May you throw them away, walk in the new life, and never look back. Amen and a thousand more amens.

Verse: John 11:44

> The dead man came out, his hands and feet wrapped with strips of linen, and a cloth around his face. Jesus said to them, "Take off the grave clothes and let him go."

Exercise: Prayer and Journaling

In response to yesterday's prayers for resurrection, what is God calling you to do to walk in the new life? Ask Him to guide you and write down ways you can encourage new life both within yourself and in the lives of others. Take action today by taking practical steps and reaching out to others.

April 11

God's Purpose (P)

Today, I will be neither persuaded nor distracted from Your exact purpose for my life. Father, remind me that my life is not about the future, but today. Holy Spirit, live in me and through me right this instant. Make me more like You and teach me to be obedient with what you have given me. I will not rush but remain in You. Amen and a thousand more amens.

Verse: Micah 6:8

> He has shown you, O mortal, what is good. And what does the Lord require of you? To act justly and to love mercy and to walk humbly with your God.

Exercise: Evangelism, Service, Worship

Don't get distracted by a vague, grand calling that takes away your peace and focus. Instead, live intentionally today. Spend time in worship. Tell someone about Jesus. Stop and smell the roses. Through this intentional living, you will bring God's Kingdom to your world.

April 12

The Father Cares (Ex)

May you know that God is focused upon you today. He is interested and He cares. He cares relentlessly and desperately. You are worth it. And as He hones in on you, may the shame and the pain and the hurtful baggage of the past be burned away and vaporized. . .GONE. His gaze is penetrating, surgical and healing. Once again, on this day, you will be made new by the Maker of New Things. I rejoice with you. . .the new you. Amen and a thousand more amens.

Verse: Psalm 25:4–7

> Show me your ways, Lord, teach me your paths. Guide me in your truth and teach me, for you are God my Savior, and my hope is in you all day long. Remember, Lord, your great mercy and love, for they are from of old. Do not remember the sins of my youth and my rebellious ways; according to your love remember me, for you, Lord, are good.

Exercise: Meditation

After reading today's prayer, read Psalm 25 slowly. Meditate on the fact that God wants to take your burdens and make you new in Him. As we look more like Christ, we bring glory to God and experience the fulfillment that is only found in Him. Since we are made righteous because of the faithfulness of Jesus, we experience the love and faithfulness of God (v.10). Read the Psalm several times and focus in on a specific verse or passage that you believe God wants to speak to you through today.

April 13

Joy (P)

God, would You fill my soul with Your joy today, that I may see You more and rejoice in You. And then, may that joy be contagious and get all over those with whom I live life. Use me to bring Your joy to the world around me for Your glory. Amen and a thousand more amens.

Verse: Psalm 16:11

> You make known to me the path of life; you will fill me with joy in your presence, with eternal pleasures at your right hand.

Exercise: Memorization and Meditation

Commit today's Scripture verse to memory. Read the entirety of Psalm 16 three times, taking a minute between each reading to listen for God's voice through His Word. Following your devotional time, place a small rock or similar object on your person (in a pocket or a place where you will see or feel it often). Every time you see or feel the object, repeat Psalm 16:11 in your mind. Ask God what He wants to show you through it, or how He wants to bring that heavenly joy to others through you today.

April 14

Delivered in Your Thought Life (Ex)

Today I am praying for the renewal of your mind. May the things that haunt and taunt you be dealt with by Him who is able to cast sin as far as the east is from the west. May Jesus hunt down and terminate the haunter and mocker of your soul. May He heal and renew that which has been broken and stolen and make his abode in that place that was formerly inhabited by fear and dread. Come Lord Jesus, come and live in our minds so Your healing can flow through us. Think your thoughts through us this day. Amen and a thousand more amens.

Verse: Isaiah 26:3

> You will keep in perfect peace those whose minds are steadfast, because they trust in you.

Exercise: Journaling

What do you fear? What worries you? What causes knots to form in your stomach? Write these down. Ask Jesus what He says about these things. He cares for our concerns, but He also casts out anxiety and fear. Pray over each area, surrender them to Jesus again, and receive His peace. Remember, this may be a process and you may not feel immediate relief, but God is with you and working in your heart. He is faithful. Trust in Him.

April 15

The Heavenly Song (Ex)

May you hear the melody of Jesus' deliverance song all day today. May its music bring peace to your storm and joy to your troubled soul. May the very voice of your God singing over you heal every ailment in your being and cause you to sing too. Yes, sing the song of deliverance today, my friends. Sing in unison with your Maker. He has overcome and you are redeemed. Amen and a thousand more amens.

Verse: Psalm 32:7

> You are my hiding place; you will protect me from trouble and surround me with songs of deliverance.

Exercise: Worship

Celebrate with the Father, Son, and Holy Spirit today. Celebrate with the heavenly hosts that continually pour out their praises to the Most High. Celebrate the new life you have received. Celebrate, for He is worthy! Turn on music, read a Psalm, write a poem. Do whatever necessary to glorify His name and join in the thanksgiving that is due to His name.

April 16

Prayer for the Government (P)

I BRING MY NATION before you, God. I pray that Your Kingdom would come and Your will would be done in my country as it is in Heaven. I pray that Your peace and order would prevail and that the plans of the enemy would be thwarted at every turn. I pray that the fire of God would burn away the rubbish that has collected in all facets of our culture; yet at the same time, warming all who are cold and forgotten, shamed and in fear. Yes, visit this land O Lord of Heaven and Earth, guiding our leaders so they will lead us in your ways. In the name of Jesus the Christ. Amen and a thousand more amens.

Verse: 1 Timothy 2:1–4

> I urge, then, first of all, that petitions, prayers, intercession and thanksgiving be made for all people— for kings and all those in authority, that we may live peaceful and quiet lives in all godliness and holiness. This is good, and pleases God our Savior, who wants all people to be saved and to come to a knowledge of the truth.

Exercise: Prayer

Today, pray for those that are in leadership positions in your nation. Pray for their health, for wisdom, and a heart to submit to God. Regardless of their views, we have been called to pray for those in authority, even when we do not agree with everything they do. In this time, pray specific prayers. Name individuals, certain issues, or areas in the nation that need a touch from on high. This week, continue this practice by choosing a small rock or similar trinket that you can keep on your person. Every time you feel or see the object, pray for the nation again.

April 17

God's Direction (Ex)

In these uncertain and fearful times, I am asking for God to bring clarity, specificity and His best into your day. Yes, you can know for sure, because He does. He is the Ancient of Days. He has seen many of them and has an opinion as to how yours could be lived best. So, may you know God's best today in all areas of your existence. Amen and a thousand more amens.

Verse: Psalm 90:2

> Before the mountains were born or you brought forth the whole world, from everlasting to everlasting, you are God.

Exercise: Journaling

Think about your day: the responsibilities, challenges, interactions, etc. With a pen and paper ready, listen for God's direction. How does He want you to approach each event? Is there someone He wants you to encourage today? Is there an area or responsibility you have not given to Him? Have you placed anything above God today? Listen and write.

April 18

Freedom (Ex)

I AM PRAYING THIS morning for you to be free. Free from all heaviness. May there be nothing holding you back. Yes, in the name of Jesus, may you fly today. May your spirit, mind and body get above it all and soar. You were made to be free, so today may you do what you were made for. Freedom to you. Life to you. Altitude to you. Amen and a thousand more amens.

Verse: Isaiah 40:30–31

> Even youths grow tired and weary, and young men stumble and fall; but those who hope in the LORD will renew their strength. They will soar on wings like eagles; they will run and not grow weary, they will walk and not be faint.

Exercise: Prayer

Pray today's prayer over someone in your life whom you know is going through a difficult season. Use the prayer as a template, but expand on the concepts within. Pray against the things that bring heaviness. Pray for a greater understanding of Christ. Pray for renewed hope. Intercede and rejoice for God's work in the individual's life.

April 19

Kindled Fire (Ex)

I pray a fire be kindled in your heart. A consuming fire. One that warms the cold and melts the frozen. A fire that instills a passion to live and love without bounds. A boundless living and loving that incites others to follow, yes a fire that kindles fire. Fire in you, on you and around you today in the name of the one who gives God's fire: Jesus. Amen and a thousand more amens.

Verse: Matthew 3:11

> I baptize you with water for repentance. But after me comes one who is more powerful than I, whose sandals I am not worthy to carry. He will baptize you with the Holy Spirit and fire.

Exercise: Meditation

If possible, spend your devotional time outside. Go on a walk or sit on the porch. Take this time to reset from the busyness or boredom of life (depending on the season you are in). After a few minutes, ask Jesus to fill you with His fire and passion. Remain in that place for 5 to 10 minutes, meditating on His fire. Regardless of whether you feel it or not, He has given you all you need. Scripture tells us that we receive when we ask. You have asked, so you have received. Continue to pursue this intimate time with Christ and spread His fire to all those you come in contact with.

April 20

God Holding You (Ex)

May you sense the hand of God holding you today. Holding you tight enough to be secure, yet loose enough to move. Yes, to live and move and be. To live and move and be full of Jesus. . .not religion. Religion is tight and suffocates and kills. God holding you in Jesus is living and breathing. . .real and total life; and then more life upon that life. . .more life than any one body can contain. So much life that it will take an eternity and then some to live it. There's an infinite amount of life in Jesus. Yes, enough to go around and then some. God, please hold us in Jesus today, all day and every day. Amen and a thousand more amens.

Verse: John 10:28

> I give them eternal life, and they shall never perish; no one will snatch them out of my hand.

Exercise: Meditation and Reading

Read John 10:1–30. Realize that you are one of the sheep that Christ talks about. Other things will come and try to steal you away, but Jesus holds you and died so you may have His life. Read this passage and meditate on the words of the One who keeps you.

April 21

Going on the Offensive (Ex)

Holy Spirit, use me today to advance your Kingdom. I cannot tolerate the darkness around me. Please guide me to shine your light on the darkness today. I will not be apathetic. I will not cower. I will step forward with You and for Your glory. Your Kingdom come and Your will be done. Amen and a thousand more amens.

Verse: Romans 13:12

> The night is nearly over; the day is almost here. So let us put aside the deeds of darkness and put on the armor of light.

Exercise: Service and Prayer

Be bold today. Take your devotional out your doors into the world. If you feel assaulted by the enemy of your soul, strike back with a vengeance. Do something intentional for the Kingdom of Heaven. I mean, get a vision from God and do something that will advance the cause of Jesus. Display His love, put others before yourself, care for the forsaken, pray for the miraculous. Record your experiences from today

April 22

Peace (Ex)

HEAVEN'S PEACE TO YOU. May a palpable peace that overshadows the storm descend upon you. May the storm be chased by Peace, leaving a quiet healing balm in its wake. Yes, healing and comfort to you who are weary. Shalom of Heaven be with you, in the name of the Prince of Shalom, Jesus. Amen and a thousand more amens.

Verse: 2 Thessalonians 3:16

> Now may the Lord of peace himself give you peace at all times and in every way. The Lord be with all of you.

Exercise: Prayer

Pray today's prayer over your life. Proclaim the verse over your mind and your surroundings. Expand on the concepts and still yourself to simply be with the Father. Then pray this over 2 to 3 other people in your life who need the Prince of Peace today.

April 23

Slaying Giants (Ex)

May the same Spirit that covered David as he slew Goliath cover you this day. Giants will fall. Those foul, intimidating and evil forces that have sought to beat you down will be felled today as you sling God's Word at them. Sling the Word. Sling prayer. Sling worship of King Jesus and watch them fall, dust rising in their wake. You are a champion in Christ Jesus and you were made for this day. Step up and sling away my friends. . .sling away. . .giants will go down by your hand. Your hand in God's hand. Amen and a thousand more amens.

Verse: 1 Samuel 17:45–46

> David said to the Philistine, "You come against me with sword and spear and javelin, but I come against you in the name of the Lord Almighty, the God of the armies of Israel, whom you have defied. This day the Lord will deliver you into my hands, and I'll strike you down and cut off your head."

Exercise: Fasting and Journaling

Fast either a meal or food for the entirety of today if possible. During these set aside times, write down the giants in your life or in the lives of those around you. Bring them to the Father and pray against them with the same mindset David displays: with no other expected outcome but victory. Pray David's prayer over those things and thank God for delivering you from the attacks of the enemy.

April 24

Covered by God (P)

Lord, please cover me today. I know that You go before me, behind me, beside me, above me, and below me. Your presence surrounds me. Protect me today and use me to bring Your peace into the world. I am never alone. Thank you for being with me. Amen and a thousand more amens.

Verse: Isaiah 58:8

> Then your light will break forth like the dawn, and your healing will quickly appear; then your righteousness will go before you, and the glory of the Lord will be your rear guard.

Exercise: Meditation

Read the entirety of Isaiah 58. The prophet is discussing what true fasting and worship looks like to God. When we remain in His will, we remain in His covering. Read the chapter and then ask God to reveal His will to you today. Ask Him to open your eyes to His presence. Intentionally seek Him today and be aware of His leading.

April 25

Health (Ex)

Today I am praying for your health. May you be healthy in your body, your mind and your spirit. May you be blessed in all of who you are. Health to you as you think. Health to you as you drive and as you walk. Health to you as you sit and as you move. Health to your soul. May you laugh today. Yes, may you burst out with peals of laughter that strike all around you and electrify your surroundings with joy unspeakable. May the joy of Heaven descend upon you and rest there, in the name of Jesus our living and joyful Lord. Amen and a thousand more amens.

Verse: 3 John 1:2

> Dear friend, I pray that you may enjoy good health and that all may go well with you, even as your soul is getting along well.

Exercise: Prayer

Receive this prayer over your life. As you pray, touch or think of any parts of your body that need healing. Place your hand on your head if your thoughts need God's touch. Then, pray the same over one or two people that need God's healing today in their bodies or spirits. Proclaim this prayer over those that God brings to mind.

April 26

Discernment (P)

Lord Jesus, guide me in the light today. I want to know your will in the situations in which I find myself, both big and small. May Your wisdom be in me and all around me. I ask that Your will would be brutally obvious and that I have peace about moving in any direction because You are with me. I receive Your peace, discernment, and strength so I may reflect, love, and glorify Your name. Amen and a thousand more amens.

Verse: Psalm 32:8

> I will instruct you and teach you in the way you should go; I will counsel you with my loving eye on you.

Exercise: Memorization and Meditation

After praying today's prayer and reading the Scripture, commit Psalm 32:8 to memory. Read it several times, slowly. What does it actually mean? How does God see you? Why does God want to guide you? Afterwards, take a small rock or similar item that you can keep on your person throughout the day. Every time you touch or see the object, repeat this verse and ask God to reveal more of Himself to you.

April 27

Protection (Ex)

I AM PRAYING THAT you would be protected today. That you and your people will sense that the Great Shepherd is tending you and keeping the enemy at bay. And not only will he keep the enemy at bay, but your Shepherd will beat the fire out of him if he dares come close. Safety to you. Rest to you. You are loved and watched over. Amen and a thousand more amens.

Verse: John 10:14–15

> I am the good shepherd; I know my sheep and my sheep know me— just as the Father knows me and I know the Father—and I lay down my life for the sheep.

Exercise: Prayer

Pray today's prayer over your schedule, your travel, and your mind. Then, pray for the Lord's protection and guidance over your people: your spouse, children, siblings, parents, friends, coworkers, etc. Proclaim that each and every one of them is covered by the Most High. The enemy cannot have any influence in their lives today because of the Good Shepherd who keeps watch.

April 28

God's Kingdom Come (Ex)

May God's Kingdom come and His will be done in you, on you, about you and through you today. Let this not be just some flippant prayer, but a reality. You will be involved in the Kingdom of God happening on this planet, in a specific geographic location and for a strategic purpose. You, your life and your very existence matter, not only to the people in your world, but to the God who made the entire universe. May His Kingdom be expanded through you as He displays His love and power in your life. Amen and a thousand more amens.

Verse: Matthew 6:9–13

> This, then, is how you should pray: "'Our Father in heaven, hallowed be your name, your kingdom come, your will be done, on earth as it is in heaven. Give us today our daily bread. And forgive us our debts, as we also have forgiven our debtors. And lead us not into temptation, but deliver us from the evil one."

Exercise: Prayer and Meditation

I do not know your past interaction with the Lord's Prayer, whether you have prayed it every day or have never heard it before, but it is Christ's instruction for coming before the Father. As such, we should pay attention. Read and pray this prayer slowly, thinking about each sentence, each word. What did Jesus mean in each section? How should we approach God? How does He interact with us? Answer each of these questions, but take your time.

April 29

A Blessing (Ex)

I am praying today that you would be blessed. I mean that you would know that you have been touched and winked at by the Creator of Heaven and Earth. That you would be blown away by the fact that God would do something so amazing and powerful for you. Be ready. Be poised. And when your blessing comes (and it will come), just know that you have been noticed, picked out and focused upon by your Maker. Yes, the Supreme Creator of ALL that is GOOD, singled you out and moved towards you this day. May you receive all that He has for you today as you submit your ways to Him. Amen and a thousand more amens.

Verse: Ephesians 1:3

> Praise be to the God and Father of our Lord Jesus Christ, who has blessed us in the heavenly realms with every spiritual blessing in Christ.

Exercise: Prayer

Know today that you are chosen. You are blessed. You are seen. You are loved by the Most High with a perfect love. A love that goes beyond reason and any amount of love that we experience on this earth. Allow today's prayer to remind you of this, as well as what God wants to do for you today. He shows His love when we don't deserve it in amazing ways. You don't have to be perfect for Him to smile at you. Rest in His delight for you once again. He loves you.

April 30

A Word From God (Ex)

In the middle of the noise and chaos of our clanging culture, I am asking that God sends you a real and substantive Word. May it be direct, peaceful and life-giving. This will set it apart from the sensual, base and consumeristic noise that permeates so much of the world and constantly vies for your attention. May it bring real hope and real life to you and a real Word to you. Listen intently my friends as your Word may have already left the lips of God and been spoken over your life. May it empower you to know Christ and see His Kingdom come today. Amen and a thousand more amens.

Verse: Colossians 1:27

> To them God has chosen to make known among the Gentiles the glorious riches of this mystery, which is Christ in you, the hope of glory.

Exercise: Journaling and Prayer

With a pen and paper in hand, sit with God and listen for His voice. Remember that His Words will not contradict Scripture, will lead to His glory, and will ultimately build up and encourage. Write down what you believe you hear God saying. Share with a respected friend or mentor.

May 1

Knowing God's Love (Ex)

May you have no doubts about God's love for you. His is a large love. May it fill every square inch of you. His is a hopeful love. May it allow you to see the light in a dark time. His is a curious love. May it drive you to live and love in places about which you thought you would only dream. His is a deep love. May it carry you through times that you thought would kill you. His is a funny love. May it breathe into you a laughter so roarous and soul cleansing that you sleep with a smile on your face. His is an absurd love. May the absurdity of it drive you to your knees and spawn in you a life of living, loving absurdity as well. I pray these things In the name of our large, living, loving, hopeful, funny and absurd savior, Jesus. Amen and a thousand more amens.

Verse: Ephesians 3:14–19

> For this reason I kneel before the Father, from whom every family in heaven and on earth derives its name. I pray that out of his glorious riches he may strengthen you with power through his Spirit in your inner being, so that Christ may dwell in your hearts through faith. And I pray that you, being rooted and established in love, may have power, together with all the Lord's holy people, to grasp how wide and long and high and deep is the love of Christ, and to know this love that surpasses knowledge—that you may be filled to the measure of all the fullness of God.

Exercise: Meditation and Worship

Today's passage of Scripture is the Apostle Paul's prayer for the church in Ephesus. In the same way he encouraged the believers of that city, may you be encouraged today, Read this prayer and Scripture three times through, pausing between each reading. Go slow and ask God what each portion means and that you would "have power, together with all the Lord's holy people, to grasp how wide and long and high and deep is the love of Christ, and to know this love that surpasses knowledge." After this, take time throughout your day to thank and worship Jesus for this amazing love.

May 2

Temptation (P)

May the fires of lust and desire that burn in me be extinguished. May their ravaging effects be averted as You show me the darkness and pain that their fulfillment would bring. May any and every appetite for people and things and power be satisfied in Jesus and Him alone. May the evil hold of the flesh be crucified and entombed, never to be resurrected. May freedom be my cry. Free to be fully alive in Christ. Jesus, be Lord of my life. Make my lusts bow to You and then slay them. Amen and a thousand more amens.

Verse: 1 Corinthians 10:13

> No temptation has overtaken you except what is common to mankind. And God is faithful; he will not let you be tempted beyond what you can bear. But when you are tempted, he will also provide a way out so that you can endure it.

Exercise: Journaling

After reading today's prayer, what did you think about? Did a specific weakness or situation come to your mind? Did several? Write these down and talk about them with the Father. How long have these been in your life? Do you know why? Is there a wound from your past that you are trying to cope with? Talk about these questions with Jesus and allow Him to speak into the hurt and the temptations. Write down any ideas or words you receive.

May 3

Christ's Redemption (Ex)

Be free from fear, right now, in the name of Jesus. Be free from shame, in the name of the one who died because of it. Be free from the regular beatings that you inflict upon yourself because of stupid decisions; He died for those too. He redeems stupidity, shame, regret, pain, fear, and all other things that seek to keep you down. Let Him hide you, heal you and hold you. Jesus is good and big and able to deal with all that you have been trying to handle yourself. May He show you how able He is today. Amen and a thousand more amens.

Verse: Psalm 103:2–5

> Praise the Lord, my soul, and forget not all his benefits— who forgives all your sins and heals all your diseases, who redeems your life from the pit and crowns you with love and compassion, who satisfies your desires with good things so that your youth is renewed like the eagle's.

Exercise: Meditation and Silence

It is easy to focus on the wrong, both in the world and in ourselves. But Christ offers newness, life, and restoration. If you have said yes to Him, those old things are not you anymore. Spend 5 to 10 minutes after reading today's prayer, so the Holy Spirit can remind you that you are a beloved child of the Most High. You don't need to run or clean yourself up first. Breathe in. Breathe out. Be with your Father.

May 4

Being with Jesus (Ex)

May Jesus Christ, the face of Grace, look straight into yours today. May you know that He is not mad at you. May you know that He wants you close. May you sense that your shame is not from Him and that you have a place at His table. Yes, you belong there. He is also not worried about how you are going to turn out. He has the utmost confidence in His ability to keep you and finish His purpose in you. He has no doubt that you will do mighty things for the cause of the Kingdom, but that's not why He loves you. He loves you because He does. He just does. That's Grace. You have been picked out, selected, set apart, focused upon. Why? Just because. May the "just because" of His Grace move you to be overwhelmed by His presence and then look with Grace upon others.

Verse: Acts 4:13

> When they saw the courage of Peter and John and realized that they were unschooled, ordinary men, they were astonished and they took note that these men had been with Jesus.

Exercise: Meditation

Peter and John stood before the Jewish rulers and boldly defended the message of Christ. They did this not out of personal strength or wisdom, but through their relationship with the One they talked about. Since they knew Jesus, they knew who they were in God and could stand with certainty. The Holy Spirit seeks to give you that same certainty: that you would know who you are because of Christ and that you would live boldly because of it. Read today's prayer several times. Have you felt unworthy? Have you felt shame? Let Christ take these away, along with any accompanying sin in your life. After this time, take a small rock or similar object that you can keep on your person. Every time you see or feel that item today, remind yourself that you are in Christ and that He is with you. Tell Jesus that you love Him and pause to listen for His voice.

May 5

God is With You (Ex)

I AM PRAYING FOR God to give you a very tangible sign that He cares about your current struggle. You are not alone. Whether physical or emotional, I am believing at this moment that you will know this day that He is on it and has not forgotten you. Hold on, my friend. Latch on with your faith and don't let go. In the next several days, be looking for God to encourage and affirm you in both little and great ways. May your trust in Him increase even when the physical circumstances are slow to change. He is the Faithful One, and He will never leave you. Amen and a thousand more amens.

Verse: Psalm 27:13–14

> I remain confident of this: I will see the goodness of the Lord in the land of the living.
> Wait for the Lord; be strong and take heart and wait for the Lord.

Exercise: Journaling

Write out your own prayer to Jesus. If you have been experiencing difficulty and stress lately, address them. If you have not had these, pray for another person in your life who needs today's prayer. In your written prayer, declare that God is faithful. Remind yourself of who the Father is; that He is all-powerful, all-good, and all-knowing. What has He brought you through in the past? What has Christ done both in His earthly ministry and through your life? How has the Holy Spirit encouraged and empowered you before? After answering these questions, compare the difficulties you are facing with the God you just described. Your struggles are real, but so is He.

May 6

Past Hurts (Ex)

I am praying today for hearts that have been hurt. May Jesus heal your heart. May He heal those deep wounds that continue to cause you much pain. Many of the wounds even have faces tied to them. Faces that represent loss, fear, regret, and doubt. If you continue to focus upon those faces, deep pains will persist, weighing on you and taking up residence in your mind. Stop this! Now!! Ask Jesus to take over the real-estate of your mind. Yes, He has saved your heart, but you have not allowed Him to live in your mind. Think about Him. Pray to Him. Read His Word. Speak His Word. Listen to His Word and before long, you will see that the faces have been evicted and hold no power. Jesus is now Lord of all that you are. O Jesus Christ, Lord of all that we are, please exercise your authority. Amen and a thousand more amens.

Verse: Psalm 147:3–5

> He heals the brokenhearted and binds up their wounds. He determines the number of the stars and calls them each by name. Great is our Lord and mighty in power; his understanding has no limit.

Exercise: Worship

Jesus gives His presence and we receive it. Be an active member of this divine romance. Instead of focusing on the hurt or those that caused the scars on your heart, look to the one who has scars Himself. Get caught up in His delight and presence. He sees your hurts and brings about redemption and healing. Join Him in the process. Take 10 to 15 minutes today to focus on Christ. To praise His name. To sit quietly with Him. To read the Word with Him. To enjoy nature with Him. Whatever you do during this time, live in the healing that is Jesus. Give Him the space that the enemy has tried to take through your hurts. Jesus will meet you in the middle of it.

May 7

Peace (Ex)

Today I am praying that those things in your life that are consistently inconsistent and causing you much anxiety and confusion be calmed by the One who is neither anxious nor confused. May the unchangeable God, the Sustainer of all that is good and right and peaceful, overwhelm you with shalom today and then overwhelm you again. Amen and a thousand more amens.

Verse: Psalm 139:16–18

> Your eyes saw my unformed body; all the days ordained for me were written in your book before one of them came to be. How precious to me are your thoughts, oh God! How vast is the sum of them! Were I to count them, they would outnumber the grains of sand—when I awake, I am still with you.

Exercise: Reading

Read the entirety of Psalm 139. Speak this prayer of David over your life and the things that have caused you worry and stress. He has already ordered your days. Nothing in your life will surprise God. Pray this Psalm and sit before God as He speaks its truths to you.

May 8

Peace With Yourself (Ex)

I am praying for healing today. Healing between you and you. Yes, may you be restored to yourself. The alive, happy and fully alive you. The you before the stupid things. The you before the pain. The you before your innocence was taken, or given away. You have hidden and winced in the shame of these things far too long and today is the day that you lift up your head! Shame be gone in Jesus' name. Look up. Lift up your head and see Jesus reaching for you. He is smiling. He is laughing even. He is happy today to extend grace to you and make you new. Stop trying to pay for it by beating yourself. You and every other descendant of Adam deserve to be punished, but He dealt with it and He reaches to restore. He has a restoring reach and it is long. You have been reached for. Unashamedly so. Be healed in Jesus' name and be free to share that healing with your world. Amen and a thousand more amens.

Verse: Colossians 3:15

> Let the peace of Christ rule in your hearts, since as members of one body you were called to peace. And be thankful.

Exercise: Meditation

If available, find a mirror. Look in your own eyes for twenty seconds. What do you think of the person looking back at you? Is it difficult to keep eye contact? Do you see past mistakes? Jesus came so we may have peace, even within ourselves. As He makes us whole we also display His character and power in the world around us. So, if you are not at peace with yourself today, ask yourself why? What words would you use to describe yourself if you were brutally honest? Allow the Holy Spirit to show you which of these opinions are right and which are wrong. Sit in silence with a pen and paper and record what you hear.

May 9

Focusing on the Good News (Ex)

My prayer is that you would not listen to the bad news today, for it is not the real news. The real news is that God is in control. "His Kingdom come" means just that. Yes, there is a very real hope that is for another day, but Jesus is Lord of today as well. In fact, He is Lord all day, every day. That news will never change and every other piece of news must be weighed against it. And when weighed against it, it has no weight. Jesus is our true substance and weight and that substance and weight is our faith that is not void. Our faith is in Him and His Kingdom. Now. Today. Go and live on behalf of your very now, very real, very much alive King Jesus. He is Hope, He is Light, He is Weight, He is Life. Amen and a thousand more amens.

Verse: Psalm 86:11

> Teach me your way, LORD, that I may rely on your faithfulness; give me an undivided heart, that I may fear your name.

Exercise: Bible Reading

Spend time in the Bible today. If you have a current reading plan or book you are studying, read in those for 10 to 15 minutes. If you do not have a passage of Scripture that you are going through, read Psalm 86. Get the Good News inside of you. God is good and He saves. We have no need to fear. There is a difference between fear and wisdom. Wisdom is awareness of one's surroundings and living thoughtfully, not brashly. Fear is the same, but tainted by worry and stress in such a way that one becomes paralyzed, no longer living the abundant life God has freely given.

May 10

The Light of Christ (Ex)

I am praying for the light of Jesus to shine in your dark places. May you be able to see in order to walk again. May the darkness over you from fear be dispelled. May intimidation be itself intimidated. May sin, sickness, and the dark plans of the enemy be exposed this day, so that you might make choices that are good and right and prosperous. May you do the same to everyone you come into contact with: dispel darkness, drive out fear, expose the plans of the enemy. Light to you. Hope to you. Jesus to you. Amen and a thousand more amens.

Verse: John 1:4–5

> In him was life, and that life was the light of all mankind. The light shines in the darkness, and the darkness has not overcome it.

Exercise: Evangelism

Jesus is the light of all mankind. Share that light throughout today. During this devotional time, write down what you believe the Gospel to be. How would you explain what God has done through Jesus? If possible, talk about this with another believer or mentor. Also, share this with someone today. This could be a stranger in a store or a friend who does not know the Light yet. Record any main points from your discussions about the Gospel.

May 11

Not About You (Ex)

My prayer today is that you would realize that your life is not about you. As a servant of Jesus, you are at His behest. He is Master, Lord, Savior, and King. You exist to do His bidding. He is about spending His life on others, so we should be as well. Our marching orders on this day come from Him and I can guarantee that they will be focused upon giving in some form or fashion. So give! Don't just stand there. Give something to somebody. Don't just sit there. Pray for somebody. In Jesus' name, come fully alive and exist for the sake of others. Amen and a thousand more amens.

Verse: Matthew 20:25–28

> Jesus called them together and said, "You know that the rulers of the Gentiles lord it over them, and their high officials exercise authority over them. Not so with you. Instead, whoever wants to become great among you must be your servant, and whoever wants to be first must be your slave— just as the Son of Man did not come to be served, but to serve, and to give his life as a ransom for many."

Exercise: Prayer and Service

Christianity is not about self. It is not about comfort. It is not about personal gain. It is about Christ and showing Christ to the world. Read Jesus' command from Matthew 20. Are you aware of the needs of others? Do you care about them? Spend 10 to 15 minutes praying for two people: First, a family member or friend that is in need. Second, a person that you do not get along with. We have been called to love all as Christ loved all. While in prayer, ask God if there is anything that you can do for either or both of these individualsfor whom you prayed today.

May 12

Whole Relationships (P)

I am praying that dead and ailing relationships might live today, in Jesus' name. That marriages would re-ignite with the life of God. That the hearts of fathers would be turned back towards their sons, causing them to speak blessing, peace and life over them. And may mothers and daughters be knit together in a love that is incomparable in this life. May families be drawn towards a unity in Christ that is contagious and viral, spreading to neighbors and neighborhoods, cities and states. Jesus, please light the fire of love in us. A consuming fire. A worship filled fire. A fire that burns away the selfishness that clings to us. O fire of God, burn us, cleanse us, engulf us, inflame us. Use us as kindling for a fire that will cause those around us to come and see what is burning. May they see your fire of love consuming us. Amen and a thousand more amens.

Verse: John 13:34–35

> A new command I give you: Love one another. As I have loved you, so you must love one another. By this everyone will know that you are my disciples, if you love one another.

Exercise: Prayer

Christ taught that love is the defining factor of Christian relationships. Intercede for your family today that they may reflect this love. If there are members who do not know Jesus, pray that they would be drawn by the love those who are believers show to one another. After praying for your family, pray for your community. Lift up fathers and mothers, spouses, children, and family units as a whole, so that they may experience the wholeness that comes from the unity in the Spirit. Pray for the Holy Spirit to revive dead and broken relationships through the love of Christ.

May 13

A Fire in Your Heart (Ex)

I am praying for a fire to be ignited in your heart. A passion from Heaven, A compulsion that will drive you towards seeking Jesus like never before. Spontaneous and unsolicited prayer. Random and unplanned acts of kindness and love. Words coming out of your mouth that are not yours. And an anger towards darkness that moves you to action. His Kingdom coming and His will being done in you today is your sustaining creed. May it be so in each of your lives, my friends. Fire of Heaven descends upon you and consumes you now. Be consumed today by the Holy Spirit. Amen and a thousand more amens.

Verse: 1 Kings 18:36–39

> At the time of sacrifice, the prophet Elijah stepped forward and prayed: "Lord, the God of Abraham, Isaac and Israel, let it be known today that you are God in Israel and that I am your servant and have done all these things at your command. Answer me, Lord, answer me, so these people will know that you, Lord, are God, and that you are turning their hearts back again." Then the fire of the Lord fell and burned up the sacrifice, the wood, the stones and the soil, and also licked up the water in the trench. When all the people saw this, they fell prostrate and cried, "The Lord—he is God! The Lord—he is God!"

Exercise: Reading and Meditation

Read 1 Kings 18 once to understand the context of today's passage. Then read it again. In this story, may your life be like the sacrifice: that when you are consumed with fire from heaven, others recognize the sovereignty of God. How does God want to ignite you today? Listen for His direction, record anything you hear, and then go burn in your world.

May 14

Sinful Habits (P)

Father, I am praying that You will set me free again. That You would reveal the thoughts, habits, and relationships that hinder Your life inside me. Please forgive me for giving them a place in my life, but I want you, Jesus. Breathe life over these areas and bring death to anything not of You. Death to the old ways of thinking, the old ways of acting, and the old ways of living. I have been created to be a living house of God in Christ Jesus, and so I will be for Your glory. Amen and a thousand more amens.

Verse: Psalm 139:23–24

> Search me, God, and know my heart; test me and know my anxious thoughts. See if there is any offensive way in me, and lead me in the way everlasting.

Exercise: Journaling

What thoughts, habits, or relationships have been drawing you away from Christ? What began as a good or small thing and has turned into a burden? What is God calling you to cut out from your life? Ask these questions after praying through today's prayer and write down the answers. Take time to process with the Holy Spirit. Allow Him to search your heart, test your motives, and reveal your thoughts.

May 15

Forgiveness (Ex)

I PRAY TODAY THAT Jesus will help you forgive. That He will go to that place of offense, dress your wounds, and do His work there. May it be a cleansing work. May it be a work that will root out all of the bitterness and pain that still reside in you, so many years later. May it be a work that will release you from something that was wrought upon you and was not even your fault. May it be a work that is a rebuilding work. One that will see something built where there was formerly only the burned out shell of a relationship. May you release the pain and allow your Father to hold you. Amen and a thousand more amens.

Verse: Matthew 18:21–22

> Then Peter came to Jesus and asked, "Lord, how many times shall I forgive my brother or sister who sins against me? Up to seven times?" Jesus answered, "I tell you, not seven times, but seventy-seven times.

Exercise: Prayer

If you have any notes or names from previous devotionals on forgiveness, look at them today. Who had God brought to your mind to forgive? Pray for these people again. If you have not read the previous entries on forgiveness, start anew. Who is God calling you to forgive? What do you need to let go of, even if you think you can't? Ask the Holy Spirit to give you the strength to do this. Take time to process these hurts in prayer to the Father..

May 16

Rejection (Ex)

My prayer today is that we would not let others' rejections of us define us in our own minds. We must not reject ourselves, because God doesn't. He has promised to never leave us, mislead us, or ignore us. His love goes deep, so let it do its deep work. Let it go to that place of rejection, unwarranted blame, and incessant accusation and do its healing work. O love of God, whose name is Jesus, please enter the pain of our rejections and their vexing presence in our minds. Please go to those places and build a house. Take up residence there, so that when we travel down those paths in our mind again, it will be you and your house that we see. And to see you is to see freedom, affirmation, and love. O to see you Jesus. Amen and a thousand more amens.

Verse: Isaiah 53:3

> He was despised and rejected by mankind, a man of suffering, and familiar with pain. Like one from whom people hide their faces he was despised, and we held him in low esteem.

Exercise: Journaling

The Prophet Isaiah spoke of Jesus in this passage. Christ was familiar with rejection, having been deserted by His closest friends and sentenced to death by the people He came to save. Because of this, He can relate to our pains, hurts and rejections.. Allow Him to speak into your past moments of rejection and feelings of inadequacy. If the rejection came from a parent, allow God to be your Father. If it came from a friend, allow Christ to be your friend. If it came from a significant other in the past, allow God to reveal His love for you. He is enough and can heal all wounds.

May 17

Receiving and Giving Love (P)

Lord Jesus, I receive and delight in Your love right now. I can only love others as deeply as I have experienced Your love. I want to love You and others well, so please show me more of Your love today. Overwhelm the insecure places of my heart. Go into the places that I have locked up and held only for myself. I ask You to love me there. Those bitter and hateful places. Let Your grace through Jesus go there and saturate them with Your love. Turn hatred into intense and passionate worship and bitterness into sweet praise. In the name of Jesus, may Your love become my greatest reality so I can delight in You and share it with everyone I interact with. Amen and a thousand more amens.

Verse: Matthew 10:7–8

> As you go, proclaim this message: 'The kingdom of heaven has come near.' Heal the sick, raise the dead, cleanse those who have leprosy, and drive out demons. Freely you have received; freely give.

Exercise: Meditation and Service

After praying today's prayer, sit with the Father and meditate on His love. Go for a walk, sit with a cup of coffee, watch a sunrise. Quiet your life for a few minutes to just sit with God and think about His great love. Talk with Him. Marvel at the wonderful gift you have been given. Thank Him for this awe-inspiring love. Then, bring that love to those you come in contact with. Keep a small rock or similar item on your person today. Every time you feel or see this object, think back to your conversation with Jesus about His love and ask Him how you can share that love in that moment. If you are around others, serve them. If you aren't, send an encouraging message or let someone know you are praying for them. Tip extra at the restaurant with a smile. Learn a stranger's name. Notice the mundane and shock the selfishness of culture with the selfless love of Christ.

May 18

Relatives Who Don't Know Christ (Ex)

Today I am praying for my relatives who don't know You, Jesus. Show Yourself to them soon. And may their encounter with You be so powerful that they call on You immediately. Come to them, Lord Jesus. Use other believers, challenges, and circumstances to open their eyes to You. Unify our family in You. Amen and a thousand more amens.

Verse: 2 Peter 3:9

> The Lord is not slow in keeping his promise, as some understand slowness. Instead he is patient with you, not wanting anyone to perish, but everyone to come to repentance.

Exercise: Prayer

God is faithful. He is love. He has been pursuing your loved ones since the moment they were born. Even when it doesn't seem like it, the Father is revealing Himself. The Spirit is moving. Join with Christ's heart today and pray for those in your family who do not know Him yet. Pray specifically for individuals and their situations. Ask for a heart to love them with God's love. Pray that they would come to know the life that is found in Jesus alone.

May 19

Victory Over the Enemy (Ex)

May any advances that the enemy is trying to make against you be thwarted by the host of Heaven. May God's forces rally to your defense today. You are not alone, and may that be more than evident before the sun sets. Yes, before the sun sets, may you have the smile of victory on your face and the satisfaction that His Kingdom has come and His will has been done in you. Amen and a thousand more amens.

Verse: Psalm 121:5–8

> The Lord watches over you— the Lord is your shade at your right hand; the sun will not harm you by day, nor the moon by night. The Lord will keep you from all harm— he will watch over your life; the Lord will watch over your coming and going both now and forevermore.

Exercise: Worship

At no point in the Bible is God ever unsure of His victory, sovereignty, or power. He has won, is winning, and will eternally continue to win. We can rest and rejoice in this fact. Take 10 to 15 minutes to focus on the victory of Christ, that He is King over all. For this time, do not think of your needs or challenges; He will be with you through them. Instead, focus on who Jesus is, how He is worthy of praise, and simply adore Him. We do not achieve victory through our own efforts, but by remaining with and in Him.

May 20

Pain in the World (Ex)

I am praying today that God would ease the pain. Many people carry a deep and residual pain. It is a pain to which they have grown accustomed and have resigned themselves to live with. God, give some soul care today. May the pain in people's souls be eased and dealt with by the One who not only saves souls, but can heal them too. Use me to heal others today and to restore them so they in turn can be messengers of Your healing. Amen and a thousand more amens.

Verse: Isaiah 61:1–3

> The Spirit of the Sovereign Lord is on me, because the Lord has anointed me to proclaim good news to the poor. He has sent me to bind up the brokenhearted, to proclaim freedom for the captives and release from darkness for the prisoners, and to proclaim the year of the Lord's favor and the day of vengeance of our God, to comfort all who mourn, and provide for those who grieve in Zion— to bestow on them a crown of beauty instead of ashes, oil of joy instead of mourning, and a garment of praise instead of a spirit of despair. They will be called oaks of righteousness, a planting of the Lord for the display of his splendor.

Exercise: Prayer

Jesus quoted this passage from the Old Testament at the beginning of His earthly ministry. His work was about bringing healing and freedom. We have been called to join Him in this work. Take this time to pray for specific individuals, your community, and your nation, that they may all experience the healing and freedom that can be found in Christ alone. Pray for restoration, peace, and a greater relationship with the Father, who is the source of all life.

May 21

Refreshed in Him (P)

Holy Spirit, refresh my spirit. Come restore all that is worn and torn in me. I do not want to get so caught up in the business and worries of life that I miss You. I can't do this by myself. I'm not meant to. I come back to You again. You are my breath and heartbeat. Thank you for taking my burdens and speaking Your life in me. Amen and a thousand more amens.

Verse: Luke 10:41–42

> "Martha, Martha," the Lord answered, "you are worried and upset about many things, but few things are needed—or indeed only one. Mary has chosen what is better, and it will not be taken away from her."

Exercise: Meditation and Silence

Slow down. Breathe easy. Release the tension in your muscles. Read Luke 10:38–42. Breathe. Don't get so caught up in doing good things that you become overwhelmed apart from the best thing: Jesus. During this time, sit at His feet. If you feel led to read, read. If to stay quiet, stay quiet. If to put worship music on, put worship music on. Just take a breath. We are dependent on Christ and we suffer when we do not stay with Him.

May 22

Against Offense (Ex)

My prayer is that God would help you to keep standing in the truth, with love. And never, ever pick up the weight of offense, hatred, and retribution. That you would display Christ through your grace and mercy, seeing even enemies through the lens of the cross. May your eyes be so fixed upon Jesus that anything that would offend "self" have no effect on you. Remain in His peace today and reflect God's divine humility and power. Amen and a thousand more amens.

Verse: Matthew 5:39

> But I tell you, do not resist an evil person. If anyone slaps you on the right cheek, turn to them the other cheek also.

Exercise: Journaling

Think of the events of the past week. Has anyone done anything that has annoyed or offended you? Write these things down. Then, ask yourself why these things bothered you? Why did they matter? Write down your answers. Next, ask the Father to tell you what He thinks of these things. Should you allow yourself to be offended by them, or do they ultimately not matter? This is not to negate your feelings, but rather to recognize ultimate realities. If a rude remark attacks your identity, rest in what Jesus says about you. If you were overlooked or forgotten, seek belonging in the God who always chooses you. Your ultimate inner peace is found in Him alone, and, as you grow in this area, other things that used to bother you will have less hold over your mind as you rest in Christ.

May 23

Speak Truth (Ex)

May God give you the grace to speak the truth in love and then stand. May you clearly know right from wrong and share God's truth with the world. Yes, may you stand in Him, for Him, and through Him. His Kingdom come through your words and actions today. Amen and a thousand more amens.

Verse: Ephesians 4:14–15

> Then we will no longer be infants, tossed back and forth by the waves, and blown here and there by every wind of teaching and by the cunning and craftiness of people in their deceitful scheming. Instead, speaking the truth in love, we will grow to become in every respect the mature body of him who is the head, that is, Christ.

Exercise: Evangelism

Either through a conversation or a message, share the Gospel with someone today. Do so with love. Seek relationship, not just another tally on your spiritual scoreboard. Understand where people are coming from, meet them in the middle of their story, and show the genuine, audacious love of Jesus. Afterwards, record your experiences.

May 24

Grace (Ex)

I am praying that His grace will be palpable to you today. Yes, may you feel it. Feel it in the depths of your soul. And may you know that He will make everything good and right, just because. Just because He chose to. He chose to love you, indwell you, and live with you and He will show up for you again and again and again. I thank Him for His grace in you. Delight in it today and rest in your Father. Amen and a thousand more amens.

Verse: 1 Corinthians 15:10

> But by the grace of God I am what I am, and his grace to me was not without effect. No, I worked harder than all of them--yet not I, but the grace of God that was with me.

Exercise: Worship and Prayer

What is grace? Grace is God giving us all of the good things that we don't deserve. Grace is salvation. Grace is a relationship with Him. Grace is having the honor of taking part in God's redemption plan for His creation. Take time to think about all of the gifts that He has given to you, simply because of His love and not because of anything you've done. Worship Him for these. Then, end with a time of prayer that others in your life might understand God's grace, as well.

May 25

Peace (Ex)

May the "peace of God, which transcends all understanding" show up for you today. Yes, so much peace coming your way that it confounds the confusion, pain, and formerly present anxiety. All of those things leave today. In the face of the storm, may you have peace. In the face of your former fears, may you have confidence. In the face of danger, may you rest in Him. Amen and a thousand more amens.

Verse: Philippians 4:4–7

> Rejoice in the Lord always. I will say it again: Rejoice! Let your gentleness be evident to all. The Lord is near. Do not be anxious about anything, but in every situation, by prayer and petition, with thanksgiving, present your requests to God. And the peace of God, which transcends all understanding, will guard your hearts and your minds in Christ Jesus.

Exercise: Meditation

The reason we can have peace beyond what makes sense, is because the "Lord is near always". He is not distant, but close and personal. He listens, speaks, protects, and blesses. Read today's passage of Scripture several times slowly. Pause at the end of each reading to thank God for His presence and ask Him to open your eyes to the beauty and comfort that He always offers. Allow His peace to fill you.

May 26

Hope (Ex)

I am praying for hope to well up in you. That it would explode into eruptions of spontaneous and joyous laughter throughout the day. May you laugh as you eat breakfast, as you are on the way to work and at school. May heaven's expectant joy follow you to the market, the gas station, and the gym. It will be a contagious elixir to those around. You will be an evangelist for the Gospel of Christ through your hope in formerly sad places. Amen and a thousand more amens.

Verse: Romans 15:13

> May the God of hope fill you with all joy and peace as you trust in him, so that you may overflow with hope by the power of the Holy Spirit.

Exercise: Prayer and Service

What places or people with whom you interact lack hope? Are your coworkers just trying to get to the weekend? Are family members despairing over the current political state? Is a friend tired of the pointlessness of life? Write down each of these and lift these people up to God. Pray specifically that their lives would be rejuvenated by the resurrecting power and hope of Christ. Then, ask the Father to use you to bring hope to them today. If there is a specific way you believe this should happen, write it down. Be a messenger of hope today.

May 27

The Presence of Christ (P)

May your level of faith skyrocket as you realize He is there. Yes, Jesus is with you, in you, around you, and through you. He is living, breathing and moving in your person. Not just partially. The entirety of the infinite God is living inside you. When you pray for His kingdom to come and His will to be done in you and through you today, remember that He is the one completing His will through your life. It is not a product of your own efforts. Embrace His presence today and walk with the Spirit as you naturally push back the darkness and bring hope, light, and life to your world. Amen and a thousand more amens.

Verse: Galatians 5:24–25

> Those who belong to Christ Jesus have crucified the flesh with its passions and desires. Since we live by the Spirit, let us keep in step with the Spirit.

Exercise: Silence and Journaling

Begin your devotional time in silence. Sit with the Holy Spirit. As you are with Him, release every other distraction and worry for the day. As you breathe in, imagine breathing in His presence. As you breathe out, release your distractions and self centered mindset. Ask God to fill you once more with His presence so that you may know, love, and serve Him in a greater way. After 5 to 10 minutes of silence, take out a pen and paper. Ask Him to reveal to you the areas that you have not submitted to Him. Where have you not kept "in step with the Spirit"? Surrender these areas to Christ again and ask Him to enter every facet of your life.

May 28

Redeeming Your Past (Ex)

May your darkness be turned to light and made into something alive. And those things that were orchestrated for your fall be re-routed by the powerful hand of God into a story of salvation and hope. Yes, salvation and hope to you all this day. What was meant to crush you in the past is redeemed in the name of Jesus. Do not be afraid to confront those things but allow the Holy Spirit to wash your past wounds and mistakes. Shame and guilt and inadequacy are not of the Father. May you receive His grace and share it with your world for His glory. Amen and a thousand more amens.

Verse: Ephesians 5:13

> But everything exposed by the light becomes visible--and everything that is illuminated becomes a light.

Exercise: Meditation

We have been called to wholeness in Christ. When we are redeemed, our past no longer defines us. Instead, Christ's sacrifice redeems our past, so that we can now face it and share it with others. Do you have this freedom in yourself? If not, ask the Father to help you release the pain or shame of your life. Listen for His voice and simply be with Him. After this time of self reflection, pray for 1 or 2 people whom you know that have allowed their past to define them. Pray that Christ would shine His light on their lives.

May 29

Experiencing Love (P)

I am praying that you would experience real love. The kind that is grace-based and true. Authentic, pure, selfless, sure. God-given, Spirit-driven, Jesus-placed. A love in which you can be safe and truly yourself. No need to strive or measure up. Receive that kind of love from the Father today and bring that kind of love to your world. Amen and a thousand more amens.

Verse: Luke 15:21–24

> The son said to him, "Father, I have sinned against heaven and against you. I am no longer worthy to be called your son." But the father said to his servants, "Quick! Bring the best robe and put it on him. Put a ring on his finger and sandals on his feet. Bring the fattened calf and kill it. Let's have a feast and celebrate. For this son of mine was dead and is alive again; he was lost and is found." So they began to celebrate.

Exercise: Reading and Meditation

Read the parable of the prodigal son in Luke 15:11–31. Do you feel the same as the wayward son, unworthy of love because of the mistakes you have made? Or do you have those in your life who have made mistakes and you are more tempted to act like the older brother? Ask the Father what He wants to speak to you now. How are you called to live out the love of this parable?

May 30

The Power of Jesus (Ex)

I am praying for the power of Jesus to inhabit your actions. May the power of the gospel be there when you speak, touch, smile at and pray for those whom you meet today. You reach, He inhabits. Do not overlook the divine potential in your life. Jesus is with you and goes before you. May you see the realities of heaven and call forth His Kingdom in your life today. Amen and a thousand more amens.

Verse: Ephesians 1:18–21

> I pray that the eyes of your heart may be enlightened in order that you may know the hope to which he has called you, the riches of his glorious inheritance in his holy people, and his incomparably great power for us who believe. That power is the same as the mighty strength he exerted when he raised Christ from the dead and seated him at his right hand in the heavenly realms, far above all rule and authority, power and dominion, and every name that is invoked, not only in the present age but also in the one to come.

Exercise: Prayer and Service

The very same power that the Apostle Paul describes in this passage is living in you. Any thought to minimize what Jesus can do through you is from the enemy. Pray over your day that the Holy Spirit would interrupt your schedule and display His power through you. Expect the miraculous today. Speak blessings over others. Listen for prophetic words of encouragement. Pray for the infirm. Allow your life to be the conduit for God's divine power. Record anything that happens today afterwards.

May 31

The Fruit of Life (Ex)

May the life of God in you exchange laughter for pain, hope for fear, and dancing for darkness. You are no longer of this world. You are in it, but your identity is wrapped up in Christ. May His life renew yours today and bring to fruition every good and perfect gift from above. Amen and a thousand more amens.

Verse: John 17:16–17

> They are not of the world, even as I am not of it. Sanctify them by d the truth; your word is truth.

Exercise: Reading and Meditation

Read John 17:6–26. This is Jesus' prayer for both His disciples and all who would believe.. Read His prayer over your life, specifically over the areas of pain, fear, and doubt. Those things must bow their knees to Christ. Join with Jesus in this prayer over your life and then over the lives of others. Pray for friends and family and then those you disagree with and who annoy you. Allow Christ's life to permeate and flow through you today.

June 1

Strength (Ex)

I am praying for strength to come your way in waves. May waves of strength roll over you. So much of it that you have to share it. The eternal strength of God deposited into your earthly vessel. You can't just hold it either. It wasn't given to be kept. Go now and be strong for someone. Pray for them, touch them, give to them, have faith for them, love them well. May you embody the divine power of the Most High. Amen and a thousand more amens.

Verse: 1 Corinthians 15:56–58

> The sting of death is sin, and the power of sin is the law. But thanks be to God! He gives us the victory through our Lord Jesus Christ. Therefore, my dear brothers and sisters, stand firm. Let nothing move you. Always give yourselves fully to the work of the Lord, because you know that your labor in the Lord is not in vain.

Exercise: Prayer and Service

During your devotional time, ask the Father to give you the strength needed for yourself and others today. Intentionally be aware of those around you and share the love of Christ. As you go about your responsibilities, be in prayer, either out loud or in your mind. Declare God's promises and strength over the challenges you face, and pay attention to the challenges of others. Record anything that happens in this area at the end of the day and pray over each situation listed.

June 2

Divine Focus (Ex)

I AM PRAYING THAT God's purposes in your life would be obvious, blatant, and focused. Gone are the days of confusion and bewilderment. You are focused, locked and loaded. A heat seeking missile for the Kingdom of Heaven. Now go out and explode somewhere in the name of our Resurrected Lord. Amen and a thousand more amens.

Verse: Deuteronomy 11:22–23

> If you carefully observe all these commands I am giving you to follow—to love the Lord your God, to walk in obedience to him and to hold fast to him— then the Lord will drive out all these nations before you, and you will dispossess nations larger and stronger than you.

Exercise: Journaling

Do you have a dream or a calling that you believe God has given you? Or are you not sure what your life should ultimately look like? In either case, your first call is to love the Lord and be faithful to Him. Spend time thinking and praying about the first two questions. If you have an answer to the first, ask the Holy Spirit if there is a specific action you should take this day. If you do not know an overarching, specific calling for your life, this does not make you less. Instead, ask the Father how you might join in His work today by bringing His Kingdom to earth. Record what you hear..

June 3

Distractions (P)

May the things that blind and obstruct others from seeing the hand of God in their lives be moved, dealt with, vaporized. Jesus, I know You are living, moving, and more active in them than they realize. Yes, You are closer to them than themselves. A very present help in trouble. A comforter. Bringer of peace. The Way, the Truth, and the Life. Open their eyes to Your beauty, holiness, and sovereignty today. I ask this in the name of Jesus Christ. Amen and a thousand more amens.

Verse: 2 Corinthians 4:6

> For God, who said, "Let light shine out of darkness," made his light shine in our hearts to give us the light of the knowledge of God's glory displayed in the face of Christ.

Exercise: Prayer

Choose one or two people in your life who do not know Jesus. Pray this verse over them that they may see the light in the darkness. At times, we may have individuals in our lives who seem so distant from God that it is hard to imagine them knowing Jesus. Do not despair or give up hope. Instead, press in. Lift up their names to the Father and proclaim the light of the Gospel to shine in their hearts.

JUNE 4

Order (Ex)

I AM PRAYING FOR order to come into the chaos. May the Creator bring the same power with which He ordered the universe into your life. Peace, solace, and rest to you. His calming breath to you. And may the cool winds of Heaven blow over you. May you be productive but not frantic, restful but not lazy, and focused but not impersonal. Grace, peace, and love to you my friend. Amen and a thousand more amens.

Verse: Genesis 1:1

In the beginning God created the heavens and the earth.

Exercise: Reading and Meditation

If possible, sit outside with a view of nature. This could be on your porch, in a park, or in a room with a window. Before you begin this time in the Word, release the worries and pressures of your day. Breathe in God's peace, breathe out any tension you are holding on to. After a minute of this practice, open your Bible. Read Genesis chapter 1 slowly. Imagine what each day of creation may have looked like. Picture light bursting into existence, the waves receding, continents ascending from the deep, and greenery sprouting over the face of the earth. Imagine the peaceful joy of this process. The satisfaction of a job well done. The symphony of nature joining together. After you finish reading, look around you. Sit quietly and simply watch nature. Take time to notice the small things in the world. After several minutes of this meditation, ask the Father to order your day with the same purpose and peace which embodied His initial creation. Enter the day with Him.

June 5

Healing (Ex)

I am praying that God will heal you now. It's time for a touch from The Maker. And may His touch be obvious, evident, and powerful. Whether this pain is physical, emotional, or spiritual, He is the great Restorer. May His hand rest on you as you wait on Him. May you feel His peace. Amen and a thousand more amens.

Verse: Psalm 107:19–21

> Then they cried to the Lord in their trouble, and he saved them from their distress. He sent out his word and healed them; he rescued them from the grave. Let them give thanks to the Lord for his unfailing love and his wonderful deeds for mankind.

Exercise: Prayer

Be honest with the Father about the ways you or others in your life are hurting. He hears you and cares deeply. Ask for healing in those areas and know that He can bring miraculous restoration into your life. Regardless of the time frame, whether you are healed immediately, over several days, through the miracle of medicine, or at the Second Coming, the Holy Spirit will be with you constantly. End this time with thanksgiving and worship for His presence and healing.

June 6

Protection (Ex)

May you be protected from all that the enemy has for you. Yes, I ask that the hand of God be there on the road, at the store, at work, and at school. And may anything evil that has been directed at you be thwarted, averted, and redirected towards the one who sent it, in the name of Jesus. Amen and a thousand more amens.

Verse: Psalm 144:2

> He is my loving God and my fortress, my stronghold and my deliverer, my shield, in whom I take refuge, who subdues peoples under me.

Exercise: Prayer

Read this prayer over yourself and your family members by name. Bless them and proclaim the Bible verse over everyone's responsibilities, actions, and thoughts so that they may reflect Jesus in every way.

June 7

Housing His Presence (Ex)

May you know without a shadow of a doubt that you are a temple for God's image. Yes, you house something of who He is inside of your body. Therefore, you are valuable, beautiful, strong, purposeful, handsome, and free. And Jesus, the God-man, causes that image to come alive in you as only He can. Ask Him to do so, buckle your seat-belt, and prepare to live life: new life, real life. Amen and a thousand more amens.

Verse: 1 Corinthians 6:19–20

> Do you not know that your bodies are temples of the Holy Spirit, who is in you, whom you have received from God? You are not your own; you were bought at a price. Therefore honor God with your bodies.

Exercise: Prayer

If the Spirit of the Most High resides in you, you have no reason to think any less of yourself: that you aren't enough, that you wish you were different, that you need to hide. Jesus made you to be as you are and chooses to impart His life into your body. Along with this truth comes a responsibility to honor God with what we do with our bodies. Take this time to repent both of thinking negatively of yourself and for using your body in sinful ways. Admit both to the Lord, ask for His forgiveness, and receive His Holy Spirit to empower you to live a holy life.

June 8

Divine Awareness (P)

Holy Spirit, allow me to see spiritual realities. To see the hand of God moving in my life. And to know that I am covered, guided, shielded, stopped, moved, and turned by You. I know that You are with me in ways that are more real than I am with myself. I want to see beyond this physical world to what You are doing and how I can join. Thank you for allowing me to be a part of Your redemptive plan. Amen and a thousand more amens.

Verse: 2 Kings 6:15–17

> When the servant of the man of God got up and went out early the next morning, an army with horses and chariots had surrounded the city. "Oh no, my lord! What shall we do?" the servant asked. "Don't be afraid," the prophet answered. "Those who are with us are more than those who are with them." And Elisha prayed, "Open his eyes, Lord, so that he may see." Then the Lord opened the servant's eyes, and he looked and saw the hills full of horses and chariots of fire all around Elisha.

Exercise: Reading

Read the story of Elisha the prophet in 2 Kings 6:8–22. After reading, pray for the same awareness to see the power of God surrounding and working in the world. Commit to joining His work today so that the attacks of the enemy may fail, look foolish, and stop altogether.

June 9

Vengeance is the Lord's (Ex)

May the intimidator of your soul be intimidated himself. His offenses against you have not gone unnoticed, they will be dealt with soon. You have been robbed and stolen from. Retribution is on its way in the form of The Lion of The Tribe of Judah. The Lion will roar for you this day. And when He does, the intimidator will flee as his strength is shown to be the shadow that it is in the light of Christ. May the victory come today in your life. Amen and a thousand more amens.

Verse: James 4:7

Submit yourselves, then, to God. Resist the devil, and he will flee from you.

Exercise: Silence and Meditation

Christ is the one who has and will completely defeat our spiritual enemy. According to this verse, the devil flees when we submit to God and draw near to Him. Take 10 minutes in silence to meditate on this verse. Listen. What does God say about it? Are you remaining in Him? Allow Him to be King of your life and watch the attacks of the enemy fail.

June 10

Personal Renewal (Ex)

May your pained heart be healed and your tired mind renewed. "Healing" and "renewal" are your words for today. Be healed and renewed by the power of the only one who can do these deep works: Jesus. He is the worker of deep things, in deep places. May His deep call to your deep. Amen and a thousand more amens.

Verse: Psalm 42:7–8

> Deep calls to deep in the roar of your waterfalls; all your waves and breakers have swept over me. By day the Lord directs his love, at night his song is with me— a prayer to the God of my life.

Exercise: Worship

Personal renewal is a result of spending time in the Father's presence. After reading today's prayer and Scripture, take the next 10 to 15 minutes to worship Jesus. Praise Him for His faithfulness and presence. Delight in Him and who He is as you allow Him into your worn and weary mind.

June 11

Against Gossip (Ex)

I am praying today that you do not get pulled into the vortex of gossip, slander, and ignorant babble that surrounds you. Focus upon what God is speaking and let that penetrate your heart and redeem your mind. He will bring healing, hope and life. Yes, healing, hope and life to you today my friends. Amen and a thousand more amens.

Verse: Ephesians 4:29

> Do not let any unwholesome talk come out of your mouths, but only what is helpful for building others up according to their needs, that it may benefit those who listen.

Exercise: Journaling

How do you think and talk about others? Do you point out others' shortcomings or analyze their drama? Do you share this with others? Think about the interactions with your family, friends, and coworkers. Ask the Holy Spirit to reveal to you any area in which you have compromised with gossip or slander, even in the moments where you have remained quiet instead of speaking up. Don't pass by this topic lightly, for this sin is an easy one to slip into. Pause for several minutes as you think about each area with the Holy Spirit and write down any specific instances He brings to your mind. Repent and receive His forgiveness.

June 12

The Ultimate Reality of Christ (P)

Holy Spirit, when the shadows of fear and doubt try to taunt and haunt me, I will ignore them. Shadows have no authority, they're only shadows. Powerless figments of something in another place and time. I know that You are the reality, the light on the other side of the shadow. So I choose to walk towards the light. May I see Your face and hold on to Your truth. Holy Spirit, help me. Amen and a thousand more amens.

Verse: John 8:31–32

> To the Jews who had believed him, Jesus said, "If you hold to my teaching, you are really my disciples. Then you will know the truth, and the truth will set you free."

Exercise: Prayer and Service

What has Jesus called you to today? Is there someone that He wants you to specifically bless or a job that you have been called to work with excellence? Follow the Holy Spirit today in obedience and the lies of the enemy will fall away.

June 13

Wounded Hearts (Ex)

May those hurt places in your heart be filled in by the Healer of Hearts. This is His specialty. He fills in and takes away hurts. It is His art, His medicine, and His passion. Ask Him and He will do it. And then, that which was formerly a place of pain, and darkness will be transformed into a place of life and love and dancing. May it be so. Amen and a thousand more amens.

Verse: Revelation 21:4

> "He will wipe every tear from their eyes. There will be no more death' or mourning or crying or pain, for the old order of things has passed away."

Exercise: Prayer

Jesus will come back and erase every pain and form of brokenness in the world. As those who have His life, we can also experience this because of His great love and grace. Join the heart of Christ and pray today's prayer over a specific person in your life who needs healing in his or her heart. It could be from a recent loss, a past painful event, or a hopeless future. Walk with Christ to that hurting place in prayer and cover it with His love.

June 14

Vision of Hope (Ex)

May hope shine on you. And as it does, may the fog and haze dissipate and leave you clear, very clear. Clear about the fact that God is with you, that He cares, and that it will ALL work out. Yes, it will ALL work out my friends. May you rest in Him today. Amen and a thousand more amens.

Verse: Romans 8:28

> And we know that in all things God works for the good of those who love him, who have been called according to his purpose.

Exercise: Reading

Read Romans 8:18–30 as the Apostle Paul discusses the hope that we have as Christians. It does not deny present hardship or weakness, but gives hope in spite of what we see. This hope is given to those who are being conformed into the image of Christ. If you have not had hope lately, have you been spending time with Christ? Read this passage two more times slowly, and ask the Holy Spirit to speak through Scripture. Record any verses or ideas that catch your attention.

June 15

Grace (Ex)

May you live yet another day covered with God's grace. And may you get used to it, but not take it for granted. Let grace become the order of the day. The way you live, love, and play. The way you speak, the way you look, the attitude you carry. Yes, grace, grace, and more grace to you today. Amen and a thousand more amens.

Verse: Romans 11:5–6

> So too, at the present time there is a remnant chosen by grace. And if by grace, then it cannot be based on works; if it were, grace would no longer be grace.

Exercise: Meditation

In order to understand today's prayer you must answer the question "what is grace?" Read the passage of Scripture that discusses a remnant of people chosen by God to be saved. What does it say about grace? How is one saved by grace? What is the opposite of being saved by grace? After answering these questions, read the prayer again over yourself and your people.

June 16

A Blessing (Ex)

May the Lord bless you and keep you and put His hand on you. And may that hand direct you and guide you through the murky and the dark, into a new place of light, life and purpose. Life, light and purpose to you. Amen and a thousand more amens.

Verse: Numbers 6:24–26

> The Lord bless you and keep you; the Lord make his face shine on you and be gracious to you; the Lord turn his face toward you and give you peace.

Exercise: Meditation

There are times in which we are called to intercede for others, to do good battle in the spiritual realm, and to bring God's miraculous power to the world around us. There are also times we are called to simply receive from God and delight in His presence. It can seem like a ridiculous thought since God is all of the omni's and the infinite deity over all of creation, yet He still chooses to reveal His love to us. Take 10 to 15 minutes to read these prayers over your life and the lives of others.

June 17

Holding on to God's Word (Ex)

I am praying that you will hold on to what you know God has said to you. Grab it. Hold it. Relentlessly embrace it. Passionately keep it. Do not let go. He will show up. He will deliver and He will honor what He has said. May you be caught up in a divine perseverance in chasing after God's will. Amen and a thousand more amens.

Verse: James 1:12

> Blessed is the one who perseveres under trial because, having stood the test, that person will receive the crown of life that the Lord has promised to those who love him.

Exercise: Journaling

Today is a day of reflection. If you have journals from your past, grab one or two to look through. If you do not have a past journal, think through the process you have gone through in the last several years. Choose a time frame to reflect on your life. This could be the past year, 5 years, 10 years, or several decades. During this time, look back on the past challenges God has walked with you through and the words that He has given you. What ones have been fulfilled? What ones have not yet? Remind yourself of God's faithfulness and return to your past experiences with Jesus, encouraging yourself to keep persevering by the power of the Holy Spirit.

June 18

Emotional Healing (Ex)

May Jesus touch the places that hurt. Those raw, sensitive, and bruised places. You will be healed there. I am not sure when you will feel it, but you will be healed. That is what He does. Thank you Jesus for meeting us in our hurt. Amen and a thousand more amens.

Verse: Matthew 8:3

> Jesus reached out his hand and touched the man. "I am willing," he said. "Be clean!" Immediately he was cleansed of his leprosy.

Exercise: Silence and Meditation

If you have been experiencing emotional pain, read the prayer over those wounded areas. Sit in silence with Jesus, only repeating Matthew 8:3 in your mind or out loud. What is God saying to you? How does He see you?

If you do not have emotional pain that comes to mind, ask the Holy Spirit if there is any past wound that He wants to address. If so, do the same as above. If not, pray this prayer over another person in your life.

June 19

True Life (Ex)

May real life just descend upon you today. Nothing fake or drummed up. Authentic, vibrant, and palpable. That is what I am asking the Creator to give each of you. May it fire you up and calm you down. May it enhance your days and deepen your nights. May it propel you into your purpose and establish you in knowledge of who you are and what you are here for. Real life through the Lord of Life. Amen and a thousand more amens.

Verse: Romans 6:23

For the wages of sin is death, but the gift of God is eternal life in Christ Jesus our Lord

Exercise: Journaling

Eternal life does not begin at death, but includes this very moment. Have you allowed present situations to determine your perspective on life? This life will pass in the blink of an eye. Do not allow the life of Christ to be stifled through focusing on temporary difficulties or gains. Take this time to write down anything that you have focused on more than Jesus, both good and bad. Then, give these back to Him and read the prayer for the day again slowly, thinking about the meaning for each part in your life.

June 20

A New Day (Ex)

May despair be cast out of your heart and very far away from you. No despair, no gloom, no doom. I am asking God to fill you all with what I call "morning life". That life that is eye opening, bird singing, wind blowing, flowers blooming kind of life. Colors coming alive out of the dark kind of life. Life that proclaims that this is a new day and the night is gone. That kind of life. Life to you, hope to you, morning to you. Amen and a thousand more amens.

Verse: Psalm 65:8

> The whole earth is filled with awe at your wonders; where morning dawns, where evening fades, you call forth songs of joy.

Exercise: Worship

The earth is filled with life. Countless plants and animals interact with the world around them and God sees them all. He sees you too. You are special in that God chose to allow you to know Him too. Allow this truth to rest on you. Enter into a time of worship and adoration, thanking the Father for this beautiful reality. Also, if possible in the next several days, wake up early to see the sunrise. Listen and watch as the world is roused from sleep for a new day. Enjoy it with the One who made it.

June 21

Worry (Ex)

I pray that worry and fear would leave you alone immediately. May the dread and panic that haunt you be chased away by the Lord of Life himself. May the real, vibrant, joy-filled, grace bursting, fear stomping life of Jesus be infused into every fiber of your being right now. Amen and a thousand more amens.

Verse: 1 Peter 5:7

> Cast all your anxiety on him because he cares for you.

Exercise: Prayer and Journaling

If Christ is holding your anxiety, you no longer have to. What is bringing you worry today? What is wearing you down? Write these in your journal. Say out loud, "Jesus, I give you______." Read through each item and give it to Christ.

June 22

Heaven (Ex)

I pray that you sense Heaven today. May you understand that it is not out there somewhere, but where you are. Jesus with you and in you is Heaven on earth. So take Heaven to work with you and to school. Take some Heaven to the store and to your neighbor's house. His Kingdom come and His will be done on earth as it is in Heaven. This brings Heaven here through the Holy Spirit. Amen and a thousand more amens.

Verse: Ecclesiastes 3:11

> He has made everything beautiful in its time. He has also set eternity in the human heart; yet no one can fathom what God has done from beginning to end.

Exercise: Meditation

Take 10 to 15 minutes to prayerfully meditate on eternity. What will it be like? How long will you be there? Who will you be with? Imagine living for ten thousand years where there is no sin, sickness, or death. Every moment is permeated by God's presence. It will never end. Ever. It can be hard to fully grasp, but after this reflection, think of your life today. How should the knowledge of eternity shape your thoughts and actions? What does it mean for you today?

June 23

The Authority of the Enemy (Ex)

The enemy has no authority over you, so walk in freedom right now. I stand with you and for you this day. You are no longer bound by, defined by, shamed by, or shackled by former sins and mistakes. They no longer exist. The power of sin in your life is broken in the name of Jesus Christ. Amen and a thousand more amens.

Verse: Psalm 103:11–12

> For as high as the heavens are above the earth, so great is his love for those who fear him; as far as the east is from the west, so far has he removed our transgressions from us.

Exercise: Reading and Prayer

After reading the day's prayer and Scripture, open your Bible to Psalm 103. Read it in its entirety. Pause for a minute to listen for God's voice in response. Then, read it again, this time reading a verse at a time and praying it over your life. Apply the Word to your situation and to the lives of those around you.

June 24

Health (Ex)

I pray for your health today. May you be wholly healthy. May the life of God in you be health to your bones, laughter to your soul, and quickness to your mind. And then, at the end of this day, may you sleep deep and well. Amen and a thousand more amens.

Verse: Daniel 1:15–17

> At the end of the ten days they looked healthier and better nourished than any of the young men who ate the royal food. So the guard took away their choice food and the wine they were to drink and gave them vegetables instead. To these four young men God gave knowledge and understanding of all kinds of literature and learning. And Daniel could understand visions and dreams of all kinds.

Exercise: Prayer

When we allow God's commandments to shape our lifestyle, we will be blessed. Daniel and the other Jewish captors displayed this in Daniel 1. We can pray for favor, but it will not come when we live outside of God's will. Satisfaction is found in Christ alone. So, pray today's blessing over you and your household, along with the request that each member may live in God's will.

June 25

The Fruit of Faithfulness (Ex)

May you see the miraculous as a result of the mundane. Yes, may the simple and small things that you do have monumental and profound effects. Mustard seed kind of stuff. Little things. May they turn into a consuming Kingdom fire. May the Lord open your eyes to the value of consistency. Amen and a thousand more amens.

Verse: Luke 16:10

> Whoever can be trusted with very little can also be trusted with much, and whoever is dishonest with very little will also be dishonest with much.

Exercise: Journaling

What has God trusted you with in this season of life? What relationships, jobs, or mundane responsibilities do you have? Have you been faithful with excellence in these areas? Ask these questions to the Holy Spirit. Then write what comes to your mind.

June 26

Being with Jesus (Ex)

I am praying for Jesus to show Himself to you today. May He be in your eating and your talking, your driving and your walking. May He laugh with you and may He smile often. And may the two of you connect in soul changing, life giving fashion. The soul and life of Jesus to you, for you and in you today. That's what I'm praying for. Amen and a thousand more amens.

Verse: John 15:9–11

> As the Father has loved me, so have I loved you. Now remain in my love. If you keep my commands, you will remain in my love, just as I have kept my Father's commands and remain in his love. I have told you this so that my joy may be in you and that your joy may be complete.

Exercise: Memorization and Meditation

We are to remain in Christ and His love. This is a beautiful, awe-inspiring truth. He is with you at all times, the good and the bad. He wants to be your best friend, Lord, Savior, King, and love. Meditate on this reality during your devotional time. Then, commit John 15:9–11 to memory. Take a small rock or similar object with you wherever you go this week. Keep it on your person in a place that you will see or feel it often. Every time you do, repeat these verses and thank Him for being with you and loving you perfectly.

June 27

Spiritual Attacks (Ex)

May you be impervious to the incoming arrows being shot at you. They will not hit their marks. You are covered. Faith is your shield and it is locked with the shields of those of us who love and stand with you. Shields locked, faith loaded. Amen and a thousand more amens.

Verse: Ephesians 6:16

> In addition to all this, take up the shield of faith, with which you can extinguish all the flaming arrows of the evil one.

Exercise: Prayer

As the enemy tries to attack you today, ask the Holy Spirit for greater trust in Him and for the power to remain faithful and obedient. Ask Him to show you any areas in which you have not lived out faith to its fullness.

June 28

Great Crowd of Witnesses (Ex)

My prayer today is that you would know you are not alone. Because of Jesus, you are part of a great crowd of witnesses. A great crowd that is ancient, yet now. You have an innumerable amount of family and friends that care for, stand for and pray for you. . .now. The power and love that is the body of Christ knows no geographical nor time imposed bounds. You are lifted up, covered and thought about right now. Ignore the voices that say otherwise. They are the voices of liars. Live in the light and in the community of believers today through the headship of Jesus Christ. Amen and a thousand more amens.

Verse: Hebrews 12:1–3

> Therefore, since we are surrounded by such a great cloud of witnesses, let us throw off everything that hinders and the sin that so easily entangles. And let us run with perseverance the race marked out for us, fixing our eyes on Jesus, the pioneer and perfecter of faith. For the joy set before him he endured the cross, scorning its shame, and sat down at the right hand of the throne of God. Consider him who endured such opposition from sinners, so that you will not grow weary and lose heart.

Exercise: Prayer and Service

After reading the prayer and passage for the day, read them again. Don't rush. Allow the words to rest on, not run through, your mind. Be encouraged by this and then take your devotional time to reach out to other believers. This could be a message in which you state the ways in which you see Jesus in them, telling them that you are praying for them, or asking if they need any prayer today. You could call on the phone or write a letter. Whatever you do, join with the cloud of witnesses in lifting up the arms of others as you pursue Christ in community.

June 29

Lies from the enemy (P)

I am praying that the insidious lies and whispers of the enemy that are aimed at my family will miss their mark. That they will gain no traction in their minds and be seen for the sham that they are. Jesus, you offer redemption, righteousness, and life. May my family accept nothing but the fullness of Your love. Wake us up to Your spirit. Amen and a thousand more amens.

Verse: 2 Timothy 1:14

> Guard the good deposit that was entrusted to you--guard it with the help of the Holy Spirit who lives in us.

Exercise: Prayer

The Apostle Paul is encouraging Timothy to guard the calling of God on His life and the truth entrusted to him. You have a similar responsibility to do your part with the Holy Spirit to guard the callings and truth in your family. Take this time to pray for each family member by name and for their specific situations in life.

June 30

A Prayer for Peace (Ex)

Praying for peace to descend upon you, like a fog. May peace actually cloud and cover your reality. That's what peace that passes understanding does. It takes what is real, and makes it not only bearable, but livable, passable, and forgettable. Yes, may a peaceful heavenly fog envelop you, cover you, and help you this day. Amen and a thousand more amens.

Verse: Romans 8:6

> The mind governed by the flesh is death, but the mind governed by the Spirit is life and peace.

Exercise: Prayer

Having a mind that is "governed by the flesh" does not only mean a mind that is set on sinful desires. It is also holding on to the belief that one can handle life's challenges under one's own strength. Reliance on God is diminished or nonexistent, and this takes away His heavenly peace. Ask yourself if you have been guilty of either thought process and repent of the areas that have not been submitted to Christ. Pray today's prayer over a leader in your life. Lift up their name to the Father that He may guide and comfort them. This could be at your work, your church, or a person who is not directly connected to you, such as, a missionary or government official.

July 1
Action and Rest (Ex)

May the life of God in you stir the lethargic places and rest the weary ones. Yes, that is what His life can do. It does not allow the sickness that comes from no motion, but also restores when there has been too much of it. So, may the restorative presence of you Maker stir you and still you. Amen and a thousand more amens.

Verse: Exodus 20:8–11

> Remember the Sabbath day by keeping it holy. Six days you shall labor and do all your work, but the seventh day is a sabbath to the Lord your God. On it you shall not do any work, neither you, nor your son or daughter, nor your male or female servant, nor your animals, nor any foreigner residing in your towns. For in six days the Lord made the heavens and the earth, the sea, and all that is in them, but he rested on the seventh day. Therefore the Lord blessed the Sabbath day and made it holy.

Exercise: Journaling

How has your work and rest balance been? Have you found yourself doing too much of one and not enough of the other? Today's passage is taken out of the Ten Commandments. God thought that it was important enough to have a healthy, productive approach to work that He included it in this historic list. Write down how you believe you have been doing in this area by responding to these questions: How much free time do you have? What do you do with that free time? How often do you work? Do you bring your work home? Do you have a day in which you intentionally rest? You are called to be productive and a responsible steward of the abilities that God has given you, but do not make an idol out of the work of your hands. On the other hand, don't let your hands remain idle or only work for your own enjoyment. Ask the Holy Spirit to reveal to you what your schedule should consist of.

July 2

Armed with Faith (Ex)

I pray that faith would grab you. Yes, may a real, life sustaining, mountain moving faith latch onto you and not let go. And may you and faith become so energized by being with each other, that you go giant hunting today. Giants will hide because of you and faith. Run at them and take them down. Amen and a thousand more amens.

Verse: Deuteronomy 7:2

> And when the LORD your God has delivered them over to you and you have defeated them, then you must destroy them totally. Make no treaty with them, and show them no mercy.

Exercise: Prayer and Service

This passage was the command given to the Israelites when they were going to enter the Promised Land. There can be no compromise with darkness. Since we serve the all-powerful God, anything less than complete rejection of sin and its fruit is disobedience on our part, not inability on His. Take time to receive the Holy Spirit's direction and insight for the day and pray over areas in which you see darkness in the world around you. Then, ask Jesus how you can join Him in pushing back the enemy today.

July 3
Offensive Christianity (Ex)

I pray today that you will be attuned and ready in the Spirit, so that you will know when to strike the enemy. Pray against the evil one and then prey upon him. Yes, he seeks whom he may devour, but I challenge you to devour him first. Rescue those in fear. Take back and tend to those whom he has wounded. You are a lion hunter. That's what you do. Listen, pray, and move towards the roar. You are more than a conqueror through Jesus Christ, our Risen King. Amen and a thousand more amens.

Verse: 1 John 5:2–5

> This is how we know that we love the children of God: by loving God and carrying out his commands. In fact, this is love for God: to keep his commands. And his commands are not burdensome, for everyone born of God overcomes the world. This is the victory that has overcome the world, even our faith. Who is it that overcomes the world? Only the one who believes that Jesus is the Son of God.

Exercise: Prayer and Service

In your devotional time, focus on people in your life that are not within your inner circle: the acquaintances, coworkers, etc. Now ask God which one of these people He wants you to pray for and/or speak into today. This may include encouraging them in a specific area, getting to know them better, or sharing the Gospel with them. Simply be available for the Holy Spirit to work through you. By this you will plant seeds, water, or harvest the fruit of God's work in their lives. Jesus interacted with the crowds, but He focused on individuals. Do the same today.

July 4

Healing in Your Mind (Ex)

I pray today for healing in your mind. May those old things that haunt, taunt, and mock you be dealt with by the renewing of your mind. May He haunt and chase them ruthlessly today on your behalf, so that your mind would be clear about this: you are new. Yes, you are not those old things. Those passed away. They are deceased. Think on new things today my friends, for that is what you are.

Verse: Philippians 4:8–9

> Finally, brothers and sisters, whatever is true, whatever is noble, whatever is right, whatever is pure, whatever is lovely, whatever is admirable—if anything is excellent or praiseworthy—think about such things. Whatever you have learned or received or heard from me, or seen in me—put it into practice. And the God of peace will be with you.

Exercise: Journaling and Meditation

The truest, noblest, most right, purest, loveliest, most admirable, excellent, and most praiseworthy thing is Jesus. Take this time to simply be with Him. Reflect on who He is, turn on worship music, draw a picture, or write a poem for Him. Whatever you do, allow this time to be unrushed and intentional as you dwell on Christ.

July 5

Battle Prayers (Ex)

May your prayers be like flaming arrows that explode with the life of God upon impact. May they be like lightning bolts sent from Heaven for the purposes of The Kingdom. And may they repulse and thwart the advances of the enemy on all fronts. Yes, "He trains (your) hands for war and (your) fingers for battle." (Ps. 144:1) So, fight today, pray today, draw your bow today! Amen and a thousand more amens.

Verse: Psalm 144:1

Praise be to the Lord my Rock, who trains my hands for war, my fingers for battle.

Exercise: Prayer and Fasting

Intentionally engage with the Holy Spirit in praying offensive prayers against the enemy. Speak death to sin in your life and in the lives of others. Speak against the injustices in your community and nation. Speak death to broken relationships, sickness, and hopelessness in the world around you. Choose a meal to set aside for fasting and prayer if possible. Take this time to sit with the Holy Spirit and join Him in condemning the attacks of the enemy.

July 6
A Holy Fire (Ex)

My prayer today is that the fire of God would be kindled in your heart. And may the swift wind of His Spirit stoke those mysterious flames that burn away impurity and warm frozen places. Be cleaned, be warmed and be moved. O kindling fire of God, burn in us now! Amen and a thousand more amens.

Verse: Deuteronomy 4:23–24

> Be careful not to forget the covenant of the Lord your God that he made with you; do not make for yourselves an idol in the form of anything the Lord your God has forbidden. For the Lord your God is a consuming fire, a jealous God.

Exercise: Meditation

What is a fire like? Think back to a time you just sat and watched a fire burn (a campfire with family, a summer bonfire, etc.) Close your eyes and watch the flames again in your mind. Or light a fire if it is possible, safe, and legal. This could be in a fireplace, a candle, etc. Watch the fire for 5 to 10 minutes while asking God how He wants to be a fire in your life. Slow down, sit with Jesus, and listen.

July 7

Mercy and Grace (Ex)

I pray that the offenses waged against you would be turned into a grace filled reservoir inside you. Grace to you, grace from you, grace over you. No hurt, no longing, and no offense will be able to breathe, stand against, or survive as it will be drowned, swamped, drenched, and swept away by an overwhelming surge of grace. I pray this over your life through the power of the Holy Spirit. Amen and a thousand more amens.

Verse: Proverbs 10:11–12

> The mouth of the righteous is a fountain of life, but the mouth of the wicked conceals violence. Hatred stirs up conflict, but love covers over all wrongs.

Exercise: Journaling

How have you been offended recently? By specific individuals or situations? Write these down. Talk about each instance with the Holy Spirit. Give these feelings to Him, ask Him to inform your reaction, letting Him remind you of who you are.

July 8

Listening and Watching (Ex)

May you hear with your heart and see with your soul. Know that your ability to hear has nothing to do with your ears, but is about Him speaking to you deep in your heart. And your sight is not really about your eyes, but His work in your soul and in the souls of others. Listen, watch, and wait. Then listen, watch, and wait again. His word will not be conventional, nor will it be clamorous. Still, small, soft and reverberating. He is speaking and moving. May you discern His voice clearly. Amen and a thousand more amens.

Verse: Isaiah 30:21

> Whether you turn to the right or to the left, your ears will hear a voice behind you, saying, "This is the way; walk in it."

Exercise: Memorization and Meditation

It is through the faithful walking with God that we gradually come to know Him and fulfill His will for our lives. Meditate on this concept, along with today's verse and ask the Father to speak to you. Then, commit Isaiah 30:21 to memory. Keep a small rock or similar object on your person this week. Whenever you see or feel the item, repeat the verse and ask God to guide you in the moment, in the small steps.

July 9

God's Whisper (Ex)

May God whisper to you with much specificity today and may you get close enough to hear. Yes, may His still small voice reverberate all of the way through you and be so clear that it takes your breath away and then fills you with life and more life. Life upon life to you all, through the power of your Father's whisper. Amen and a thousand more amens.

Verse: 1 Kings 19:11–13

> The Lord said, "Go out and stand on the mountain in the presence of the Lord, for the Lord is about to pass by." Then a great and powerful wind tore the mountains apart and shattered the rocks before the Lord, but the Lord was not in the wind. After the wind there was an earthquake, but the Lord was not in the earthquake. After the earthquake came a fire, but the Lord was not in the fire. And after the fire came a gentle whisper. When Elijah heard it, he pulled his cloak over his face and went out and stood at the mouth of the cave.

Exercise: Reading and Silence

Choose a chapter in the Bible to read. This could be a part of a current reading plan, a favorite Psalm, or 1 Kings 19 if you don't have a specific text in mind. Then, read the chapter in its entirety once. After finishing, take a deep breath in, hold it for 3 seconds, and release. Listen for God's voice through the verses. Write down anything you hear. Then repeat, reading slower and paying attention to any verse or verses that might stick out. Take note of these. After finishing the chapter, look at your selected verse or verses and repeat the post-reading process: take a deep breath in, hold it for 3 seconds, and release. Listen for God's voice through the verses you chose. Finally, read your selected verses again, this time paying attention to any specific words or phrases that catch your attention. Repeat the process again and record anything that you feel God says to you during this time.

JULY 10

God Speaking (P)

HOLY SPIRIT, I KNOW that You are always speaking, even when there is nothing being said. May I hear You clearly. Teach me to wait on You. Amen and a thousand more amens.

Verse: Psalm 46:10

> He says, "Be still, and know that I am God; I will be exalted among the nations, I will be exalted in the earth."

Exercise: Silence and Meditation

Focus on being in God's presence today, not on receiving any specific answers or meeting any needs. These will come in time. Instead, pursue a greater understanding of God's holiness. Take your Bible and open up to Psalm 46:10. With nothing else around and no distractions present, take a humble posture such as being on your knees if possible. Say this verse out loud. Breathe in. Breathe out. Read it again. Breathe in. Breathe out. Read it again. Repeat this process for 10 to 15 minutes, pausing to meditate on what it actually means and how you might respond.

July 11

Covering Your Loved Ones (P)

Lord Jesus, I lift up my loved ones to You today. I ask for peace, hope, love, and power to be in, on, with, and around them. Cover them today by Your power. Amen and a thousand more amens

Verse: Psalm 67:1–2

> May God be gracious to us and bless us and make his face shine on us— so that your ways may be known on earth, your salvation among all nations.

Exercise: Prayer

Take 20 minutes to talk with Jesus about the ones closest to you in your life. What are they going through? Do they know Him? How is your relationship with them? Pray a blessing over them and listen for God's voice. Write any thoughts down and share these with your loved ones when possible.

July 12

Those That Don't Know Jesus (Ex)

I AM PRAYING THAT your friends and loved ones who don't know Jesus will know Him soon. May the light of the life of Christ pierce through the darkness and open their eyes. May the impossible people who seem so far from God become living testimonies of His miraculous power. May the hopeless find hope, the blind find sight, the weak find strength, and the cold find warmth. May they find Jesus. Amen and a thousand more amens.

Verse: Isaiah 9:2

> The people walking in darkness have seen a great light; on those living in the land of deep darkness a light has dawned.

Exercise: Prayer

The Prophet Isaiah is speaking about the coming of Christ several centuries before the life of Jesus. In the same way that Jesus shared God's light during His earthly life, He can and will do the same thing today. Pray specifically for those you are close to and seem the farthest from God. Pray that they might see Jesus and their walls would come crashing down. Pray and watch for the victory.

July 13

The Miracle of Christianity (Ex)

I asked God to do a miracle in your life. He said that is what He is. He is your miracle. Spend some time with your miracle today and see what comes of it. May you see Jesus as your everything. Amen and a thousand more amens.

Verse: Psalm 63:2–5

> I have seen you in the sanctuary and beheld your power and your glory. Because your love is better than life, my lips will glorify you. I will praise you as long as I live, and in your name I will lift up my hands. I will be fully satisfied with the richest of foods; with singing lips my mouth will praise you.

Exercise: Worship

Jesus is worthy of everything we have and everything we are. He is the Risen King, the Lord of lords, the Great I Am, the Alpha and Omega, the Beginning and the End, the Lamb that was Slain, and the Lion of Judah. Remind yourself of His identity. Worship Him for who He is, not because of any need you have, or a situation on your mind right now. These are valid, but the ultimate reality is how worthy our God isand how He deserves our adoration and praise. Take 15 to 20 minutes to humble yourself. Simply adore Him. Give Him the honor that He deserves.

July 14

Heavenly Passions (Ex)

I am praying for your heavenly passions to be kindled. Yes, may a fire for God's purposes and plans explode in you, on you, and around you this day and forevermore. Amen and a thousand more amens.

Verse: 1 Corinthians 10:31

So whether you eat or drink or whatever you do, do it all for the glory of God.

Exercise: Silence, Evangelism, Worship, Reading, Meditation, Service, Prayer

Heavenly Passions are sometimes given during prayer, but are always developed and exercised through action. Ask God how He wants you to spend this time today. Do you need to sit quietly before heaven? Do you need to share the Gospel with that person on your mind? Have you not spent much time worshiping Jesus lately? Should you spend this time reading and meditating on God's Word? Is there a church outreach or non-profit where you might serve? Ask, listen, and act.

July 15

Where Healing Comes From (Ex)

I asked God to heal your body today. He said that He is your healing. Yes, He is all you need. He is the point of our existence and the reason for our being. So, be healed in Him my friends. Amen and a thousand more amens.

Verse: Isaiah 41:10

> So do not fear, for I am with you; do not be dismayed, for I am your God. I will strengthen you and help you; I will uphold you with my righteous right hand.

Exercise: Prayer

Is there any part of your body, mind, or spirit that needs healing? To clarify, by body I mean your physical person and any pains or sickness that is present. By mind, your emotions, sleep quality, relationships, and cognitive abilities. By spirit, your relationship with God, your ability to hear His voice, or an area that is not surrendered to Him, such as a sinful habit or a lack of time with Him. Pray through any identified areas and talk about them with Jesus. Ask for His presence to be over you, for Him to walk with you through each of these things, and for Him to guide your thoughts and actions.

July 16

Fear's Fear (Ex)

I asked God to calm your fears. He said that fear fears Him. May you see the fear in your life tremble, fall, and fade away. And in the process, may the fear in the lives around you do the same. Amen and a thousand more amens.

Verse: Joshua 1:9

> Have I not commanded you? Be strong and courageous. Do not be afraid; do not be discouraged, for the LORD your God will be with you wherever you go.

Exercise: Meditation and Prayer

Joshua receives this command before entering the Promised Land with the Israelites. God did not say this expecting Joshua to rely on an inner strength and personal bravery to carry Him through the conquest. No, he could be strong and courageous because God was going with Him. The hero of the story is God and His power to fulfill His promises, not on the might of the Israelites. It is the same for you and me. We are not the hero of the story. After reading the prayer and the verse, think of specific situations in which you have seen fear in others. Pray for God's presence to guide and encourage all those involved, so that these fears might melt away in His presence.

July 17
Praying for Others (P)

How might I pray for others? What would you have me pray for today, Holy Spirit? I love you and want to join You in Your work today. Amen and a thousand more amens.

Verse: Ephesians 6:18

> And pray in the Spirit on all occasions with all kinds of prayers and requests. With this in mind, be alert and always keep on praying for all the Lord's people.

Exercise: Prayer

Take time to be quiet and listen for God's direction. Who does He want you to pray for today? There may be some situations that you think need prayer, but listen for God's direction. Take 15 to 20 minutes and focus specifically on others.

July 18

The Ultimate Blessing (Ex)

I asked God to shower you with many blessings. He said that you only need one . . . Him. Be blessed today my friends with the Ultimate Blessing. Amen and a thousand more amens.

Verse: Matthew 6:33

> But seek first his kingdom and his righteousness, and all these things will be given to you as well.

Exercise: Reading and Worship

Read Matthew 6:25–34. The things that Jesus lists are not bad in and of themselves. We need clothes, food, and provision, but we need God infinitely more. Spend this time with God today, recognizing your dependence on Him and submitting to Him once again. This could include a time of listening for His direction, reading and meditating on this passage of Scripture, or taking time to worship Him.

July 19

The Ultimate Help (P)

Holy Spirit, I know that You are my present help. A help that is here, now, always and ready. I depend on You. Apart from You, what am I? A mist that is here for a moment and then gone. May I know You more and rely on You more for my very life today. Amen and a thousand more amens.

Verse: Psalm 121:5–8

> The Lord watches over you— the Lord is your shade at your right hand; the sun will not harm you by day, nor the moon by night. The Lord will keep you from all harm— he will watch over your life; the Lord will watch over your coming and going both now and forevermore.

Exercise: Meditation and Journaling

After reading the prayer and Scripture, read them again and ask yourself how they apply to you. Do you rely on God for your life, or do you take it in your own hands? When you succeed, do you keep the credit for yourself? When there is pain, do you find yourself losing hope quickly? Write down your answers to these questions and ask the Father to help you rely on Him more.

July 20

Total Healing (Ex)

I AM PRAYING FOR healing in every aspect of your being. In your body, soul and spirit. Totally healed . . . totally free. Yes, healed and free you shall be. Amen and a thousand more amens.

Verse: 2 Corinthians 3:17–18

> Now the Lord is the Spirit, and where the Spirit of the Lord is, there is freedom. And we all, who with unveiled faces contemplate the Lord's glory, are being transformed into his image with ever-increasing glory, which comes from the Lord, who is the Spirit.

Exercise: Prayer

The freedom that Christ grants is healing: relational, physical, spiritual, and complete healing. We are made right before Him and will spend eternity experiencing that wholeness. As His children, we can begin to experience this complete life now. Read this verse over your life and receive all that God has for you today: strength, hope, insight, humility, awe, love, power, etc. Then, pray this prayer and verse over one or two others.

July 21

Constantly Hearing His Voice (Ex)

Father, come speak to me this day. I know that You are always speaking, even while I sleep. But help me hear You clearly today. I give You room. This time is Yours. I come sit with you again. Amen and a thousand more amens.

Verse: Proverbs 2:1–5

> My son, if you accept my words and store up my commands within you, turning your ear to wisdom and applying your heart to understanding— indeed, if you call out for insight and cry aloud for understanding, and if you look for it as for silver and search for it as for hidden treasure, then you will understand the fear of the Lord and find the knowledge of God.

Exercise: Meditation, Silence, and Journaling

During this time, have a pen and paper on hand. Take a minute or two to slow down from the day. Breathe slowly. When you breathe in, imagine you are breathing in the Holy Spirit. When you breathe out, release distractions. Then for the next 15 to 20 minutes, sit with God. If specific people or situations come up in your mind, write them down. If an area of your life comes to mind, ask for His perspective on the subject. If nothing specific is happening, continue to listen and just be with the Father.

July 22

Being Jesus in Your World (Ex)

May visions and thoughts of His life in your life flood your mind. Yes, may you be inundated with ideas as to how to be Jesus to those around you. He in you, you in Him. Light in dark places, hope in heavy ones, and life where death seeks to cast its evil pallor. Amen and a thousand more amens.

Verse: John 14:12

> Very truly I tell you, whoever believes in me will do the works I have been doing, and they will do even greater things than these, because I am going to the Father.

Exercise: Prayer, Service, Evangelism

You have been empowered by the Holy Spirit to be Christ in your world, to display His love and redemption through your thoughts, words, and actions. In your devotional time, read the prayer over your life and commit to be intentional with your time. Be listening and watching for opportunities to share Jesus through word or deed.

July 23

Seeing God in a New Way (Ex)

I am asking God to reveal Himself to you in a new way. Yes, may you see Him like you never have before. And when you do, may new life follow. Boundless, new and fresh life to you all. Amen and a thousand more amens.

Verse: Luke 10:22–24

> All things have been committed to me by my Father. No one knows who the Son is except the Father, and no one knows who the Father is except the Son and those to whom the Son chooses to reveal him." Then he turned to his disciples and said privately, "Blessed are the eyes that see what you see. For I tell you that many prophets and kings wanted to see what you see but did not see it, and to hear what you hear but did not hear it."

Exercise: Meditation and Prayer

Although Jesus was talking to the Twelve disciples who had lived and interacted with Him for three years, Christ still reveals His and the Father's character today. Take this time to think about who God is. What is He like? Ask Him to open your eyes to His holiness and beauty in new ways today.

July 24

Out of Complacency (Ex)

I pray that you would be stirred. Yes, may He move you out of complacency and beyond comfort. You and your God in a place where good battle will be fought on behalf of the Kingdom. His Kingdom come and His will be done in you and through you this day. May laziness and selfish motives fall off you today. Amen and a thousand more amens.

Verse: 1 Corinthians 9:24–27

> Do you not know that in a race all the runners run, but only one gets the prize? Run in such a way as to get the prize. Everyone who competes in the games goes into strict training. They do it to get a crown that will not last, but we do it to get a crown that will last forever.Therefore I do not run like someone running aimlessly; I do not fight like a boxer beating the air. No, I strike a blow to my body and make it my slave so that after I have preached to others, I myself will not be disqualified for the prize.

Exercise: Journaling

After reading the prayer and the passage, ask the Holy Spirit to enter this moment. It is easy to get caught up in complacency and comfort. Ask him to reveal the areas in which you have acted in your own interests or have neglected the needs of others. You have been called to live a sacrificed life. Write down areas where you see the need for improvement and repent.

July 25

Holy Passion (Ex)

I AM PRAYING THAT a fire would be kindled in your heart. Yes, that you would feel a passion and energy for life that is not of this world. That's because it came from the Lord of Heaven. Amen and a thousand more amens.

Verse: Acts 2:1–4

> When the day of Pentecost came, they were all together in one place. Suddenly a sound like the blowing of a violent wind came from heaven and filled the whole house where they were sitting. They saw what seemed to be tongues of fire that separated and came to rest on each of them. All of them were filled with the Holy Spirit and began to speak in other tongues as the Spirit enabled them.

Exercise: Prayer

The Holy Spirit not only calls you to a holy life, He empowers you to bring the life of Christ to your world. Ask Him to fill you with His fire today in a new way. Listen for His direction, ask for His power, and remain in His presence. Make this time unique between you and Jesus. Put on music, open the Bible, or take out your journal as you listen. Lay down your desires and ask Him to give you His.

July 26

Happiness (Ex)

I am praying for happiness to well up in you and burst. Random explosions of happiness all day long. And at the end of it, may you lay your head down, face tired from smiling. May it be a good and happy day for you because of Christ in you. Amen and a thousand more amens.

Verse: Hebrews 12:2

> Fixing our eyes on Jesus, the pioneer and perfecter of faith. For the joy set before him he endured the cross, scorning its shame, and sat down at the right hand of the throne of God.

Exercise: Prayer and Meditation

Regardless of your circumstances or challenges today, you have reason to have joy: the empty tomb of Jesus. Take several minutes to meditate on the death and resurrection of Christ. What does it mean for you? How can you react to your day because of it? Sit quietly and ask Him to open your eyes to this infinite source of joy. Whenever you are tempted to get frustrated or upset today, remind yourself of Christ.

July 27

Strength (Ex)

I am praying that strength would come your way, and that it would affect your mind, body and spirit. Yes, strength to every part of you in the name of Jesus. His strength in you, to you, through you. May you know what His strength looks and feels like today. Amen and a thousand more amens.

Verse: 2 Corinthians 12:9

> But he said to me, "My grace is sufficient for you, for my power is made perfect in weakness." Therefore I will boast all the more gladly about my weaknesses, so that Christ's power may rest on me.

Exercise: Journaling

In what areas of your life are you experiencing weakness? Where do you feel inadequate or worried that things will not go your way? Write these areas down. Be honest with God on how they make you feel and what you are worried about. Then, ask the Holy Spirit to show His strength in these places through out this week.

July 28

Kingdom Battle (Ex)

I am praying that you will engage in good Kingdom battle today. Speak, touch, walk, and move on His behalf. Ask Him what He wants you to do, then listen and do. May you take back what the enemy has stolen from you, your family, and your community by the power of Christ. Amen and a thousand more amens.

Verse: Ephesians 6:12–13

> For our struggle is not against flesh and blood, but against the rulers, against the authorities, against the powers of this dark world and against the spiritual forces of evil in the heavenly realms. Therefore put on the full armor of God, so that when the day of evil comes, you may be able to stand your ground, and after you have done everything, to stand.

Exercise: Prayer and Service

Being a Christian is not about personal gain or comfort. There is a spiritual struggle occurring constantly in the world. Jesus is our King and has won the ultimate victory, but that reality has not yet reached completion. Take time to listen for God's direction. Who should you pray for today? Who needs to hear the Gospel message? Where has the enemy been attacking you or your family lately? Bring these to the Holy Spirit and listen for any steps that need to be taken today to partner with what Jesus is doing around you.

July 29

Spiritual Protection (P)

Lord Jesus, cover me in this day of war. Yes, may all the efforts of the enemy against me be thwarted, repulsed, and turned back upon him. Display Your omnipotent power in audacious fashion. Amen and a thousand more amens.

Verse: Psalm 28:7

> The LORD is my strength and my shield; my heart trusts in him, and he helps me. My heart leaps for joy, and with my song I praise him.

Exercise: Prayer, Worship, and Memorization

After reading this prayer over your life and being informed by the passage of Scripture, worship Jesus for how wonderfully He loves you and protects you. You are not alone, you are not at the mercy of your circumstances, and you are not defined by mistakes or wounds. Either turn some worship music on to sing to Him, or adore Him in your own words through prayer and praise. Then, commit Psalm 28:7 to memory. Keep a small rock or similar object on your person. Whenever you feel or see the item, repeat the verse and thank God for His wonderful love and protection. You are His child and He will cover you.

July 30

God's Presence on Your Body (Ex)

I AM PRAYING FOR your body today. May you feel God in it. Yes, may the One who created you touch, heal, and empower your physical person in a manner that only The Creator can. May it function better than it ever has and may you clearly experience heaven's blessing on it today. May the Holy Spirit meet you in the midst of pain and give you peace. Amen and a thousand more amens.

Verse: 3 John 1:2

> Dear friend, I pray that you may enjoy good health and that all may go well with you, even as your soul is getting along well.

Exercise: Prayer

Identify any physical ailments you have. Jesus cares about the pain or discomfort you experience. Bring these to Him again, praying for two things. First, ask for healing. He is the Healer and Comforter and can take away your sickness or pain. Take several minutes to talk with Him about them. Second, ask God to be with you, that His presence would rest on you. It is a beautiful thing when God miraculously heals an individual, but it is equally inspiring for someone to receive God's peace and joy in the midst of suffering. All disease and pain will be taken away when Jesus returns, and He will heal many before then.

July 31

Impossible Desires (Ex)

I am praying that the deepest desires of your heart come alive. Yes, may those things that have seemed utterly impossible begin to look highly probable. May you bring these people or situations to Jesus again and experience His power anew. Amen and a thousand more amens.

Verse: Matthew 19:26

> Jesus looked at them and said, "With man this is impossible, but with God all things are possible."

Exercise: Prayer and Journaling

Read Matthew 19:16–30 to see the context of this passage. It seems impossible that anyone can be saved, but Jesus reassures His disciples that there are no limits on the ability of the Father. If He can redeem a broken creation such as humanity, all other things can be achieved within Him as well. Write down the desires in your heart that you have hoped for and held onto for a long time. Then, ask yourself these questions: Are the desires biblical? Will their fulfillment bring honor to Jesus, or result in only personal gain? Why do I want these in the first place? Does God want to shift them at all to line up with His will? Am I supposed to do anything to see this come to pass? Ask each of these while in dialogue with the Holy Spirit, write down the responses, and pray over each one specifically.

August 1

Peace Like a River (Ex)

May peace come your way. Yes, peace like a river. A river that sweeps you away, invigorates, and carries you for days upon end. The peace of Heaven in your earthly space. Amen and a thousand more amens.

Verse: Psalm 23:1–2

> The Lord is my shepherd, I lack nothing. He makes me lie down in green pastures, he leads me beside quiet waters.

Exercise: Reading and Meditation

Read the entirety of Psalm 23. Imagine what this scene would be like. Utilize all five senses. What do you see? What color is the water? How does the grass look? What do you hear? Are there birds? How loud is the stream? What do you feel? Are you sitting in the grass, against a tree, or something else? What do you smell? What do you taste when you breathe in? Take 5 to 10 minutes for this meditation. Ask the Father to give you the same peace that this Psalm describes, and that He would help you share it with others.

August 2

The Final Word (Ex)

Be encouraged, you can't fail. In Him, all things are made new. Your mind, your plans, your purpose, your body . . . yes your whole person. Jesus is the Great Redeemer. Redemption to you all this day. Right here, right now. Amen and a thousand more amens.

Verse: Galatians 2:20

> I have been crucified with Christ and I no longer live, but Christ lives in me. The life I now live in the body, I live by faith in the Son of God, who loved me and gave himself for me.

Exercise: Prayer and Meditation

Read both the prayer and Scripture out loud to yourself. Pause. Breathe in. Breathe out. Read them out loud again. Jesus has the final word on who you are and your value. Breathe in. Breathe out. Read. Repeat. Spend this time with the Father and allow Him to remind you of how He sees you.

August 3

New Desires (P)

God, I am asking You to renew my mind. Yes, a total new mind. Not just an overhaul of the old either. Fresh thoughts, dreams, and visions that would honor You and help Your Kingdom come in and through my life. I want to know You more and share Your heart. Amen and a thousand more amens.

Verse: Ezekiel 36:26–27

> I will give you a new heart and put a new spirit in you; I will remove from you your heart of stone and give you a heart of flesh. And I will put my Spirit in you and move you to follow my decrees and be careful to keep my laws.

Exercise: Journaling

What have your desires been lately? What desires does God want to give you? His Word tells us that His Spirit will move us to follow Him. Ask Him to speak to you during this time. Does He want to change any of your plans, or reignite your passion for past directions? Listen, write, and abide.

August 4

Consistency (Ex)

I AM PRAYING THAT your words will have weight. And for that to happen, you must be living what you speak. Live truth and your words will carry it into the lives of others. May the Holy Spirit transform you to look more and more like Jesus in this way and show you any areas that need change. Amen and a thousand more amens.

Verse: Hebrews 13:7–8

> Remember your leaders, who spoke the word of God to you. Consider the outcome of their way of life and imitate their faith. Jesus Christ is the same yesterday and today and forever.

Exercise: Meditation and Journaling

Ask the Holy Spirit to show you the ways you have been consistent and the areas which need growth. Examples include your attitude, consistent time with Jesus, how you treat others, and how you use your free time. Take 2 to 3 minutes to identify these and write them down.

August 5

Hearing Your Name (Ex)

May God whisper your name. Yes, may you know without a shadow of a doubt that your Heavenly Father has called to you. Be quiet long enough to hear it. He knows you and loves you like no other. May you understand this in a greater way today. Amen and a thousand more amens.

Verse: Isaiah 43:1

> But now, this is what the LORD says-- he who created you, Jacob, he who formed you, Israel: "Do not fear, for I have redeemed you; I have summoned you by name; you are mine."

Exercise: Meditation and Silence

Sadly, many have experienced rejection and a lack of intimacy from those who should have loved them most, such as parents or significant others. This pain can leave wounds within that hinder one from being able to receive love and affirmation. Take 10 to 15 minutes to listen for God's voice calling your name today. Read Isaiah 43:1 over yourself and be reminded that you are worthy of love because the Father has chosen you.

August 6

God with You (Ex)

I asked God to be with you today. He said that there was no way, no place, and no time where He could be otherwise. That's what the "OMNI" in omnipresent means. You are covered, not alone. You are taken care of, not lost. Thought about, not forgotten. You are Fathered, not orphaned. Amen and a thousand more amens.

Verse: Psalm 139:7–10

> Where can I go from your Spirit? Where can I flee from your presence? If I go up to the heavens, you are there; if I make my bed in the depths, you are there. If I rise on the wings of the dawn, if I settle on the far side of the sea, even there your hand will guide me, your right hand will hold me fast.

Exercise: Prayer and Meditation

Think about the past year. What have been the hardest moments you have experienced in the year? How about the best? Have you had any significant changes to your lifestyle? Reflect on how much God has brought you through. He has never left you and He is still with you. Thank Him for bringing you through all of your past mountains and surrender again to Him the current struggles you face.

August 7

Protection (Ex)

I asked God to protect you today. He said that it's done. He has gone before you into time and taken care of business on behalf of you and your people. The Timeless One can do these sorts of things. Blessings to all of you. Amen and a thousand more amens.

Verse: Exodus 13:21–22

> By day the Lord went ahead of them in a pillar of cloud to guide them on their way and by night in a pillar of fire to give them light, so that they could travel by day or night. Neither the pillar of cloud by day nor the pillar of fire by night left its place in front of the people.

Exercise: Prayer

After asking the Holy Spirit to go before you throughout your day, pray the same over your family. Bless each of their days specifically and pray that just as the pillars of cloud and fire guided the Israelites, so too would the Holy Spirit direct your people.

August 8

Doubts (P)

Father, remind me of how many times You have taken care of my doubts through a greater understanding of Jesus. Jesus is the Doubt Killer and Life Giver. May any doubts give birth to new life and fresh vision through interaction with You. I don't have to understand everything, but just let me know You more. Thank you for opening my eyes to You. Amen and a thousand more amens.

Verse: Isaiah 55:9

> As the heavens are higher than the earth, so are my ways higher than your ways and my thoughts than your thoughts.

Exercise: Journaling

What things with God have been hard to understand? Has there been a tragedy or deep question that can't seem to be resolved? Write these down and ask for God's answer. Listen with a pen in hand and a Bible nearby if any verses come to mind. However, if no answers seem to present themselves, ask God for the ability to trust Him in the midst of the confusion. Not everything makes sense and there are some things that are difficult to process with God. Don't shrink away from these things, but be honest with the Father and trust that He knows best. He is not obligated to explain Himself, but He does promise to be with us through everything.

August 9

God is Bigger (Ex)

This morning I prayed that you would realize God is bigger than your biggest issue, problem, or struggle. Yes, I asked Him to deal with whomever or whatever is stealing from, intimidating, or hampering you from living life to the fullest. May you see breakthrough soon in those areas. Amen and a thousand more amens.

Verse: 1 Timothy 1:17

> Now to the King eternal, immortal, invisible, the only God, be honor and glory for ever and ever. Amen.

Exercise: Worship

Challenges and difficult people can be common in life. They can take away peace, distract from your purpose, and steal the joy of life if you let them. Instead, take this devotional time today to remind yourself of who God is. Read the verse. Meditate on God and ask Him to reveal Himself in a greater way. Worship His name and humble yourself as you focus on Him. Those other distractions may be real, but they are fleeting when compared to God.

August 10

Encouraged Inspite of the World (Ex)

I AM PRAYING THAT you would be encouraged today. May Jesus in you overpower the life-draining effects of the world around you. Jesus vs. the world=no contest. Life to you my friends and overflowing amounts of it! Amen and a thousand more amens.

Verse: Colossians 3:1–4

> Since, then, you have been raised with Christ, set your hearts on things above, where Christ is, seated at the right hand of God. Set your minds on things above, not on earthly things. For you died, and your life is now hidden with Christ in God. When Christ, who is your life, appears, then you also will appear with him in glory.

Exercise: Reading

It can be hard at times to remain hopeful and focused on Christ in the midst of a crazy world. Read Colossians chapter 3 in its entirety. Pause after the first reading, asking God to speak to you through His Word. Spend a minute thinking and listening. Read the chapter again, slowly. Take note of any verses that catch your attention specifically. Take another minute or two to listen for God's voice. Read the passage one more time, listening for what God says to you about this world and the mindset you should have in it.

August 11

Fearless (Ex)

I am praying for fear to lose its grip on you, in the Name of the One who knows no fear. Fear can't grip Him, neither can it grip those who are His. So, may you walk, rest, reside, and live in the powerful, fearless place that is Jesus. Fearless and grip free you shall be. Amen and a thousand more amens.

Verse: 1 John 4:18

> There is no fear in love. But perfect love drives out fear, because fear has to do with punishment. The one who fears is not made perfect in love.

Exercise: Journaling and Prayer

What are you afraid of? Does fear paralyze you at times? If not, do you know anyone who is held in fear? Take this time to write out a prayer over these fears, asking Jesus to take them away and replace those feelings with an overwhelming awareness of His perfect love.

August 12

Understanding God's Power (Ex)

I AM PRAYING THIS morning that you would feel God's power. Yes, that you would feel fired up, fueled up, rested up and ready to assault the enemy. A fiery and relentless assault upon the enemy you shall be. Amen and a thousand more amens.

Verse: 1 Chronicles 29:11

> Yours, LORD, is the greatness and the power and the glory and the majesty and the splendor, for everything in heaven and earth is yours. Yours, LORD, is the kingdom; you are exalted as head over all.

Exercise: Worship

In this passage, King David is recounting the nature and sovereignty of God. He is able to deliver and is over all things. Take this time to remind yourself of God's power through worship. What has He brought you through? How much does He know? What is beyond His reach? This time could include prayers of adoring Him, journaling the answers to these questions, or reading all of David's prayer in 1 Chronicles 29:10–20.

August 13

Affirmed by God (Ex)

I am praying today that you feel affirmed by God. Yes, affirmation from Heaven that will make your day on earth so much better. May God's thoughts invade your space and open your eyes to His presence and approval. Amen and a thousand more amens.

Verse: 2 Corinthians 10:18

> For it is not the one who commends himself who is approved, but the one whom the Lord commends.

Exercise: Prayer

Regardless of how your life has been lately, or where you are at with God, ask Him, "How do you see me?" Find a quiet place without any distractions for 10 to 15 minutes. Listen for any specific verses or songs. Allow Him to speak into any brokenness or false ideas you have about yourself. Allow Him to speak into any striving or attempts to earn His approval.

August 14

Redeeming Anxiety (Ex)

I am praying that the fear, panic, and anxiety you have recently been vexed with will be turned by God into fuel for Hope to burn bright, long, and strong in you. Yes, burn Hope, burn. In the name of The Hopeful One, Jesus. Amen and a thousand more amens.

Verse: Hebrews 6:19–20

> We have this hope as an anchor for the soul, firm and secure. It enters the inner sanctuary behind the curtain, where our forerunner, Jesus, has entered on our behalf. He has become a high priest forever, in the order of Melchizedek.

Exercise: Meditation

Jesus has entered God's presence to intercede on our behalf. He has become like Melchizedek, an Old Testament king and priest, holding both roles before the Father. Christ's work is the anchor for your soul, as even now He prays for you. Think about that amazing fact: Jesus is talking to the Father about YOU at this very moment. Meditate on this truth. What does it mean for you? How should you approach today because of it? How should you react to challenges or sorrow or success? Ask the Holy Spirit to help you grasp the awe-inspiring fact of Jesus' prayers over your life.

August 15

Diminishing Fear (P)

Lord God, I know that in You there is no fear. May Your overwhelming presence eradicate any and all fears that try and intimidate today. May You become more real today and show fear to be the lie that it is. Thank you for bringing peace and safety, Holy Spirit. Amen and a thousand more amens.

Verse: 2 Timothy 1:7

> For the Spirit God gave us does not make us timid, but gives us power, love and self-discipline.

Exercise: Prayer

Who in your life battles fear? How well do they know Him? Pray that the Father would become so real in the lives of the people you are thinking of that they cannot deny Him any longer. Pray that their doubts and insecurities would vanish in Jesus name. Read the prayer and verse over their situations and thank God for revelation in their lives.

August 16

Covered by the Holy Spirit (Ex)

May the Spirit of the Lord cover you. And may you know that He has got your back, your front, your sides, above and below you. Yes, God has got you covered this day, all day. When you feel Him and when you don't, His faithfulness supersedes our finite ability to perceive Him. May you rest in His love and power today in the face of any situation or challenge that comes your way. Amen and a thousand more amens.

Verse: Psalm 32:7

> You are my hiding place; you will protect me from trouble and surround me with songs of deliverance.

Exercise: Meditation and Prayer

The Holy Spirit goes ahead of you and remains with you. What does this actually mean? How does He go ahead of you? Think of your schedule and ask God to work before you even enter the situations you will face today. Pray specifically for places, people, and responsibilities. Think about how God will go before you. Don't just pray the prayer, but think about what you are saying and allow that to encourage you as you enter your day.

August 17

The Word (P)

Jesus, You are my Word, my logic and my truth. So, in your name, may I speak, dwell upon, and rest in The Word today. May Your truth flow through my thoughts and actions into the lives of others and the challenges I face. May I represent You well today. Amen and a thousand more amens.

Verse: Hebrews 4:12

> For the word of God is alive and active. Sharper than any double-edged sword, it penetrates even to divide soul and spirit, joints and marrow; it judges the thoughts and attitudes of the heart.

2 Timothy 3:16–17

> All Scripture is God-breathed and is useful for teaching, rebuking, correcting and training in righteousness, so that the servant of God may be thoroughly equipped for every good work.

Exercise: Journaling

On a piece of paper, answer these questions: How often do you read the Bible? How many days out of the week? Where have you been reading lately? Do you remember what you have been reading about? Do you have a plan you have been following, or a book you have been going through? Consistent time in Scripture is of the utmost importance. It is our weapon. Ask the Holy Spirit what this discipline should look like and make a plan. If you have been consistent with your reading, use this time to put what you have been learning to words. Write what you believe God is teaching you through His Word.

August 18

Guided Through Relationship (Ex)

To know Christ is to be guided. May you draw close to Him and be directed to the right places, at the right time, with the right people, for the right reasons. May divine appointments be yours today for His glory. Amen and a thousand more amens.

Verse: Proverbs 16:9

In their hearts humans plan their course, but the LORD establishes their steps.

Exercise: Prayer and Journaling

After praying that your day would be guided by the Holy Spirit, pray the same for your loved ones and those you work with. Pray for these people specifically, that the Lord would establish their steps. Then at the end of the day, record any moments in which you saw God at work, either in your life or in the lives of those around you.

August 19

Living in Christ (Ex)

The Hope, Light, and Life of Jesus to you this day. Yes, may you be filled with His Hope, guided by His Light, and sustained by His Life. May all despair, darkness, and death be driven back from you and your people in the name of Jesus Christ. Amen and a thousand more amens.

Verse: 1 Thessalonians 5:8

> But since we belong to the day, let us be sober, putting on faith and love as a breastplate, and the hope of salvation as a helmet.

Exercise: Prayer and Worship

Pray specifically for the areas you see in which the Hope, Light, and Life of Christ are needed. Is there difficulty? Is there uncertainty? Is there discouragement? Pray against these things in your life and in the lives of those around you. Then, spend the last 5 to 10 minutes of your devotional time just being with Jesus and thanking Him for who He is.

August 20

Take Our Eyes Off of Ourselves (Ex)

May you take your eyes off of personal gain or feelings and focus once more on the cross. May the Holy Spirit remind you that this life is not about what you can get out of it, but instead is about Jesus and loving those that God has put in your life. May this become ever more real to you today as you fall deeper in love with Jesus. Amen and a thousand more amens.

Verse: Luke 9:23

> Then he said to them all: "Whoever wants to be my disciple must deny themselves and take up their cross daily and follow me."

Exercise: Prayer

Have you fallen in love with yourself: your appetites, your aspirations, your desires, your career, your hobbies? As we take up our cross, we must remember that saying "yes" to Jesus is ultimately saying "no" to self. Reflect on your life and your motivations recently. Ask the Holy Spirit to mentally walk with you and show you any areas that have been more concerned with yourself than Him.

August 21

Speaking God's Word (Ex)

May you say what God wants you to and then do what you say you will do. God will be with you and will help you be a person of integrity and truth. May distractions melt away as you receive a clear understanding of who you are in Him. You are a child of God. Act like what you are today. Amen and a thousand more amens.

Verse: Philippians 2:12–13

> Therefore, my dear friends, as you have always obeyed—not only in my presence, but now much more in my absence—continue to work out your salvation with fear and trembling, for it is God who works in you to will and to act in order to fulfill his good purpose.

Exercise: Meditation and Memorization

The Holy Spirit lives in you and helps you live the Christian life. Yes, effort and sacrifice are needed, but we will not succeed without relying on God's strength in our lives. Read the prayer and verse again, listening for God's voice concerning any of the areas discussed. Does He want any habit or mindset to change in you? Afterwards, commit Philippians 2:12–13 to memory. Keep a small rock or similar object on your person. Every time you see or feel the item this week, repeat the verse and pause as you think about it.

August 22

Giants in Culture (Ex)

May the giants intimidating our culture be terrified and miserable that you are near. Yes, be on the prowl for them and push them out of their strongholds. May the Holy Spirit open your eyes to their influences so you can exert the power of heaven in driving them off. Victory and breakthrough to you today. Amen and a thousand more amens.

Verse: Ephesians 1:18–21

> I pray that the eyes of your heart may be enlightened in order that you may know the hope to which he has called you, the riches of his glorious inheritance in his holy people, and his incomparably great power for us who believe. That power is the same as the mighty strength he exerted when he raised Christ from the dead and seated him at his right hand in the heavenly realms, far above all rule and authority, power and dominion, and every name that is invoked, not only in the present age but also in the one to come.

Exercise: Prayer and Reading

Take 5 minutes to listen after reading today's prayer and passage of Scripture. What area or stronghold of the enemy does Jesus want you to join Him in praying against? Is there a certain evil in society that angers you or hurts your heart to see? This could be the presence of drugs, broken families, pornography, etc. After identifying this area, pray Ephesians 1:18–21 over it. Read each verse and pray the message of it over the situation. For example, you could ask for eyes to be opened, people to be set free, and Christ's power to be known.

August 23

Living in Resurrection (Ex)

I AM ASKING GOD today for your hopes to be resurrected. Your thoughts to be resurrected. Your faith to be resurrected. Your plans to be resurrected. Your health to be resurrected. Your potential to be resurrected. Your visions to be resurrected. Your dreams to be resurrected. Your relationships to be resurrected. Your desire to be resurrected. May the Resurrected One resurrect these things. Amen and a thousand more amens.

Verse: 1 Peter 1:3–4a

> Praise be to the God and Father of our Lord Jesus Christ! In his great mercy he has given us new birth into a living hope through the resurrection of Jesus Christ from the dead, and into an inheritance that can never perish, spoil or fade.

Exercise: Prayer

Spend time praying this prayer over those in your life who are not living in Jesus' resurrection. These people may not know Jesus yet, or have lost sight of His authority and need to be renewed. Read the prayer and passage from 1 Peter over their lives.

August 24

He Speaks to You (Ex)

May you hear Jesus speak your name today. I don't mean this in some cute little metaphysical way either. I am asking that He call your name and that both you and He know that He has done so. Like He called Mary's name at the tomb and Peter's name by the seashore, I pray that He does so to you. And when He does, may you feel singled out, focused upon and loved by the King of Kings. Amen and a thousand more amens

Verse: Isaiah 43:1

> But now, this is what the LORD says-- he who created you, Jacob, he who formed you, Israel: "Do not fear, for I have redeemed you; I have summoned you by name; you are mine."

Exercise: Meditation and Journaling

Ask God to clearly show His presence in your life so, that you may be reminded of His call. His love is so amazing, He continues to lavish more and more love in both small and great ways. Be on the lookout for His calling your name today. When you hear it, write down where, when and how it happened. it will encourage you in the future.

August 25

The Breath of God (Ex)

May God breathe life into your spirit today. Yes, may His breath fill you fully and bring life to the lifeless places. And may those lifeless and hurting places be restored, healed, and renewed. Life to you, breath to you, hope to you right now. Breathe on us O God, breathe on us all. Amen and a thousand more amens.

Verse: Job 33:4

The Spirit of God has made me; the breath of the Almighty gives me life.

Exercise: Memorization and Meditation

After reading the prayer, commit Job 33:4 to memory. For the next three days, keep a small rock or similar item on your person. Every time you see or feel the item, think of the life that Christ has breathed in you because of His Resurrection. Think about it with the Holy Spirit and ask Him to make that truth your ultimate reality.

AUGUST 26

Friends (Ex)

SEEING OLD FRIENDS BRINGS new joy. A joy rooted in the heart of God. May you experience this joy today and enjoy the fellowship of other believers. You have entered the family of God and belong here. May you be reminded of this and remind others of it as well because of the unity you have in Christ. Amen and a thousand more amens.

Verse: Matthew 19:29

> And everyone who has left houses or brothers or sisters or father or mother or wife or children or fields for my sake will receive a hundred times as much and will inherit eternal life.

Exercise: Community and Prayer

During this time, call a fellow believer. Thank him or her for the encouragement they have been and ask if they need prayer for anything. Share the things that you need prayer for and spend time praying for one another. Our brothers and sisters in Christ are one of the greatest gifts we receive as Christians. Don't take them for granted, but encourage and cultivate these relationships.

August 27

Loved by God (Ex)

May you realize that you are loved by God more than you will ever know. Unfathomable, grace-based, and boundless. Jesus is the physical and real picture of it. Look to Him today. May you be reminded of how He feels for you and what He did so you could know Him. Amen and a thousand more amens.

Verse: John 3:16–17

> For God so loved the world that he gave his one and only Son, that whoever believes in him shall not perish but have eternal life. For God did not send his Son into the world to condemn the world, but to save the world through him.

Exercise: Meditation and Silence

Repeat the prayer and verses out loud to yourself. Remind yourself of the cross and the beautiful relationship and purpose that have been in your life since you accepted Jesus. Take this time to sit quietly and reflect on who Jesus is and your relationship with Him since you met Him. Who were you before? What has He brought you through? Who would you be without Him? Take 15 to 20 minutes with Jesus and gratefully acknowledge who He is and what He has done for you.

August 28

Carriers of Grace and Truth (P)

God, make me a living example of grace and truth. Full of graceful, truthful fire is what I want to be. Reveal Yourself through me today so that others may see You. Thank you for revealing Yourself to me. Here I am, send me. Amen and a thousand more amens.

Verse: Isaiah 6:8

> Then I heard the voice of the Lord saying, "Whom shall I send? And who will go for us?" And I said, "Here am I. Send me!"

Exercise: Fasting and Journaling

Choose to either fast a meal or all of today if possible. During the time you would have eaten, sit quietly with Jesus and ask Him to speak. It is more important that your heart and character are developed than knowing what to do. Allow Him to speak to you about who He wants you to be and what He is calling you to do. If you don't receive any specific instructions, don't lose focus or motivation. Press in. Listen. Be with Him. Learn His heart. Die to yourself. If you are looking to make this discipline a normal occurrence, choose a day out of the week to fast in some capacity. It is a great way to intentionally pursue God and His will.

August 29

Fear Overwhelmed by Hope (Ex)

I AM PRAYING FOR you to see that God is bigger than your biggest. Yes, whatever it is that is intimidating, shaming, or haunting you will be swallowed up by the power of God. And then, hope will be your constant companion and forever friend. Fear swallowed by hope. Amen and a thousand more amens.

Verse: Philippians 2:9–11

> Therefore God exalted him to the highest place and gave him the name that is above every name, that at the name of Jesus every knee should bow, in heaven and on earth and under the earth, and every tongue acknowledge that Jesus Christ is Lord, to the glory of God the Father.

Exercise: Prayer

Every knee must bow at the name of Jesus, including the spiritual forces of the enemy. Think of a person in your life that has lived in fear and worry for far too long. Spend the next 15 to 20 minutes praying for that person intentionally and with the knowledge that the all-powerful God is with you. Don't be content for a quiet, orderly prayer. Allow Jesus' passion to flow through you to see that person set free, delivered, and living in the full calling and purpose that God has for them.

August 30

Feeling God's Grace (Ex)

I AM ASKING TODAY that God would help you to feel grace. Yes, may you feel His love for you, just because. Just because He decided to pick you out especially as one of His. You have been selected, prized, and focused upon by God. Grace to all of you, in the name of grace incarnate, Jesus. Amen and a thousand more amens.

Verse: Romans 8:15

> The Spirit you received does not make you slaves, so that you live in fear again; rather, the Spirit you received brought about your adoption to sonshiP And by him we cry, "Abba, Father."

Exercise: Meditation

After reading the prayer and passage, read them again. Ask yourself what they actually mean. What are the implications and how does that affect how God sees you? What is the difference between a slave and a child? Which have you been acting like? Read Romans 8:15 again and ask the Holy Spirit to open your eyes. Sit quietly with your Father and let Him reveal His love for you again.

August 31

All for Him (P)

I love Jesus. He is my Master, I am His slave. I exist to do His will, He does not exist to do mine. His will, my purpose. May I be completely obedient to You today as Your servant and child. Amen and a thousand more amens.

Verse: Romans 6:18

You have been set free from sin and have become slaves to righteousness.

Exercise: Prayer and Worship

Take a humble posture in prayer, such as kneeling or laying prostrate if possible. Pray today's prayer to God and ask Him to be Lord of your life again. This means that everything you do and everything you are is His. After this, enter into a time of repenting for the ways that you have not been obedient to Him or trusted Him with your life. Ask Him to take it all once more. Finally, end this time by worshipping Him.

September 1

God On and Over You (Ex)

I AM PRAYING FOR your body. Yes, may the God who made you touch every cell of you. And may those cells respond in lively, hope filled, and powerful fashion. Be healed and be filled today through the power of Christ. Amen and a thousand more amens.

Verse: Matthew 4:23

> Jesus went throughout Galilee, teaching in their synagogues, proclaiming the good news of the kingdom, and healing every disease and sickness among the people.

Exercise: Prayer

God is still moving in our world in miraculous fashion. Join Him today in this work through praying for the sick, both in your devotional time and in person. Step out in faith and ask Jesus to do the same works He did during His earthly ministry. Take this time to pray for those that you know are sick or hurting and send them a message or give them a call to let them know that you are doing so.

September 2

Faith to Come Alive (Ex)

I pray that your faith will come alive. Yes, may all that is dormant, stale, and lifeless in you be dealt with by the power of The Living One. May Jesus' life explode in you today and may the reverberations be felt for days and weeks and months and years. Hallelujah to the Resurrected One! Amen and a thousand more amens.

Verse: Romans 10:17

> Consequently, faith comes from hearing the message, and the message is heard through the word about Christ.

Exercise: Community

If you have found your faith in and relationship with God struggling lately, ask yourself how much time you have spent with other believers simply talking about Jesus. Not just a Sunday morning service, but intentional conversations that challenge and encourage those involved to pursue Christ. We are meant to pursue Christ, both as a community and individually. Our spiritual health suffers if we neglect either of these. Are you pursuing Him with others?

September 3

Order in Your Chaos (Ex)

May the God who has ordered eternity speak peace into your chaos. He isn't intimidated, confused, or scared by your perceived mountains and tsunamis that are actually molehills and puddles. His presence equals order and peace. Amen and a thousand more amens.

Verse: Mark 4:37–40

> A furious squall came up, and the waves broke over the boat, so that it was nearly swamped. Jesus was in the stern, sleeping on a cushion. The disciples woke him and said to him, "Teacher, don't you care if we drown?" He got up, rebuked the wind and said to the waves, "Quiet! Be still!" Then the wind died down and it was completely calm. He said to his disciples, "Why are you so afraid? Do you still have no faith?"

Exercise: Prayer

The safest place a believer can be is in the center of God's will. If you have situations or challenges that worry or stress you, first ask yourself if you are in God's will. If you aren't sure, or don't believe you are, ask the Holy Spirit to make this clear to you. Commit to change what needs to be changed if you have been focusing on things that are not of God's plan. If you believe you are in God's will, read this passage again and ask the One who calms storms, to either quiet those things taking your peace or bring peace to your mind in the midst of the wind and waves.

September 4

Victory Over the Enemy (Ex)

May the enemy of your soul be stopped in his tracks. And then may those tracks be used against him by the Good Shepherd so that he might be found, bound, and severely dealt with. Yes, in Jesus' name you are covered and protected this day. Amen and a thousand more amens.

Verse: John 10:14–18

> I am the good shepherd; I know my sheep and my sheep know me— just as the Father knows me and I know the Father—and I lay down my life for the sheep. I have other sheep that are not of this sheep pen. I must bring them also. They too will listen to my voice, and there shall be one flock and one shepherd. The reason my Father loves me is that I lay down my life—only to take it up again. No one takes it from me, but I lay it down of my own accord. I have authority to lay it down and authority to take it up again. This command I received from my Father.

Exercise: Reading and Prayer

Read John 10:1–21. Since you are one of Jesus' sheep, you know His voice and He lays down His life for you. Take this time to pray over those things in your life and in your family's life that have plagued for a long time. Proclaim that the Good Shepherd has authority over the wolf and that evil has no place in you, or with your people.

September 5

Hope (Ex)

My prayer for you is that hope would flicker, flash, and then burst up in your heart like never before. Yes, levels of life altering hope are what I am praying for. Get ready to have your life altered in hopeful fashion through the power of the Resurrected Savior. Amen and a thousand more amens.

Verse: 1 Peter 1:3–4a

> Praise be to the God and Father of our Lord Jesus Christ! In his great mercy he has given us new birth into a living hope through the resurrection of Jesus Christ from the dead, and into an inheritance that can never perish, spoil or fade.

Exercise: Worship and Meditation

Make today's verse your prayer of praise to Jesus. Read it out loud and believe it for yourself. Speak it over your life, putting "me" and "my" into the passage to make it your prayer. ("God and Father of my Lord Jesus Christ. . . he has given me a new birth into a living hope. . .). Thank Him for this living hope and continue to reread and pray this passage as you meditate on its truth.

SEPTEMBER 6

Turning the Tables (Ex)

I AM PRAYING FOR a hedge of protection around you. Yes, I am sick and tired of the enemy inflicting pain, fear, and fatigue upon you. May all the forces of Heaven come to your aid and give you a respite, so that you can rest a second and then assault the same enemy who dared attack you in the first place. Turn the tables on him in the name of Jesus Christ. Amen and a thousand more amens.

Verse: Deuteronomy 28:8

> The LORD will grant that the enemies who rise up against you will be defeated before you. They will come at you from one direction but flee from you in seven.

Exercise: Prayer

Do you have a person in your life who is constantly beaten down? Pray this prayer over that person. Pray that the attacks of the enemy would completely fail.

September 7

Prioritize and Clarify (P)

You who flung the stars into space, please bring your order to our lives. There is too much to remember and not enough time to get it all done. Lead, Lord, and I will follow. Your Kingdom come and Your will be done in and through us all. Help us O God. Amen and a thousand more amens.

Verse: Luke 10:41–42

> "Martha, Martha," the Lord answered, "you are worried and upset about many things, but few things are needed—or indeed only one. Mary has chosen what is better, and it will not be taken away from her."

Exercise: Meditation

If possible, have your devotional time with a view of nature. If not possible, think of one of the most beautiful scenes you have witnessed in creation during your life. Think about what each of your senses experience. Think about them one by one. Breathe in. Breathe out. God created all of this and is with you now. He was before time and will be after time. Take a step back from your life and see from God's perspective. Life is fleeting and is gone as quickly as it appears. He has called you to be faithful, but don't lose sight of eternal realities for temporary distractions. Lastly, think about what it will be like to stand before Jesus for the first time. To hear Him say "Well done, good and faithful servant." What will you feel? What will you say? Allow what is true and lasting to inform your daily schedule, not the other way around.

September 8

Slow Down and Listen (Ex)

I pray for God to speak to you. He said that He is always doing so, but that sometimes you talk too much. Quit asking for things and listen. That for which you are praying will be dealt with fully as you hear His voice. May you realize that His voice and His presence make everything better. Amen and a thousand more amens.

Verse: Psalm 37:7

> Be still before the LORD and wait patiently for him; do not fret when people succeed in their ways, when they carry out their wicked schemes.

Exercise: Silence and Journaling

Place a pen, piece of paper, and your Bible in front of you. Take the next 10 to 15 minutes to sit quietly with God. Don't ask for anything or fill the time with your voice. The Bible tells us that He knows what we need before we ask for it. So sit and listen. If a Bible verse or thought arises that you believe is from God, write it down and seek confirmation in prayer, in circumstances, or from other believers. Quiet your mind and allow Him to speak.

September 9

Prayers for the City (P)

Lord, Your Kingdom come and Your will be done in ________ as it is in Heaven. May your Holy Spirit descend in a powerful presence very soon and draw all people to You. In the name of Jesus. Amen and a thousand more amens.

Verse: 1 Timothy 2:1–4

> I urge, then, first of all, that petitions, prayers, intercession and thanksgiving be made for all people— for kings and all those in authority, that we may live peaceful and quiet lives in all godliness and holiness. This is good, and pleases God our Savior, who wants all people to be saved and to come to a knowledge of the truth.

Exercise: Prayer

Insert the name of your city in the blank space in today's prayer. After this, pray for specific issues that are applicable to your community. Pray for the families, for the schools, for the businesses, and the government. Allow the Holy Spirit to guide you to pray for whatever area He would have you join Him in.

September 10

Peace and Order (Ex)

I pray for your peace. Yes, may the peace and order of Heaven invade the hectic nature of your day here on earth. His Kingdom come, His will be done in, on, and through every facet of your day. Be blessed and covered in the name of Jesus. Amen and a thousand more amens.

Verse: Joshua 1:8

> Keep this Book of the Law always on your lips; meditate on it day and night, so that you may be careful to do everything written in it. Then you will be prosperous and successful.

Exercise: Prayer and Memorization

Just as Joshua was to enter a new land to conquer, ask Jesus to be with you as you step out in faith today. Surrender your day and plans to Him again. Ask the Holy Spirit to guide you in following His Word, so that the blessings you live in could be used to point back to Him. Spend the remainder of this time committing Joshua 1:8 to memory. Keep a small rock or similar item on your person this week, possibly in a pocket or other accessible place. Every time you feel or see this object, repeat the verse and surrender again in that moment to God's plan in your life.

September 11

The Battle is Won (Ex)

I asked God to protect you. He said that the enemy had already been dealt with before he even tried to assault you, end of story. May you live in the victory today that is rightfully yours. Amen and a thousand more amens.

Verse: Colossians 2:15

> And having disarmed the powers and authorities, he made a public spectacle of them, triumphing over them by the cross.

Exercise: Worship

Today, worship God specifically for and over the situations in your life that have tried to come against you. Praise God over each one by name, joining Jesus in making a public spectacle of the efforts of the enemy.

September 12

A Fire for Heaven (Ex)

I am praying that a fire for Jesus would be kindled in your heart. And may it compel you to go out in public and burn. Burn in the morning, burn at mid-day, and long into the evening. Yes, a fire for Heaven you will be by the power and indwelling presence of the Holy Spirit. Amen and a thousand more amens.

Verse: Exodus 13:21

> By day the LORD went ahead of them in a pillar of cloud to guide them on their way and by night in a pillar of fire to give them light, so that they could travel by day or night.

Exercise: Prayer

Being in a fire is a painful sacrifice. Asking God to use you as a light for others to see Him is not a small matter. It is a sacrifice of comfort and desires, while also adding responsibility. If you want to be used by God, realize that it will cost you. If so, ask Jesus to refine you today and open your eyes to the things that you need to give up in order to be better used by Him. This could include bad habits, how you use your free time, and what you do with your money. Listen with open hands, that God may give to and take from your life as He wishes. God calls you to a higher standard, but, if you submit and allow Him to transform you, you will become like the pillar of fire to the Israelites: a testament of God's presence and power.

September 13

Uncompromising (Ex)

May you quit condescending to contemporary culture and find your backbone. Yes, may His backbone be yours to stand for what is right and what is true. May you hear clearly from heaven on the issues of your day so you may live with wisdom and strength for His glory. Amen and a thousand more amens.

Verse: John 17:15–18

> My prayer is not that you take them out of the world but that you protect them from the evil one. They are not of the world, even as I am not of it. Sanctify them by the truth; your word is truth. As you sent me into the world, I have sent them into the world.

Exercise: Journaling and Community

What are the controversial and tense issues that you are facing in your life, or that society is facing as a whole? Write these issues down. You have been called to reflect Jesus in everything you do. Many times big issues will become sources of division and can be tricky to navigate while trying to live in both love and truth. Take this time to ask for God's perspective on the things you face. Have your Bible present and write down any response or verses that you believe are from God. Then, plan a time to discuss these with a mentor or close Christian friend.

September 14

Private Discipline, Public Fruits (Ex)

May what you and God do in private have powerful and public effects today. Seek no one's attention but His and allow Him to empower you and provide the opportunities to reap the harvest of your private disciplines. May you be blessed by your obedience in the name of the Father, Son, and Holy Spirit. Amen and a thousand more amens.

Verse: Matthew 6:6

> But when you pray, go into your room, close the door and pray to your Father, who is unseen. Then your Father, who sees what is done in secret, will reward you.

Exercise: Prayer, Reading, and Worship

Make this time an extension of whatever you would like to make it. You could choose to pray for specific situations, study the Word, or worship Jesus. Take delight in having no other plans except being with Jesus. He will bring about increase and opportunity in His timing. Be consumed with pursuing God and allow Him to figure out the rest.

September 15

Divine Order (Ex)

I pray that He who ordered the universe would order your life today. May you hear His orders and align your life with His. Amen and a thousand more amens.

Verse: 1 Peter 1:14–16

> As obedient children, do not conform to the evil desires you had when you lived in ignorance. But just as he who called you is holy, so be holy in all you do; for it is written: "Be holy, because I am holy."

Exercise: Prayer and Journaling

It is healthy to frequently reflect with the Holy Spirit on your recent thoughts, actions, and relationships with God, yourself, and others. Set aside at least 30 minutes for this exercise as it is more contemplative than many others discussed in this devotional. Grab a cup of coffee, tea, or your beverage of choice and sit down with your journal or a piece of paper. Ask the Holy Spirit to guide this time of reflection and walk through each area of your life: your relationship with God, your relationships and interactions with others, your relationship with yourself, and how you spend your time and resources. Write down the victories and areas of growth for each on the piece of paper. Pray over these notes and ask God to direct you to grow closer to Him as He teaches you to lead a holy, complete life.

September 16

Intimidating Intimidations (Ex)

I pray the things that intimidate you lose their power. Yes, may they shrivel up and die, becoming powerless and senseless under the authority of Jesus in your life. His authority intimidates the intimidator. Amen and a thousand more amens.

Verse: Revelation 1:18

> I am the Living One; I was dead, and now look, I am alive for ever and ever! And I hold the keys of death and Hades.

Exercise: Prayer

Write down the things that are intimidating you and those closest to you. The things that are taking away peace and sleep. Say the first thing on your list, and then read Christ's words in Revelation 1:18 over it as a prayer. Command it to bow to the Living One and be silent in His presence. Repeat this for each situation and intimidation that you wrote down.

September 17

Only Jesus (Ex)

Yes, Jesus in the morning, Jesus at noon, Jesus at the end of the day. I speak Jesus to you, over you, and around you my friends. Amen and a thousand more amens.

Verse: John 14:23

> Jesus replied, "Anyone who loves me will obey my teaching. My Father will love them, and we will come to them and make our home with them."

Exercise: Prayer and Journaling

When you read today's prayer, what did you think? What does it actually mean? With a pen and paper, write down your responses to these questions. Apply this prayer to your life. Don't just read it, get warm, fuzzy feelings inside, and move on. Seek to understand and interact with who Jesus is. Read the prayer and the verse again. Ask Jesus to reveal to you how He wants to be in your morning, noon, and night. Write down His response and what it looks like for you today.

September 18

Seeing God Around You (Ex)

I asked God to show Himself to you today. He said that you should look in the mirror, at your neighbor, and the closest need you can fill. He will be in those places. May you seek Him and find Him as you follow Him for His glory. Amen and a thousand more amens.

Verse: Jeremiah 29:13

> You will seek me and find me when you seek me with all your heart.

Exercise: Prayer and Service

If possible, look in a mirror. Ask Jesus to show you how you have grown in Him since becoming a Christian. Remember that this is not to glorify how good you are, nor is it to downplay how much Jesus has done in your life. Attempt to have an honest reflection informed by the Holy Spirit. Spend 5 minutes looking at yourself and reflecting on the person you were, the person you are, and the person you are becoming. Thank God for your growth and surrender to Him the areas that can look more like Him. Then, ask God to show you a need that you can fulfill for someone else today. Be ready to respond to whatever that is, having money on hand, opening up your schedule, or coming up with some other practical step to act when you feel God say "this is it."

September 19

Going on the Offensive (Ex)

May you take it to the enemy today. Yes, engage him, stomp him, and give God the glory. God battle, good God, good day. May you have no compromise with darkness but choose to slay any and every enemy that comes against God's plan in your life and in the lives of others. Amen and a thousand more amens.

Verse: 1 Thessalonians 5:4–6

> But you, brothers and sisters, are not in darkness so that this day should surprise you like a thief. You are all children of the light and children of the day. We do not belong to the night or to the darkness. So then, let us not be like others, who are asleep, but let us be awake and sober.

Exercise: Prayer

Take your stand against the strategies of the evil one today. Specifically, think about your family and your work. Spend this time praying against what the enemy is trying to do in your house and in the lives of your family members. Pray for your immediate family by name and any others that you believe need to be covered in prayer today. Then, pray for your place of work. If you are in school or a stay at home parent, you can pray for these as well. Pray for those you work with to know Jesus, for God to be reflected in your work, and for unity in that place. Add any other needs that you see, as well. Allow the Holy Spirit to guide these prayers and to help you continue in them as you interact with your family and your job.

SEPTEMBER 20

Dependent On Jesus (P)

I LOVE YOU, JESUS. I need Your help in my life. You are my Help and Life. May I love and know You more today. That is the cry of my heart. Jesus. Jesus. Jesus. Amen and a thousand more amens.

Verse: Psalm 84:2

> My soul yearns, even faints, for the courts of the LORD; my heart and my flesh cry out for the living God.

Exercise: Prayer and Meditation

Take a humble posture in prayer if possible. This could be sitting down, kneeling on the floor, or lying prostrate. For 10 to 15 minutes, get rid of all distractions and sit in silence with the lights off. During this time, take the sentence "Jesus, I need you." Say this out loud quietly. Pause and breathe. Repeat it. Think about what that sentence means, what each word means. Say it out loud again, whispering it in prayer. Pause and meditate on it. Continue doing this practice for 10 to 15 minutes or longer if you would like.

September 21

Order Over Your World (Ex)

I pray this morning that the One who ordered the universe would bring order to your world. Order, peace, and hope to all of your worlds, in the Name of Jesus. Amen and a thousand more amens.

Verse: Psalm 144:12–15

> Then our sons in their youth will be like well-nurtured plants, and our daughters will be like pillars carved to adorn a palace. Our barns will be filled with every kind of provision. Our sheep will increase by thousands, by tens of thousands in our fields; our oxen will draw heavy loads. There will be no breaching of walls, no going into captivity, no cry of distress in our streets. Blessed are the people of whom this is true; blessed are the people whose God is the Lord.

Exercise: Reading and Prayer

Read Psalm 144 in its entirety. Then, pause and listen for a minute, looking at the text in front of you for any verses or words to stick out. Write these down. Then, read the psalm again. Pause again after reading and listen for a minute. At this time, identify the words or verses that caught your attention. Pray these over your schedule, order, and challenges today.

September 22

Not About You (Ex)

For the believer, life is not about you, your comfort or, for that matter, your opinion. It's about His purpose and His plan. May you realize this and submit all of your ways to Him. He is God, you are not. May you rest in this fact and be free to live focused on Him today. Amen and a thousand more amens.

Verse: Isaiah 55:8–9

> "For my thoughts are not your thoughts, neither are your ways my ways," declares the Lord. "As the heavens are higher than the earth, so are my ways higher than your ways and my thoughts than your thoughts."

Exercise: Prayer

Have you made any part of your life focused on self, even unknowingly? Take the first 5 minutes to reflect on your life and motives. Identify situations, responsibilities, and relationships that you have kept separate from God. Ask Jesus to forgive you of this pride and repent of holding on to these things for yourself. Listen for His direction in each area listed.

September 23

Jesus is the Thesis (P)

Jesus, may I realize more and more that this is all about You. You are the thesis of The Book. You are the reason I am alive. May all I am and all I do point back to You. I don't need my name to be known or to understand everything, just let me honor You. Amen and a thousand more amens.

Verse: Revelation 22:13

I am the Alpha and the Omega, the First and the Last, the Beginning and the End.

Exercise: Worship

This life is not about you. It is not about your dreams, experiences, or advancement. It is 100% completely about Jesus. He is Lord and King, Savior and God. Take your eyes off of yourself and those around you. Spend this time looking to Christ and worshipping Him. This time can look however you would like, just focus on Him. Humble yourself as you honor Him.

September 24

Such a Time as This (Ex)

May you know that you were made for such a time as this. So quit complaining about how bad things are. Yes, you were supposed to be here, so live like it: purposefully, hopefully, and focused. May you not give in to the temptation to despair or be cynical, but remain steadfast in Jesus regardless of outside circumstances. Amen and a thousand more amens.

Verse: John 15:4

> Remain in me, as I also remain in you. No branch can bear fruit by itself; it must remain in the vine. Neither can you bear fruit unless you remain in me.

Exercise: Prayer and Journaling

Think about the things in your life that seem dark. Write these down. Remember that none of them have surprised God and that He put you where you are for a reason. Pray for His will to be done in these situations and to have a heavenly perspective with everything that comes your way. Spend the last 5 minutes in silence with your list as you listen for guidance or peace.

September 25

Filled and Overflowing (Ex)

My prayer for you today is that you will be inundated with Hope, Light, and Life; so much so, that you have too much for one person and see the need to give away a significant amount of it to someone else. May you look beyond yourself and share the life bursting from inside you. Amen and a thousand more amens.

Verse: John 4: 13–14

> Jesus answered, "Everyone who drinks this water will be thirsty again, but whoever drinks the water I give them will never thirst. Indeed, the water I give them will become in them a spring of water welling up to eternal life."

Exercise: Prayer and Evangelism

Jesus the above conversation with a Samaritan woman. It was culturally unacceptable because she was a Samaritan, (being half Jew and half gentile), and because she was a woman. Just as Christ interacted with those that normally would remain unnoticed, go and love today. Jesus has implanted you with a spring of eternal life. Ask Him to bring opportunities today that allow you to share this with others. Share what Jesus has done in your life with one person today and write about the experience afterwards. Pray for that person.

September 26

Answers to Your Prayers (Ex)

I asked God to answer your prayers. He said that He is your answer and that is really all you need. So, may you and the omniscient, omnipotent, and omnipresent One sit together and talk today. May you see the great value, unbelievable holiness, and unending love of the One always with you. And when this happens, may your trust and reliance on Him increase as you bring your prayers before Him. Amen and a thousand more amens.

Verse: Isaiah 6:1–7

> In the year that King Uzziah died, I saw the Lord, high and exalted, seated on a throne; and the train of his robe filled the temple. Above him were seraphim, each with six wings: With two wings they covered their faces, with two they covered their feet, and with two they were flying. And they were calling to one another: "Holy, holy, holy is the Lord Almighty; the whole earth is full of his glory." At the sound of their voices the doorposts and thresholds shook and the temple was filled with smoke. "Woe to me!" I cried. "I am ruined! For I am a man of unclean lips, and I live among a people of unclean lips, and my eyes have seen the King, the Lord Almighty." Then one of the seraphim flew to me with a live coal in his hand, which he had taken with tongs from the altar. With it he touched my mouth and said, "See, this has touched your lips; your guilt is taken away and your sin atoned for."

Exercise: Reading and Meditation

It is easy to get so distracted by our needs and circumstances that we forget to see the One to whom we are praying. Our God is a loving Father and caring Savior, but He is also incredibly Holy and worthy of complete honor. Read the passage in Isaiah once again, picturing each piece of imagery and imagining what each of your senses would experience in God's throne room. Take a humble posture as you do this, asking God to give you a greater understanding of Him. Then, join with the angels crying "Holy, holy, holy is the Lord Almighty."

September 27

Hope, Light, and Life (Ex)

I pray that hope, light, and life would invade your space today. Yes, may you be invaded and inundated with these things, so much so that you break out in spontaneous fits of happiness and joy that are contagious with those you come in contact with. May the chains of the past be broken as your Father reminds you that you are chosen, you are loved, and you are His. Amen and a thousand more amens.

Verse: John 15:19

> If you belonged to the world, it would love you as its own. As it is, you do not belong to the world, but I have chosen you out of the world. That is why the world hates you.

Exercise: Worship and Silence

Jesus has chosen you. He went to the cross to buy you back and resurrected to give you life in God's presence. Jesus has chosen you. Sit in silence for 5 minutes, just being with Him and listening for His voice. If you hear anything specific, feel free to write it down. Then spend the remaining time you have looking at Him and worshipping Him for who He is. Read a psalm of praise, put on a worship song, or simply tell Him how much you love Him. Hope, light, and life are just byproducts of being close to Him.

September 28

Eyes to See (Ex)

I am praying for hope to ignite your faith. Yes, may these two cause your dreams and visions to explode into reality today. Explosions of faith and hope, hope and faith. May you be expectant for the future and trust in Christ to work mightily as you remain obedient to Him. Amen and a thousand more amens.

Verse: Ephesians 6:18–20

> And pray in the Spirit on all occasions with all kinds of prayers and requests. With this in mind, be alert and always keep on praying for all the Lord's people. Pray also for me, that whenever I speak, words may be given me so that I will fearlessly make known the mystery of the gospel, for which I am an ambassador in chains. Pray that I may declare it fearlessly, as I should.

Exercise: Prayer

There are many Christians in the world experiencing persecution and pressure to compromise the Gospel. Pray today's prayer and passage over these groups of believers. Choose a specific location to pray for in which it is dangerous to be a Christian. If you are not sure, pray for the persecuted church as a whole. Pray for our brothers and sisters to remain hopeful and faithful in God's service.

September 29

Good Battle (Ex)

I ask God to lead you to some good battle today. He said that He would, but that it wouldn't look like what you think. Be looking for unconventional ways to fight evil, bring hope, and lift up the downtrodden. May your eyes be opened to the hurting and broken, both strangers you meet and those that live in your own home. Amen and a thousand more amens.

Verse: 1 Samuel 14:7

> "Do all that you have in mind," his armor-bearer said. "Go ahead; I am with you heart and soul."

Exercise: Reading and Service

After reading the prayer and Bible passage, read 1 Samuel 14:1–15. Say the same statement to Christ that the armor-bearer told Jonathan. Follow Him into battle today, staying right next to Him. Take 5 minutes to listen, asking the Holy Spirit to show you people in your life who have been oppressed by the enemy. Write these names down, pray over them, and plan to intentionally interact with them as you confront the enemy's plan for them.

September 30

Heaviness (Ex)

I ask God to lift the heaviness from your life. May you sense in resounding fashion that He has dealt with all things that were holding you down. May the burdens of the past, present, and future be gone in Jesus' name. Amen and a thousand more amens.

Verse: Isaiah 61:1–3

> The Spirit of the Sovereign Lord is on me, because the Lord has anointed me to proclaim good news to the poor. He has sent me to bind up the brokenhearted, to proclaim freedom for the captives and release from darkness for the prisoners, to proclaim the year of the Lord's favor and the day of vengeance of our God, to comfort all who mourn, and provide for those who grieve in Zion— to bestow on them a crown of beauty instead of ashes, the oil of joy instead of mourning, and a garment of praise instead of a spirit of despair. They will be called oaks of righteousness, a planting of the Lord for the display of his splendor.

Exercise: Reading and Meditation

Jesus quoted this prophetic passage at the beginning of His ministry. His work did not end when He ascended, but instead expanded. Christ wants you to know the redemption and freedom that Isaiah describes so that you can be with Him and become a vessel of this freedom. Read through the passage again, reading it out loud. Ask Jesus to reveal more of Himself through His Word. Read this passage once more, speaking it over any weight that you carry and any people that you will come in contact with.

October 1

Peace and War (Ex)

May your day be filled with periods of intermittent peace and good battle. Peace and battle, battle and peace. May you know when to do one and not the other as you walk with Jesus. You will represent His Kingdom by His power today. You have been sent on purpose, so may the holy Spirit guide your steps, thoughts, and actions to rest in Him and fight the enemy. Amen and a thousand more amens.

Verse: Ecclesiastes 3:1

There is a time for everything, and a season for every activity under the heavens

Exercise: Reading and Prayer

Read Ecclesiastes 3:1–8. Reflect on this passage as you sit with the Father. Ask for His guidance in your day, so that you may know when to rest and when to make war on the enemy, when to speak and when to remain silent. Ask for discernment both for you and other believers. Pray for a concerted effort by the family of believers to push back the darkness.

October 2

Prayers for Friends (P)

Lord Jesus, please go before and remain with my friends today. Ward off any and all attacks of the enemy against them. Instead, may the efforts of the enemy be turned into opportunities to display your power in their lives. I seal this prayer in the name of Jesus. Amen and a thousand more amens.

Verse: Isaiah 54:17

> "No weapon forged against you will prevail, and you will refute every tongue that accuses you. This is the heritage of the servants of the LORD, and this is their vindication from me," declares the LORD.

Exercise: Prayer

Pray for your family and friends by name during this time. Pray both the day's prayer and Scripture verse over their schedules and responsibilities. If you know their struggles, pray for these specifically as well. Cover them in prayer and speak the life of Christ into their days.

October 3

Covering (Ex)

He is your covering, your protection, and your safety. Yes, Jesus is your safe-room from any and every storm. Be safe today by the power of His might. Find rest in the shadow of His wings. Amen and a thousand more amens.

Verse: Psalm 63:5–8

> I will be fully satisfied as with the richest of foods; with singing lips my mouth will praise you. On my bed I remember you; I think of you through the watches of the night. Because you are my help, I sing in the shadow of your wings. I cling to you; your right hand upholds me.

Exercise: Reading and Memorization

After reading today's prayer and passage of Scripture, read Psalm 63:5–8 again out loud. Make this your prayer, thinking about each statement's meaning. Speak it over the storms in your life, in the lives of your loved ones, and in your community and nation. Then, commit this passage to memory. Keep a small rock or similar item on your person this week. Every time you feel or see the object, repeat the passage and pray for God's peace and protection in whatever situation you are in. Pray for those around you, even if they are strangers. Do this for the entire week as you meditate on His covering.

October 4

A Fire in Your Heart (Ex)

I PRAY THIS MORNING that God would kindle a fire in your heart. Yes, may His flame burn strong and hot in your soul. And may the heat of it radiate into the lives of any who come close. May you experience Christ in greater ways as others are drawn to the hope within you. Amen and a thousand more amens.

Verse: 2 Corinthians 4:7

> But we have this treasure in jars of clay to show that this all-surpassing power is from God and not from us.

Exercise: Prayer and Service

Ask God to give you opportunities to go outside of your comfort zone throughout your day. That you would have chances to display His power in ways that are beyond human abilities. Seek to love unconditionally, serve sacrificially, and speak encouragingly to those who have escaped your notice. Specifically pour into one family member or close friend that you have not gone beyond surface level interactions for some time. Ask the Holy Spirit to guide your conversation and actions so that you may reflect Him in that relationship.

October 5

His Presence in Your Life (Ex)

I am asking God to give you signs of His presence in your life today. He said that is what He is. He is The Sign. May you be on the alert for signs of Him. May you be quick to sense His presence in every moment so you may enjoy being with Him and use these moments to point others to the personal God we serve. Amen and a thousand more amens.

Verse: Revelation 12:11

> They triumphed over him by the blood of the Lamb and by the word of their testimony; they did not love their lives so much as to shrink from death.

Exercise: Prayer and Evangelism

Allow God to continue the work He started yesterday in you. Ask the Holy Spirit for a mind fixed on Christ today, so that when you are at work, with your family, or anywhere else, you can hear and see Christ working around you. Ask for prophetic words to give, encouraging actions to take, and a humility to love others with God's power while seeking no glory for yourself. Step out of your comfort zone today to speak to the heart of people and share Jesus with your world.

October 6

God's Faithfulness (P)

Today I am thankful for Your faithfulness to me. When I am fickle and stumble, You are faithful. I am blessed because of Your grace. Thank you Jesus for loving me and staying with me. You never leave and always welcome me home. With You I am complete. Amen and a thousand more amens.

Verse: 2 Timothy 2:13

> If we are faithless, he remains faithful, for he cannot disown himself.

Exercise: Worship

Take a humble posture if possible. While sitting, kneeling, laying, or whatever you choose to do, reflect on how much God has forgiven in your life and how He has brought you new life. Think of how dependent you are on His faithfulness, even to serve Him. As you reflect on your finite abilities and limited strength, thank Him again for the cross and the Holy Spirit. Spend the entirety of this time meditating on His faithfulness and worshipping Him for what He has done.

October 7

Receiving and Giving Selfless Love (P)

God, I know that You love and give. You have shown Yourself generous and caring. I love to take and focus on myself. My prayer is that You give me Your love to love. Help me die to myself today. Bless those around me and give me opportunities to serve them today in the name of Jesus. Amen and a thousand more amens.

Verse: Philippians 2:3–5

> Do nothing out of selfish ambition or vain conceit. Rather, in humility value others above yourselves, not looking to your own interests but each of you to the interests of the others. In your relationships with one another, have the same mindset as Christ Jesus.

Exercise: Prayer and Service

Pray for the efforts of others today. Ask for God's blessing on your coworkers and family members, that He would guide them, they would mature in their relationship with Him, and that God would expand their influence. Then, ask the Holy Spirit to show you practical ways you can serve and encourage others. Write down 2 to 3 specific ways you can and will do this today.

October 8

Your Passion for God's Glory (Ex)

May the Holy Spirit help you find out what fires you up and then direct you to go out and do it for God's glory. Fired up for His glory is the best place to be. May your passions be married with the purposes of God today and may you teach others to do the same. Amen and a thousand more amens.

Verse: Matthew 6:21

For where your treasure is, there your heart will be also.

Exercise: Journaling and Prayer

Time and money are two of the most significant resources we are entrusted with as people. Where have these been spent in your life? Have they been utilized intentionally or have they been spent without thought? Ask the Holy Spirit to refine how you use time and money. Record any thoughts or impressions that come to mind.

October 9

A Ruling Peace (Ex)

I AM PRAYING THAT the peace of Jesus will rule and reign in your hearts and minds today. That means that anything that is neither peaceful nor calming to you must bow to Him. So, in the name of Jesus, confusion, delusion, oppression, and depression must BOW NOW. Peace to you all. Amen and a thousand more amens.

Verse: Galatians 5:22–23

> But the fruit of the Spirit is love, joy, peace, forbearance, kindness, goodness, faithfulness, gentleness and self-control. Against such things there is no law.

Exercise: Reading and Memorization

The Apostle Paul's letter to the Galatians discusses the fruit of the Spirit and what God's presence produces in the life of a believer. Anxiety, stress, and worry are not included. Read the list of attributes again, asking the Holy Spirit to make them your reality today. Commit this list to memory so that any time you begin to feel confused or anxious, you can repeat it and meditate on the truth of Scripture.

October 10

Christ the Irresistible Force (P)

Jesus, may You show Yourself to be an irresistible force. Yes, Heaven's Vortex come to earth. Break down the walls of those that don't know You yet and pull them into Your love. Reach those that seem the farthest away from You so that You can receive the glory that You are worthy of. Amen and a thousand more amens.

Verse: John 12:32

And I, when I am lifted up from the earth, will draw all people to myself.

Exercise: Prayer

Jesus stated that He would draw all people to Himself. He is the One at work in each and every heart. Join in His work today, praying for those that do not yet know Him, that they may have their eyes opened. Pray for the people farthest from God: those involved in crime, in the adult film industry, in the "other" political party, etc. Pray that these people would have a Damascus Road experience, like the Apostle Paul and be radically converted to Jesus.

October 11

Light Into Your Life (Ex)

I ask the One who said "Let there be light" to speak light into your life. May the Lord of Light shine upon you. Yes, may He shine upon every cell of you. In the name of Jesus, Lord of Light. Amen and a thousand more amens.

Verse: Psalm 97:10–11

> Let those who love the Lord hate evil, for he guards the lives of his faithful ones and delivers them from the hand of the wicked. Light shines on the righteous and joy on the upright in heart.

Exercise: Journaling and Prayer

Are there areas of your life in darkness, either from the presence of sin, or the absence of surrender? Ask the Holy Spirit to reveal any of these areas to you, so that you may repent and remain in the light of obedience. Then, pray today's prayer over someone else. Ask Jesus to show you someone to pray over today, listen, and then speak the prayer over his or her life.

October 12

Praying for Your Nation (P)

Holy Spirit, I pray for my nation today. May Your Kingdom come Your will be done in my country as it is in Heaven. I proclaim life and redemption to this society and the political system. May Your presence rest and be glorified here. Amen and a thousand more amens.

Verse: Jeremiah 29:7

> Also, seek the peace and prosperity of the city to which I have carried you into exile. Pray to the LORD for it, because if it prospers, you too will prosper.

Exercise: Prayer

Take your devotional time today to pray for the governing authorities and people in your country. Address specific issues, ask for guidance from heaven, and speak against the attacks of the enemy in your land.

October 13

Drawing Others to Christ (Ex)

My prayer for you today is that His fire be kindled in you, so much so that many come to watch you burn. May the sacrifice of your life be pleasing to the Lord and magnetic for those you come in contact with. Amen and a thousand more amens.

Verse: Hebrews 13:15–16

> Through Jesus, therefore, let us continually offer to God a sacrifice of praise—the fruit of lips that openly profess his name. And do not forget to do good and to share with others, for with such sacrifices God is pleased.

Exercise: Worship, Service, and Evangelism

Praise is both offering worship to God and loving others. Jesus taught that all of the Law and prophets were connected to loving God and loving others. Seek to offer both kinds of praise today, spending this devotional time in humble worship of the Father and intentionally loving others throughout your day. You can choose a song to sing, a psalm to pray, or a thought to meditate on for 10 to 15 minutes. Just tell God you love Him again and again and again. Then, finish with asking Him to guide your steps to love others and plan one way that you can enact this today.

October 14

The Power of Prayer (Ex)

May you realize the power of prayer today. Prayer is a real-time connection to eternity. Yes, eternal power pulsating through earthly vessels. May you realize that it isn't just a mere discipline, but a heavenly opportunity to be with the Holy of Holies and partake in His redemptive plan for creation. May your eyes and soul be reinvigorated with this communion with heaven as you are sucked into the vortex of abundant life. Amen and a thousand more amens.

Verse: Matthew 6:9–13

> This, then, is how you should pray: "Our Father in heaven, hallowed be your name, your kingdom come, your will be done, on earth as it is in heaven. Give us today our daily bread. And forgive us our debts, as we also have forgiven our debtors. And lead us not into temptation, but deliver us from the evil one."

Exercise: Meditation and Prayer

Imagine Jesus teaching on prayer. The Lord's Prayer was the model He gave for how we should approach heaven. It is not something to be merely repeated, but experienced and delighted in. Many denominations have differing approaches to this prayer. Focus on the simplicity and beauty of Jesus' words. Read the verses as a prayer to heaven once, reading straight through. Then read it again out loud, this time pausing after each idea to think about what you are saying. Don't rush this time, but instead ask the Holy Spirit to reveal the depth of this prayer. After this time, keep a small rock or similar object on your person for the day. Any time that you see or feel this item, repeat the Lord's Prayer and reflect on your devotional time and what God showed you.

October 15

A Clear Mind (Ex)

I PRAY THAT YOU would have a clear mind. Yes, may clarity of thought rule and reign inside of your head. Death to anxiety, distractions, and the giants that seek to intimidate you. I pray this in the name of the Redeemer of Minds, Jesus. Amen and a thousand more amens.

Verse: Romans 12:2

> Do not conform to the pattern of this world, but be transformed by the renewing of your mind. Then you will be able to test and approve what God's will is--his good, pleasing and perfect will.

Exercise: Journaling

Take this time to write down everything that is on your mind. What are the positive, negative, and neutral things taking up space in your thoughts? Has your mind been racing uncontrollably, giving you no rest? Write all of this down. Mark what things are from God and which aren't. Pray over both, that the Holy Spirit would take the burden of your thoughts and help you have peace and clarity throughout your day and night. Surrender and listen for direction for both the negatives and the positives.

October 16

Hope in the King (Ex)

May you fix your eyes on Jesus, not on governmental authorities. He is Lord, they are not. Presidents, Caesars, Prime Ministers, and Kings are merely footnotes to His rule and reign. May your faith in Him contextualize everything else. Live in the truth that only He can fill the God shaped hole in us all. May you face each crisis, emergency, and headline with the assurance that Jesus is King and you are His. Amen and a thousand more amens.

Verse: Isaiah 9:6

> For to us a child is born, to us a son is given, and the government will be on his shoulders. And he will be called Wonderful Counselor, Mighty God, Everlasting Father, Prince of Peace.

Exercise: Prayer

Although we are of a different Kingdom and world, that does not mean that we should disconnect from our context. The community, nation, and time that we live in need a godly presence. Spend this time praying for those in authority and the society in which you live.. That there would be a greater awareness of Jesus, righteousness would prevail, and those in power would humble themselves before God.

October 17

God's Response to Your Deep Prayers (Ex)

Today I ask that God would give you a direct, focused, palpable answer to your deepest and most heart-felt prayer. Be expectant, observant, and ready to give thanks as He leans down from heaven to answer. May you feel His presence today as you interact with Him. Amen and a thousand more amens.

Verse: Psalm 66:17–20

> I cried out to him with my mouth; his praise was on my tongue. If I had cherished sin in my heart, the Lord would not have listened; but God has surely listened and has heard my prayer. Praise be to God, who has not rejected my prayer or withheld his love from me!

Exercise: Prayer and Worship

Do you have a prayer that you have held onto for weeks, months, or even years? If you do, write it down. Ask Jesus to speak to you concerning this thing today, whether that is an immediate resolution or an encouragement for today. Spend the remaining time worshipping Him for who He is and His faithfulness in your life. Thank Him for the situation you are praying for and trust Him in the midst of uncertainty. Read Psalm 66:17–20 as a prayer to finish your devotional time.

October 18

Hearing God's Voice (Ex)

I asked God to speak to you today. He said that He cannot do otherwise and that you should listen with your ears, eyes, nose, hands, and feet. For He can speak through anything and everything He wishes. Listen, listen, and listen some more. May your whole being be sensitive to His voice. Amen and a thousand more amens.

Verse: Psalm 19:1–4a

> The heavens declare the glory of God; the skies proclaim the work of his hands. Day after day they pour forth speech; night after night they reveal knowledge. They have no speech, they use no words; no sound is heard from them. Yet their voice goes out into all the earth, their words to the ends of the world.

Exercise: Meditation

Creation testifies of God's character. Situations point to His faithfulness. Music and beauty merely reflect Him, albeit twisted at times. This passage in Psalm 19 is an example of truth being displayed and conveyed constantly. Take 10 to 15 minutes and choose one thing to focus upon. This could be a scene in nature, an instrumental piece, or the complexities of yourself. Ask Jesus to open your eyes to His truth and character through this meditation. Utilize every sense to listen and seek His face.

October 19

Today is the Day of Action (Ex)

Holy Spirit, may today be a day of action. I choose You over my comfort and my desires. Lead me to quit talking about the future and take a leap for The Kingdom right now. I do not know what this will look like or when I will see the fruits of my faith, but I trust You and will cling to You. Amen and a thousand more amens.

Verse: 2 Corinthians 6:2

> For he says, "In the time of my favor I heard you, and in the day of salvation I helped you." I tell you, now is the time of God's favor, now is the day of salvation.

Exercise: Service, Evangelism, Prayer

We will not only receive salvation when we draw our last breath, we have it now. It has been given in full, if not yet fully experienced. Do not wait until you die or for "someday" to come before you get out of your comfort zone. Has God asked you to do something and you have been halted by fear? Have you wanted to take a step of faith, but stopped yourself each time? Have you held onto pain or a relationship because you are not sure who you are without it? Today is the day. Ask God to direct your thoughts, identify what He wants to do in you. Take the step of faith, and follow Him.

October 20

Remain Encouraged (Ex)

I am praying that you would stay encouraged. Yes, may the discouragements thrown at you be exponentially transformed by Jesus into success after success after success. Success to you this day and forevermore. Amen and a thousand more amens.

Verse: Genesis 50:20

> You intended to harm me, but God intended it for good to accomplish what is now being done, the saving of many lives.

Exercise: Prayer and Journaling

Write down the things that are causing you stress or pain. Write down what about them produces these feelings and write a prayer asking God to redeem them for His glory and for your good. Save these prayers, so that when they are resolved and produce good things, you can look back and be encouraged.

October 21

Loving Others (Ex)

My prayer is that Jesus will love others through you. So, get ready for some Samaritan-loving, leper-touching, refuse-redeeming power to come your way! A good day it shall be as you upset cultural norms, love the unlovable, and bring the Holy Spirit's power into your world. Be blessed and equipped to share the Good News of Jesus Christ today. Amen and a thousand more amens.

Verse: Philippians 2:3–4

> Do nothing out of selfish ambition or vain conceit. Rather, in humility value others above yourselves, not looking to your own interests but each of you to the interests of the others.

Exercise: Service and Evangelism

Spend your devotional time planning ways that you can love others. Write letters of encouragement, prepare bags of food to give away, open your schedule to focus on others. Ask the Holy Spirit what He wants you to do today and go do it.

October 22

Living Like What You Are (Ex)

Live like what you are . . . A NEW CREATION. So, stop acting like the old, worn out, ashamed, and depressed you. Because of the finished work of Jesus, that person doesn't . . . shouldn't exist. NEW, NEW, NEW is what you are. Amen and a thousand more amens.

Verse: Isaiah 43:18–19

> Forget the former things; do not dwell on the past. See, I am doing a new thing! Now it springs up; do you not perceive it? I am making a way in the wilderness and streams in the wasteland.

Exercise: Prayer

Jesus came so that you may have life and life to the full. He does not have a sense of disappointment or frustration when He thinks of you; but love and a holy anger towards the things that keep you from experiencing His life. What things have kept you from experiencing His life? What struggles or pain are present that He wants to address today? Sometimes Jesus instantly restores and sometimes He uses a process. Submit these areas to Him and ask Him to have control and direct you once again so you can live like the child of God that you are.

October 23

Jesus is Peace (Ex)

Right now I am praying for your peace. You need it. Jesus is Peace incarnate. So, Jesus, Jesus, Jesus to every single one of you. All day long and all night through. Amen and a thousand more amens.

Verse: Romans 8:6

> The mind governed by the flesh is death, but the mind governed by the Spirit is life and peace.

Exercise: Silence

Find a place in which you can sit and be quiet without any distractions. Keep your phone in a different room and close the door. Slow down. Jesus is with you. Take a humble posture, sitting, kneeling, or laying prostrate. Wait on Jesus. No words. No questions. Set aside 10 to 15 minutes like this. Breathe deeply. Listen closely. Only Him.

October 24

Jesus in Control (P)

Lord Jesus, I know that You are in control. Darkness, gloom, and despair are mere shadows with no ultimate power. You are The Light that outshines and dispels all that evil can muster. May Your power be displayed clearly today, and may You teach me to rest in You again. Thank you for opening my eyes to You. Amen and a thousand more amens.

Verse: 1 Chronicles 29:11–12

> Yours, Lord, is the greatness and the power and the glory and the majesty and the splendor, for everything in heaven and earth is yours. Yours, Lord, is the kingdom; you are exalted as head over all. Wealth and honor come from you; you are the ruler of all things. In your hands are strength and power to exalt and give strength to all.

Exercise: Worship and Meditation

One of the greatest ways we can remind ourselves of God's sovereignty, is to spend time thinking on and worshipping Him. Take today's Bible passage and pray through it slowly. Take each idea it presents and expand upon it in worshipful prayer. For example, take "Yours, Lord, is the greatness and the power." and think about each word: "Lord," "greatness," and "power." What does each word mean and how does that impact how you see God? Praise Him for these attributes and walk through these two verses over 15 to 20 minutes of prayer. If you finish before the time is completed, continue in the chapter or maybe repeat these verses again.

October 25

Unexpected Visit (Ex)

Today, I ask Jesus to visit you. He said that He would, but it may not look like who or what you thought. Be on the lookout for someone or something that is unexpected and beyond what you have learned from in the past. May Jesus speak to you in a new way that is clear, encourages you, humbles you, and brings glory to Him. Amen and a thousand more amens.

Verse: Numbers 22:26–31

> Then the angel of the Lord moved on ahead and stood in a narrow place where there was no room to turn, either to the right or to the left. When the donkey saw the angel of the Lord, it lay down under Balaam, and he was angry and beat it with his staff. Then the Lord opened the donkey's mouth, and it said to Balaam, "What have I done to you to make you beat me these three times?" Balaam answered the donkey, "You have made a fool of me! If only I had a sword in my hand, I would kill you right now." The donkey said to Balaam, "Am I not your own donkey, which you have always ridden, to this day? Have I been in the habit of doing this to you?" "No," he said. Then the Lord opened Balaam's eyes, and he saw the angel of the Lord standing in the road with his sword drawn. So he bowed low and fell facedown.

Exercise: Prayer

Hearing from God can be an encouraging and exciting experience. It can also be humbling as He sometimes chooses to speak through things we would not expect. After reading the prayer and passage of Scripture, ask the Father to help you remain in humility as you pursue Him today. That you would be able to see and hear Him clearly if He uses things or people that you would normally discount.

October 26

Refined In Him (P)

I NEED SOME FIRE. Heavenly fire. Kindled by the One who knows how to stir my heart. Fire that burns up weakness and kindles greatness. Bring that fire to my heart today, O God. leave nothing untouched by You as You purify me for Your glory. Amen and a thousand more amens.

Verse: Zechariah 13:9

> This third I will put into the fire; I will refine them like silver and test them like gold. They will call on my name and I will answer them; I will say, "They are my people," and they will say, "The Lord is our God."

Exercise: Journaling

A metal can only be refined by fire if it remains in the flames. The impurities and dirt are burned away as only what is pure remains. Allow the fire of God to do the same in your life today. Take 10 to 15 minutes to write down the areas in which you need His refining fire, the areas that you have tried to clean up, but have not been able to get rid of. The areas that make you feel dirty and inadequate. The areas that are sources of pain and confusion. Write these down, surrender them to Jesus, and ask Him to help you get further in the process of purification as you walk with Him.

October 27
A Personal God (Ex)

My prayer today is that God would show Himself faithful to you in an obvious way. Yes, may He do something that is so personal, powerful, and purposeful that only the two of you would know it. And when He does, please laugh out loud. Laugh loud and long and in the face of the enemy. Laugh the hell out of this day because of the all-powerful, all-holy, and all-knowing God that somehow loves to make you smile and laugh at the little things in life. May you see how beautiful this love is that you have. Amen and a thousand more amens.

Verse: Psalm 126:2–3

> Our mouths were filled with laughter, our tongues with songs of joy. Then it was said among the nations, "The Lord has done great things for them." The Lord has done great things for us, and we are filled with joy.

Exercise: Journaling

The Bible uses words like "love" and "friend" to describe God. He is also shown as holy, just, wrathful, and jealous, along with many other attributes. Look for his winks at you, or the funny moments of holy "coincidence." At the end of the day, look back on the past 24 hours (or even this week) and write down the ways He has shown up for you. Don't overlook the small things or dismiss blessings as natural occurrences.

October 28

In Awe of the Cross (Ex)

May the power of His cross dominate you today. Yes, may you be inundated with and overwhelmed by the awesomeness of what was done for you there. Saved, delivered, redeemed, empowered, and bound for glory. That is what you are by the grace of God through the cross of Christ revealed to you by His Spirit. Amen and a thousand more amens.

Verse: Colossians 2:13–15

> When you were dead in your sins and in the uncircumcision of your flesh, God made you alive with Christ. He forgave us all our sins, having canceled the charge of our legal indebtedness, which stood against us and condemned us; he has taken it away, nailing it to the cross. And having disarmed the powers and authorities, he made a public spectacle of them, triumphing over them by the cross.

Exercise: Meditation and Worship

After reading the prayer and passage of Scripture, read them again slowly. Ask the Holy Spirit to help you truly see and understand the cross in a new way. Thank God for His saving love and spend the next 10 to 15 minutes praising Him for the life you have been given. Read Colossians 2:12–15 again, worship with music, or sit in silence as you think of what He has done for you.

October 29

Invigorated by God (Ex)

My prayer for each of you today is that God would touch you. Yes and when He does, may you be energized, focused, and catapulted into life and more life. Teeming with life is what you will be through the wonderful presence of Jesus in your life. Amen and a thousand more amens.

Verse: Ezekiel 47:12

> Fruit trees of all kinds will grow on both banks of the river. Their leaves will not wither, nor will their fruit fail. Every month they will bear fruit, because the water from the sanctuary flows to them. Their fruit will serve for food and their leaves for healing."

Exercise: Reading

The Prophet Ezekiel saw a vision of a river coming from the Temple in Jerusalem that brought life to every place it touched. Read this account in Ezekiel 47:1–12. Ask the Father to produce the same effects in and through your life; that you would become a river of His Spirit, both experiencing and sharing His redemptive power in all you do. Read the passage again, taking your time to grasp each verse.

October 30

Total War (P)

I WILL FIGHT THE Enemy. I will pray against him. I will prey upon him. I will assert the Name of Jesus over him all day, every day, and in as many ways possible. Jesus is Lord of all and I receive His strength to push back the darkness today. Amen and a thousand more amens.

Verse: James 4:7

Submit yourselves, then, to God. Resist the devil, and he will flee from you.

Exercise: Prayer and Meditation

Ask the Holy Spirit to equip and empower you to stand for Him today. When you have Jesus within you, you become the enemy's weakness. Repent of any known sins and ask God to show you any areas that need to be submitted to Him again. Then, pray against any sins or temptations facing you and your loved ones today. Cover each person in prayer and make a plan to respond specifically to any attack of the enemy. For example, if you struggle with gossip, make a plan for when you are tempted to talk about others. Instead, have a verse to repeat in your mind, or change the subject of the conversation. Prepare to join Jesus in dominating the enemy today.

October 31

Death and Life (P)

I hate death and I love life. I speak death to death today and Life to life. The Life of God to my life through Jesus, the Lord of Life. Yes, may death and its effects lose their hold on every aspect of my being and may Life explode. Explosions of life that overwhelm the death of the past. Amen and a thousand more amens.

Verse: 1 Corinthians 15:54

> When the perishable has been clothed with the imperishable, and the mortal with immortality, then the saying that is written will come true: "Death has been swallowed up in victory."

Exercise: Prayer

As Christians, we have the hope that we shall live beyond our death.. The greatest weapon against finite man has been made impotent by Christ. Take your devotional time today to pray for those in your life who do not know Christ yet, or have not been living in His victory. Speak death to specific things in their lives and life to the plans of God for them. Choose two to three people to pray for in the next 15 to 20 minutes and proclaim Jesus over every aspect of their lives.

November 1

Freedom (Ex)

Freedom to you in Jesus' name. You will not be shackled by the thing that has pulled you down, shamed you, and held you back. Shackled no more. That is what you are by the power of Jesus Christ, the Lamb of God. Amen and a thousand more amens.

Verse: Galatians 5:1

> It is for freedom that Christ has set us free. Stand firm, then, and do not let yourselves be burdened again by a yoke of slavery.

Exercise: Prayer

This letter was addressed to a group of believers who were beginning to believe that they needed to earn salvation through following the Old Testament laws that God had given to Israel. Believing that we need to do more in order to be worthy of Christ's love, is an easy trap to fall into. You do not have to clean yourself up, or beat yourself up, for things that Jesus has already paid for. If you have areas of shame, or feelings of inadequacy in your life, admit them to Jesus, and ask for His forgiveness. Release those feelings so His love and purpose can renew you again.

NOVEMBER 2

Life to You (Ex)

HE IS LIFE. IN Him is Life. This is because death, hatred, and Hell could not keep Him down, nor will it prevail over you. In the name of the Living One I declare it: LIFE TO YOU. In this moment, not just when you die. Amen and a thousand more amens.

Verse: 2 Timothy 1:9–10

> He has saved us and called us to a holy life—not because of anything we have done but because of his own purpose and grace. This grace was given us in Christ Jesus before the beginning of time, but it has now been revealed through the appearing of our Savior, Christ Jesus, who has destroyed death and has brought life and immortality to light through the gospel.

Exercise: Prayer

Identify those things in your life that are attempting to hold you down and squeeze out the life of Christ from your daily existence. The Apostle Paul tells us that Jesus destroyed death and has brought light. That is your inheritance and your right as a child of the Most High. Condemn those things that have been weighing you down and bringing stress and fear. These things do not belong and must leave in the presence of the light of the Gospel: Jesus Christ.

November 3

Being Like Jesus (P)

I WANT TO BE like You, Jesus. I want to live like You, pray like You, fight like You, love like You. Please live through me today, Lord Jesus. Amen and a thousand more amens.

Verse: Galatians 2:20

> I have been crucified with Christ and I no longer live, but Christ lives in me. The life I now live in the body, I live by faith in the Son of God, who loved me and gave himself for me.

Exercise: Meditation, Reading, Worship, and Prayer

Living like Jesus is not the result of straining and personal effort. It is the product of being close to Him, loving Him, and surrendering to His life. Take 10 to 15 minutes to be with Jesus in whatever way you would like. You could spend this time worshipping with music, sitting in silent adoration, reading about Him in the Gospels, or asking Him questions with a pen in hand. Just be with Him, seek to know Him more, and He will cause His life to shine through you.

November 4

The Fights in Life (Ex)

LIFE IS A FIGHT, there's no way around it. May you fight for relationships. Fight for peace. Fight for health. Fight the enemy of your body, soul, and spirit. Fight, fight, fight. But, when you fight, may you fight like Jesus. Even more important, when He fights in you, through you and for you, may you see everything change. Keep showing up. Keep hoping. Keep praying. And keep living again and again and again by the power of the Holy Spirit as you see His victory unfold. Fight to live today. In the Name of Jesus. Amen and a thousand more amens.

Verse: Ephesians 6:13–17

> Therefore put on the full armor of God, so that when the day of evil comes, you may be able to stand your ground, and after you have done everything, to stand. Stand firm then, with the belt of truth buckled around your waist, with the breastplate of righteousness in place, and with your feet fitted with the readiness that comes from the gospel of peace. In addition to all this, take up the shield of faith, with which you can extinguish all the flaming arrows of the evil one. Take the helmet of salvation and the sword of the Spirit, which is the word of God.

Exercise: Prayer

Put on the full armor of God. Whether you are reading this at the beginning, middle, or end of your day, take 10 to 15 minutes to pray through each piece of armor and prepare for the fights you will face. Put each piece of armor on and pray for that specific area in your life. For example: "I put on the belt of truth today. I am held together by the truth because, Jesus, You are Truth. I will not allow the lies of the enemy or my finite perspective to determine my thoughts, but instead will look to You for truth." Walk through each piece and pray over the fights you will face.

November 5

Trusting Him (P)

I have nothing today. Jesus, You have everything. I empty myself again. Fill me with You. I am limited. You are not. I will trust in You. Amen and a thousand more amens.

Verse: Psalm 16:2

I say to the Lord, "You are my Lord; apart from you I have no good thing."

Exercise: Meditation

Go back to the foundation of your faith today. Remind yourself of how limited you are. Read today's prayer and Scripture and sit quietly with God. Repeat them and add similar statements to the prayer that apply to your life. We are totally dependent upon God. He is the ultimate good and all that we need. Repeat the prayer and verse. Return to the place of dependence on Him and not your own ability or strength. Ask Him to humble you and reveal your weaknesses, so His strength would be known to you in a greater way.

November 6

Jesus-Focused Thought Life (Ex)

I am praying for your thoughts today. May they be Jesus-focused. Yes, may they be full of His hope, light, and life. May you reveal His hope to everyone you come in contact with, His light to those in darkness, and His resurrection life to those who have not truly experienced life. Christ's thoughts through you today. Amen and a thousand more amens.

Verse: Matthew 5:14–16

> You are the light of the world. A town built on a hill cannot be hidden. Neither do people light a lamp and put it under a bowl. Instead they put it on its stand, and it gives light to everyone in the house. In the same way, let your light shine before others, that they may see your good deeds and glorify your Father in heaven.

Exercise: Prayer and Service

When the life of Christ was lighted in you, You received the entirety of Jesus' life.. Because of this, you can produce fruit that reflects Him. Ask that the Holy Spirit would make you more like Jesus today and give you opportunities to share His life with all those you come in contact with. He has appointed good works for you today. Be on the lookout for divine opportunities.

NOVEMBER 7

Giants Fall (Ex)

TODAY, MY PRAYER IS that you will face, confront, and speak to the giants in your life and nation in the name of the King of Giant Slayers: Jesus. In His name may they fall all over this nation. Amen and a thousand more amens.

Verse: 1 Samuel 17:45

> David said to the Philistine, "You come against me with sword and spear and javelin, but I come against you in the name of the Lord Almighty, the God of the armies of Israel, whom you have defied."

Exercise: Prayer and Journaling

Think of the giants that are intimidating your community and nation. Some examples include broken families, drug addictions, pornography, or political division. Choose a giant to pray against in the name of Jesus and speak David's declaration over them, regardless of how bad or powerful they might look. Write down this prayer and keep it on your person to read throughout the day.

November 8

Seen and Loved (Ex)

May God touch you today. Yes, may you have no doubts that you were singled out and interacted with by the Lord of It All: Jesus. And when it happens, give Him praise right then and there, regardless of where you're at. May praise come frequently and naturally in your life as you witness God's love and power firsthand. Amen and a thousand more amens.

Verse: 1 Peter 1:8–9

> Though you have not seen him, you love him; and even though you do not see him now, you believe in him and are filled with an inexpressible and glorious joy, for you are receiving the end result of your faith, the salvation of your souls.

Exercise: Worship

Peter states that we are continually receiving salvation, that it is an ongoing experience. Allow yourself to slow down and think about this wonderful fact. You are living in salvation even now. Because of this, we have been filled with "an inexpressible and glorious joy." Spend your devotional time today thanking Jesus for His gift of life and everything He gives beyond the moment you said yes to Him. Ask Him that you might see Him at work throughout your day, that you may think about and love Him more as time passes. He is an infinite God that wants to share all of Himself with us. Try to grasp that.

November 9

Winning for God (Ex)

May you win for God. More souls. More baptisms. More giants slain. More healed. More encouraged. More fire kindled. More Hope. More Light. More Life. More and more and more for Jesus. May you experience these wins and come to expect even greater victories. Amen and a thousand more amens.

Verse: Romans 8:37

> No, in all these things we are more than conquerors through him who loved us.

Exercise: Prayer

Identify any challenges or difficult situations that you have experienced recently. Pray for those in your life who do not know Jesus. Pray over each one by name and command the challenges to be resolved and to be removed. Ask Jesus to enter each area and bring about victory soon in a way that displays His supremacy. Afterwards, ask Him if there is anything else you can be praying for, then sit and listen.

November 10

Lies In Your Life (Ex)

I PRAY THAT YOU would stop believing the lies being told about you. Lies about your past. Lies about your future. Lies about today. Jesus came to give you life and more life. Life upon life cancels lies upon lies every day. So, life to you in Jesus' name. Amen and a thousand more amens.

Verse: John 16:13

> But when he, the Spirit of truth, comes, he will guide you into all the truth. He will not speak on his own; he will speak only what he hears, and he will tell you what is yet to come.

Exercise: Meditation and Journaling

Jesus promised the Holy Spirit would guide you, and He has been given to you. "He will guide you into all the truth". What lies have you told yourself about yourself or others? You may not consciously think these things, but you may act like you do. With a pen and paper, write down what you think of yourself in a letter format (Examples include. "You are a hard worker," "You should be doing better as a parent," "You're disappointing," "You are enough," etc.) What do you think about yourself? Spend 5 to 10 minutes thinking about and writing this down. At some point this week, talk about your letter with a close, Christian friend or mentor and discuss which parts are from God and which have been lies from the enemy.

November 11

Victory for the Victims of Sin (P)

In the name of Jesus, I come against every plan, activity, strategy, and thought that the enemy has against my life and my people. Now, Holy Spirit, stand up, rise up within me so I can live like what I am: a child of Jesus. Become greater and help me become less for Your glory. Amen and a thousand more amens.

Verse: 2 Corinthians 2:14

> But thanks be to God, who always leads us as captives in Christ's triumphal procession and uses us to spread the aroma of the knowledge of him everywhere.

Exercise: Prayer

Christ is already leading a triumphal procession. The victory has already happened and is in the process of being realized. Pray that it may be known in your life and in the lives of those around you. Pray specifically for those that you know who have been beaten down and have lost hope in life. Those that are wounded, broken, and searching. Pray that they may understand and believe in Christ's victory, so they can join in the procession as well.

November 12

Prayer (Ex)

May prayer become more real and powerful for you in the coming weeks. Allow it to be a conversation with God - just as real as if you were sitting down & speaking with a loving father over a meal or a cup of coffee. May you be persistent in it and experience greater depths in your walk with Christ through learning to pray. Amen and a thousand more amens.

Verse: Luke 11:1

> One day Jesus was praying in a certain place. When he finished, one of his disciples said to him, "Lord, teach us to pray, just as John taught his disciples."

Exercise: Prayer

Ask Jesus to teach you to pray just as the disciples did. They noticed something special about Jesus' prayers because the text tells us that they asked the same after He finished praying. Christ would go on to tell them a form of the Lord's Prayer. Read this passage and reflect on His prayer while also listening for His voice. Write down how you think the Holy Spirit wants to grow you in prayer.

November 13

Seeing Jesus Today (Ex)

I am praying today that Jesus would smile real big at you and that you will know without a shadow of a doubt that it wasn't luck, chance, or fate, but Him. Jesus is Lord of ALL and will erase ALL doubt, don't you doubt it for even a second. May you behold and love Him in a greater way today. Be encouraged and recharged because of Him. Amen and a thousand more amens.

Verse: Hebrews 12:1b-3

> And let us run with perseverance the race marked out for us, fixing our eyes on Jesus, the pioneer and perfecter of faith. For the joy set before him he endured the cross, scorning its shame, and sat down at the right hand of the throne of God. Consider him who endured such opposition from sinners, so that you will not grow weary and lose heart.

Exercise: Meditation

The book of Hebrews tells us that Jesus endured the terrible punishment and death of the cross for a joy that He saw on the other side. That joy was a restored relationship with humanity. With you. Read this passage slowly and ask the Holy Spirit to open your eyes to the beautiful, unbelievably good news of Jesus again. Whether you are a new believer, or have been following Christ for decades, take 10 minutes to come back to the cross, sit in awe of His love, and remember why you are His in the first place.

November 14

Assaulting the Enemy (P)

Father, may I assault the enemy on behalf of You today. You are worthy yesterday, today, and forevermore. So, let's assault with every breath, every word, every look, and every move. You are all-powerful. Advance the Kingdom today and use me in every way you want. Dispel death, darkness, and the demonic. May I do so alongside You because You are alive, You are risen, You are Lord, and You live inside me. Amen and a thousand more amens.

Verse: 2 Corinthians 10:3–4

> For though we live in the world, we do not wage war as the world does. The weapons we fight with are not the weapons of the world. On the contrary, they have divine power to demolish strongholds.

Exercise: Community and Service

One of the greatest ways to assault the enemy is through being united with other believers, either in a church body or smaller interactions like small groups or mentoring relationships. Christ has called the Church to do His work, not just as individuals. Are you involved in either of these? We are much more effective together. Pray over your efforts and those of your church, that they would be blessed and bring the light of Christ into your community.

November 15

A Holy Touch (Ex)

I ask God to touch your heart. I ask Him to fire you up. I ask Him to speak to you so deeply that you feel it in your bones. A fiery, heart moving, bone shaking touch. May comfort, complacency, and compromise be burned away. Amen and a thousand more amens.

Verse: Jeremiah 20:9

> But if I say, "I will not mention his word or speak anymore in his name," his word is in my heart like a fire, a fire shut up in my bones. I am weary of holding it in; indeed, I cannot.

Exercise: Reading and Prayer

This verse can bring inspiration or excitement at the thought of having God's Word in you so powerfully that you cannot hold it back. In reality, Jeremiah honestly had times when he wished that he could stop sharing God's Word, because it was not what people wanted to hear and he was punished for it. Read Jeremiah 20 for context. Being touched by God and following Him will cost all we have. It is a sacrifice and painful at times, but undoubtedly worth it. Ask the Holy Spirit to give you the same determination to follow Him that Jeremiah had: that regardless of your own status or desires, Jesus will be shared through your life in all you say and do. Take up your cross again today and follow the Risen Savior.

November 16

Peace in Your House (Ex)

May the shalom (peace) of Heaven descend upon you and your house and all who dwell therein. May your sensing of that peace be so profound that you have to sit down and just let it do its work in your mind, body, and spirit. Peace to you. Healing to you. Grace to you. Amen and a thousand more amens.

Verse: Proverbs 3:33

The Lord's curse is on the house of the wicked, but he blesses the home of the righteous.

Exercise: Prayer and Meditation

If you never have done so, begin this time by praying over each room in your house, that God's presence and peace would cover every inch of your home. Pray for the people who do life within your walls and pray that your place would be a place of peace and belonging. Then, sit still and listen. If God wants to say something specific, pay attention. If it is a time to just sit with Him and enjoy His company, relax with Him.

November 17

God's Unseen Work (Ex)

May you know that God is totally aware of your circumstance and moving on your behalf. You are not alone, my friends, and there is one who "sticks closer than a brother" who is working things out for your good. It may seem like He has forgotten you, but that couldn't be farther from the truth. God is growing you and will be with you through it all. Amen and a thousand more amens.

Verse: Proverbs 18:24

> One who has unreliable friends soon comes to ruin, but there is a friend who sticks closer than a brother.

Exercise: Prayer and Journaling

This verse in Proverbs juxtaposes "unreliable" with the friend that "sticks closer than a brother." We can rely on Christ because He is always with us and working. You may not see or feel Him, but He is reliable. Write down the areas that you are either trusting Him with or need to trust Him with. Write these as prayers. For example, "Lord Jesus, I trust you with my family. They don't know you and there is a lot of pain. I will hold on to You and pray You continue to work in us. Amen and a thousand more amens." Do this for each area you identify.

November 18

Used in His Kingdom (Ex)

I want for you to know how very much God wants to use you in His Kingdom efforts today. My prayer for you is: His kingdom come and His will be done with you, in you, and through you this day in Jesus' name. Amen and a thousand more amens.

Verse: Philippians 2:6–8

> Who, being in very nature a God, did not consider equality with God something to be used to his own advantage; rather, he made himself nothing by taking the very nature of a servant, being made in human likeness. And being found in appearance as a man, he humbled himself by becoming obedient to death— even death on a cross!

Exercise: Meditation and Reading

The Apostle Paul is speaking about the humility and sacrifice of Christ. We are to have the same mindset as we follow Him, our Lord and Redeemer. Read the prayer and passage of Scripture again, asking the Holy Spirit to help you understand how Jesus lived so that you can have the same mindset in your life. Read these one more time, having them in front of you as you sit quietly for a minute thinking about how Christ has given you His example to follow.

NOVEMBER 19

Seeing God's Faithfulness (P)

GOD, YOU ARE TRULY faithful. May your faithfulness be shown through my life today. You are the Living God and I believe that You crafted a plan to show Yourself faithful through me once again. Use me to encourage another today. May I be the instrument of Your faithfulness at work in my world. Amen and a thousand more amens.

Verse: Hebrews 10:23–24

> Let us hold unswervingly to the hope we profess, for he who promised is faithful. And let us consider how we may spur one another on toward love and good deeds.

Exercise: Prayer and Service

It is often so easy to get caught up in our own needs and situations, that we neglect those around us. Take this time to pray for God to show Himself faithful in the lives of others. Ask Him to show you how you can encourage and be an answer to someone's prayer today. As Hebrews 10 states, "consider how we may spur one another on toward love and good deeds." Write down any ideas that come to mind, send an encouraging message, or call someone you haven't spoken to in a while, to tell them how much you appreciate them.

November 20

Ready to Move (Ex)

May you go to someone today in the name of Jesus. I mean it. Be aware that God is going to bring someone across your path for whom you are supposed to do something on behalf of your amazing and risen Lord. Be ready and be filled with His Holy Spirit as you go. May the Holy Spirit make it clear who this is to be and guide you in that interaction. Amen and a thousand more amens.

Verse: 1 Peter 3:15

> But in your hearts revere Christ as Lord. Always be prepared to give an answer to everyone who asks you to give the reason for the hope that you have. But do this with gentleness and respect.

Exercise: Service and Evangelism

When did you accept Christ? What was your life like before and how did you meet Him? Think of the people who were involved in sharing Jesus with you. Ask Christ to be the same for someone today. Pray over your schedule, that you may be interrupted by heavenly opportunities to share the Gospel and serve others. At the end of the day, record how these opportunities went and pray for those involved again.

November 21

Desiring God First (Ex)

May your desire to serve and love God supersede all other desires in your life today. I am praying that the Holy Spirit will do His work deep in your souls, so that you will really know that you are changed on the inside. May His love be placed deep in you and become part of who you are, in Jesus' name. Amen and a thousand more amens.

Verse: Exodus 20:3

You shall have no other gods before me.

Exercise: Journaling

Reflect on what you want in life. Write down your top 5 desires. Have any of these taken away focus from God or taken His place as Lord over your life? Ask the Holy Spirit to show you if any of them have. Compromise may have happened in great or small ways; but you are to be completely God's, not having divided desires or loyalties. Write down a prayer giving these desires back to God, asking for help to repent from idolatry.

November 22

Reminded of God's Redemption (Ex)

May you be involved in the giving and the receiving of unconditional love today. May you realize how very valuable you are, and may you extend that same feeling of value to someone else in Jesus' name. You are so very valuable to the effort of seeing His Kingdom come and His will being done. Go out with Christ's love and power. Amen and a thousand more amens.

Verse: Psalm 139:13–14

> For you created my inmost being; you knit me together in my mother's womb. I praise you because I am fearfully and wonderfully made; your works are wonderful, I know that full well.

Exercise: Prayer and Service

God has orchestrated your creation and your redemption. He says that you are worth redeeming and loving. Read Psalm 139:13–14 as a prayer to the Father and thank Him again for knowing and loving you. God desires to have that same relationship with all people. Take the last 5 to 10 minutes of your devotional time to pray this prayer over someone else. Although it may be difficult, think of a person that you don't get along with, annoys you, or has hurt you in the past. Pray for them. Jesus loves and wants to redeem their lives as well. Ask for His grace to heal your heart, so you can love them as Christ does.

November 23

Lead Beside Still waters (P)

Lord Jesus, I pray that You would lead us beside still waters and that we might use the time by those waters to learn how to show others how to find the quiet place as well. Go before me and my family and friends today so that your name may be known through us. Give us rest and confidence in You. Amen and a thousand more amens.

Verse: Psalm 107:29–32

> He stilled the storm to a whisper; the waves of the sea were hushed. They were glad when it grew calm, and he guided them to their desired haven. Let them give thanks to the Lord for his unfailing love and his wonderful deeds for mankind. Let them exalt him in the assembly of the people and praise him in the council of the elders.

Exercise: Reading, Meditation, and Silence

Read Psalm 107:29–32 out loud slowly, dwelling on each syllable. Pause for a minute after finishing and allow God to speak with you in the quiet. Repeat this two more times, listening to the Word and allowing heavenly peace to become your reality. Pray the same over your loved ones today.

November 24

Peace in Every Area (Ex)

May the Shalom of Heaven invade every area of your lives today. Peace to your relationships, your finances, your body, your emotions, your mind, and every other area where you might be stressed. Amen and a thousand more amens.

Verse: 1 Thessalonians 3:16

> Now may the Lord of peace himself give you peace at all times and in every way. The Lord be with all of you.

Exercise: Prayer and Meditation

Read this verse over each area listed in today's prayer: relationships, finances, body, emotions, mind, and any other need you have. Take your time, reading the verse out loud and praying that Jesus would rule in each of these ways. Surrender them to Him again and pray for His direction.

November 25

Healer of Our Souls (Ex)

May our Lord Jesus show Himself as the Healer of your soul. May you feel healed today deep in your soul. May the thoughts and habits that have plagued you and weighed you down be lifted from you in His mighty name. Be healed in every way. Amen and a thousand more amens.

Verse: Psalm 34:17–18

> The righteous cry out, and the Lord hears them; he delivers them from all their troubles. The Lord is close to the brokenhearted and saves those who are crushed in spirit.

Exercise: Prayer and Journaling

Are there any wounds from your past that you know have not been fully healed? Ask the Holy Spirit to reveal these to you. Take 5 minutes with a pen and paper to write down any of these areas that come to your attention. After identifying these, ask Jesus to enter each of them with His healing presence, to reveal the roots of the pain and the fruit that the pain has produced in your life. This fruit could include things such as being slow to trust others, critical of yourself, or unsure about the future. Thank Him for entering these places and reflect on the wounds He has already healed. Sit with Him, receive His peace, and walk in it today.

November 26

Reconciliation (Ex)

My prayer for you today is that you will be reconciled with those from whom you have been separated through some type of offense. May the Great Healer of our souls do a work in you so that you can overcome the walls of hurt and pain and be able to walk in unity and peace. In Jesus' name, please Lord let it be so. Amen and a thousand more amens.

Verse: 2 Corinthians 5:16–20

> So from now on we regard no one from a worldly point of view. Though we once regarded Christ in this way, we do so no longer. Therefore, if anyone is in Christ, the new creation has come: The old has gone, the new is here! All this is from God, who reconciled us to himself through Christ and gave us the ministry of reconciliation: that God was reconciling the world to himself in Christ, not counting people's sins against them. And he has committed to us the message of reconciliation. We are therefore Christ's ambassadors, as though God were making his appeal through us. We implore you on Christ's behalf: Be reconciled to God.

Exercise: Prayer

May today be both a call for healing and forgiveness.. Forgiveness is a process of letting go, so take this time to ask the Holy Spirit who you need to forgive. It is a choice to let go of the hurt and offense. The Holy Spirit is inside you and will help.

November 27

Sufficiency in Jesus (Ex)

May you see in living color that Jesus is your sufficiency. May you know beyond a shadow of a doubt that He will care for you and see that you are secure in every aspect of your life. He is the image of the invisible God and He holds "ALL THINGS" together (Col. 1:17). Oh praise the One who saves and sustains. Amen and a thousand more amens.

Verse: Colossians 1:15–18

> The Son is the image of the invisible God, the firstborn over all creation. For in him all things were created: things in heaven and on earth, visible and invisible, whether thrones or powers or rulers or authorities; all things have been created through him and for him. He is before all things, and in him all things hold together. And he is the head of the body, the church; he is the beginning and the firstborn from among the dead, so that in everything he might have the supremacy.

Exercise: Prayer

Jesus is more than enough for anything we experience in life. Take this time to remind yourself that you are cared for and seen. Read Colossians 1:15–18 out loud and speak its truth over the areas of worry or lack. Regardless of present realities, the cross has the final word.

November 28

Organizing Lives (Ex)

I am believing that the Great Organizer and Creator of the universe will help you organize your life, so that you might be effective in seeing His Kingdom come and His will be done on the earth, in your home, at our school or place of work, and everywhere else that you do life. Amen and a thousand more amens.

Verse: Revelation 4:11

> You are worthy, our Lord and God, to receive glory and honor and power, for you created all things, and by your will they were created and have their being.

Exercise: Worship and Prayer

Revelation 4 describes the throne room of heaven, and verse 11 is a proclamation of praise to God. Read this chapter, spending 5 to 10 minutes meditating on it and joining with the heavenly beings in praising God. Then, pray that the One who created all and sustains all would exert His influence in each area of your life.

November 29

Who God is to You (P)

God, you are my source, my refuge, my strength, my helper, my healer, lover of my soul, my redeemer, my rock, my provider. . . Amen and a thousand more amens.

Verse: Psalm 95:1–3

> Come, let us sing for joy to the Lord; let us shout aloud to the Rock of our salvation. Let us come before him with thanksgiving and extol him with music and song. For the Lord is the great God, the great King above all gods.

Exercise: Reading and Worship

Read Psalm 95 in its entirety. Read it again, slowly, this time speaking the prayer out loud to Jesus. After finishing the second reading, pick one verse or title to focus upon either in the Psalm or from today's prayer (ie. my source, Rock of our salvation, etc). Repeat this word or phrase in your mind and think about what that actually means. Praise Him with your thoughts and simply be with and adore Him today.

November 30

Repairing Breaches (Ex)

My prayer for you today is that God will repair the breach that exists between you and someone in your life with whom you are at odds. He is an expert at doing breach repair if you will just let Him. In Jesus' name I am praying for the breaches to be gone very soon in your life. Amen and a thousand more amens.

Verse: Matthew 5:9

Blessed are the peacemakers, for they will be called children of God.

Exercise: Prayer and Service

After reading the prayer and Scripture, spend 5 minutes just being quiet with God. Ask Him to reveal the relationships that need mending or encouragement. These could either be past hurts or simply neglected relationships. Write down the names of those that come to mind and pray over each person. Ask for God's peace and reconciliation to be at work in both hearts. Ask the Holy Spirit if there are any steps for you to take today to repair the relationships.

December 1

The Christmas Season (Ex)

I AM PRAYING THAT you get a new revelation of the Christ child this year. May the power and glory of the Incarnation overwhelm you. May it stun you. May it wow you. May it humble you. And may it motivate you to live your life in yet a place of deeper commitment to Him than ever before. "And upon seeing Him, they bowed down and worshipped Him. . ." (Matt. 2:11). May you see the miracle of Christ in a greater way this year. Amen and a thousand more amens.

Verse: Matthew 2:10–11

> When they saw the star, they were overjoyed. On coming to the house, they saw the child with his mother Mary, and they bowed down and worshiped him. Then they opened their treasures and presented him with gifts of gold, frankincense and myrrh.

Exercise: Silence and Worship

Read today's passage out loud. Sit in silence for five minutes, thinking about what actually happened on that night. Repeat. Ask God to open your eyes to the beauty and holiness and awe-inspiring nature of this event. Repeat. End with a time of adoration and thanks for the greatest gift we could have ever received: Jesus Christ. Our Immanuel: God with us. After this time, grab a small rock or similar item to keep on your person for the month of December (or one week). Every time you feel or see it, come back to Immanuel. Thank Him again. Worship Him again. Delight in Him again.

December 2

God's Presence in Your Space (Ex)

My prayer today is that the presence of God invades your space. May you feel a palpable sense of His presence in your home, your car, at school, at breakfast, at lunch, and all throughout your day. May that presence give you faith that His Kingdom has come and His will is being done in your life. Amen and a thousand more amens.

Verse: Matthew 18:19–20

> Again, truly I tell you that if two of you on earth agree about anything they ask for, it will be done for them by my Father in heaven. For where two or three gather in my name, there am I with them.

Exercise: Prayer and Community

Jesus tells us that He is with each of us individually, but that we also get a clearer understanding of His character and power in the context of community. If possible, reach out to a fellow believer during your devotional time or at any point in the day. Talk about your days and pray together for God's presence to be known in your lives.

December 3

The Mind of Christ (Ex)

I pray today that you realize that you have the mind of Christ. May you think like, act like, love like, and respond like Jesus today and then watch and see what happens. May His Kingdom come and His will be done in your spheres of influence, my friends. Amen and a thousand more amens.

Verse: Acts 1:8

> But you will receive power when the Holy Spirit comes on you; and you will be my witnesses in Jerusalem, and in all Judea and Samaria, and to the ends of the earth.

Exercise: Prayer and Service

Ask the Holy Spirit to guide you and empower you to present Christ to your world. Take time to sit with Him and reflect on ways that you have not been living like Jesus. Repent of these, write them down, and ask Jesus to change you, so you can be His witness today. At the end of the day, write down the ways that you were able to reflect Christ and the things you could have done differently.

December 4

Meditating on Immanuel (Ex)

May the reality of "God WITH us" in Jesus overwhelm you this day. God WITH you. A prophetic voice from the Prophet Isaiah that still reverberates into this very instant in time, directly into your "now". You are not alone, nor will you ever be. God WITH us means that there is absolutely nothing that you will face in which He is not engaged. Jesus makes this so. He is Immanuel. He is WITH us and . . .WITH means together. He is neither apart nor away from you, but WITH. So, speak WITH Him. Walk WITH Him. Have a cup of coffee WITH Him. Laugh WITH Him. Dance WITH Him. Sit WITH Him. Cry WITH Him. Take the dog on a walk WITH Him. Have dinner WITH Him. Oh praise the One who is WITH us and ever will be. Amen and a thousand more amens.

Verse: Matthew 1:22–23

> All this took place to fulfill what the Lord had said through the prophet: "The virgin will conceive and give birth to a son, and they will call him Immanuel" (which means "God with us").

Exercise: Silence and Meditation

In prayer, find a quiet place where you will not be disturbed. Leave your phone somewhere else, or turn it off. Take a position of humility (kneeling, laying prostrate, etc.). For 5 to 10 minutes, sit in silence except for one word: Immanuel. Every few seconds, repeat this in a whisper or in your mind. Meditate on the word, what it means for you, and Who it points to. Sit and listen. Ask God to reveal what Immanuel truly means; beyond an intellectual comprehension, to an intimacy in your heart. Give Immanuel time to be with you today in the quiet and take Him with you wherever you go.

December 5

Reflecting God's Presence (Ex)

May the presence of God rest on you like a star over the manger of your heart so that seekers, drawn close by the innocent beauty of a babe, might be saved by this Lion of a Lord. May you be the hands and feet of the Holy Spirit today and draw others to the Father. Amen and a thousand more amens.

Verse: Matthew 2:9–10

> After they had heard the king, they went on their way, and the star they had seen when it rose went ahead of them until it stopped over the place where the child was. When they saw the star, they were overjoyed.

Exercise: Evangelism

Today, be willing to have your schedule interrupted and share what Jesus has done in your life. I challenge you to intentionally share the Gospel with one person. This individual could be someone you have never met, or a family member who does not yet know Christ. You have the Holy Spirit within you and can stand right before the Throne of Heaven. Do not keep this happy news to yourself!

December 6

Christ's Coming (Ex)

Today I am praying that you would prepare your heart to celebrate the coming of Jesus this Christmas. Yes, He came. . .but He still comes. Prepare to have Him come into your life in a fresh way. . .a new way. . .the way of a baby crying in the night. An invasion of your sleep that demands your attention and steals your heart. May your heart be stolen and invaded this Christmas. Amen and a thousand more amens.

Verse: Micah 5:2

> But you, Bethlehem Ephrathah, though you are small among the clans of Judah, out of you will come for me one who will be ruler over Israel, whose origins are from of old, from ancient times.

Exercise: Prayer

The Prophet Micah spoke this prophecy centuries before Christ would come. He was and is the coming King. His reign has begun, but has not yet reached fulfillment. However, we still live in submission to Him. Ask God to reveal the areas in your life that are not surrendered to Him. In what ways does Christ want to become Lord of your life once again?

December 7

He is Pleased with You (Ex)

May you rest in the fact that God is pleased with you and wants to be with you today. God, the creator of the universe, the Ancient of Days, the Great "I Am", would like some time with you. May you delight in His presence as He also delights in you. Fall in love with Him more as you grow closer to Him today. Amen and a thousand more amens.

Verse: 1 John 3:1

> See what great love the Father has lavished on us, that we should be called children of God! And that is what we are! The reason the world does not know us is that it did not know him.

Exercise: Meditation and Prayer

A parent should not want to be with his or her child because it is a duty, but because there is deep love. It is the same with our Father. Don't only approach Him with needs or a checklist, but remind yourself that the greatest gift is simply being with Him. Take your devotional time to just be with your Father. This can look however you want it to. You could get a cup of coffee, admire nature with Him, or just sit in silence. Put away the prayer lists and studies. Just be with Him and ask Him to open your eyes to Him once again.

December 8

The Favor of the Lord (Ex)

May the favor of the Lord rest upon you and may you know that it is there. May that favor result in you knowing that God is "winking" at you. May you receive unexpected blessings, gifts, healings, jobs, phone calls, and whatever else God wants to do to favor you. Blessings, favor, and the presence of God be upon you my friends. Amen and a thousand more amens.

Verse: Psalm 90:17

> May the favor of the Lord our God rest on us; establish the work of our hands for us-- yes, establish the work of our hands.

Exercise: Worship

Think about the last three months. What have been the major events, both good and bad? How have you been blessed in that time frame? Write down these blessings and thank God for them. Celebrate, sing, dance, and sit in awe of His unmerited favor. Yes, believe for new breakthroughs and pray the same for others.

December 9

Walking in Authority (Ex)

May you walk in an authority today that will help you to see His Kingdom come and His will be done in your spheres of influence. Please know that God is intent upon using you in powerful and influential ways on His behalf. He loves you and is proud of who you are becoming, just keep seeking His face. Blessings to each of you. Amen and a thousand more amens.

Verse: Matthew 28:18–20

> Then Jesus came to them and said, "All authority in heaven and on earth has been given to me. Therefore go and make disciples of all nations, baptizing them in the name of the Father and of the Son and of the Holy Spirit, and teaching them to obey everything I have commanded you. And surely I am with you always, to the very end of the age."

Exercise: Prayer and Memorization

Because Jesus has all authority and is with you, you can bring about transformation in the lives of those around you. Ask the Holy Spirit to guide you in exerting the authority of Christ in your spheres of influence today. Ask for boldness, wisdom, and humility. Listen for practical steps on how to be like Jesus. Commit Matthew 28:18–20 to memory. Keep a small rock or similar item on your person. Every time you feel or see this object this week, repeat the verse and ask God how you can bring about His Kingdom in that moment.

December 10

Heavenly Priorities (Ex)

May the Lord help you to prioritize in accordance with His Kingdom coming and His will being done in your life today. He has a perfect order for your life and I am praying today that you can hear what that is and then follow His rhythm. Order, peace, and calm to you today in the name of Jesus. Amen and a thousand more amens.

Verse: Matthew 22:36–40

> "Teacher, which is the greatest commandment in the Law?" Jesus replied: " 'Love the Lord your God with all your heart and with all your soul and with all your mind.' This is the first and greatest commandment. And the second is like it: 'Love your neighbor as yourself.' All the Law and the Prophets hang on these two commandments."

Exercise: Meditation and Journaling

On a piece of paper, write down your top 5 priorities in life based upon how much time you spend doing and thinking about them. Ask the Holy Spirit to help you be honest with yourself. For example, you may believe physical health is a top priority, but if you haven't worked out in weeks or stayed consistent with healthy foods, it may not be as high as you like. After writing these 5 down, read the passage of Scripture again in Matthew. How does your list line up with Jesus' teaching on the greatest commandment? Are your priorities right? Ask Jesus to help you change your lifestyle to reflect His priorities and alter your list as needed. Think of practical ways you can live out heavenly priorities.

December 11

Peace of Mind (Ex)

May the Lord bless you and keep you and impart His peace of mind to you. The Apostle Paul tells us that we have the mind of Christ and I don't believe that He is anxious about anything. The peace, calm, and confidence of Jesus to you my friends. May depression, anxiety, jumbled thoughts, and hysteria be cast far from you. Blessings and peace to you this day. Amen and a thousand more amens.

Verse: 1 Corinthians 2:12–16

> What we have received is not the spirit of the world, but the Spirit who is from God, so that we may understand what God has freely given us. This is what we speak, not in words taught us by human wisdom but in words taught by the Spirit, explaining spiritual realities with Spirit-taught words. The person without the Spirit does not accept the things that come from the Spirit of God but considers them foolishness, and cannot understand them because they are discerned only through the Spirit. The person with the Spirit makes judgments about all things, but such a person is not subject to merely human judgments, for, "Who has known the mind of the Lord so as to instruct him?" But we have the mind of Christ.

Exercise: Prayer

The Holy Spirit explains the heavenly realities of life in Christ. We can know Christ and His character because His Spirit dwells inside of us. We don't have to make judgments about our lives, or the world, based only on our finite perception. Ask Jesus to make His point of view clear to you in the areas that have been taking your peace. Write down each point of stress and listen for His response in each. Think about how God sees each of them from His point of view and write it down. Ask Him to give you peace in the midst of chaos today.

December 12

For Those Struggling With Stress (Ex)

I am praying today for those of you who are struggling with stress and anxiety. May the Shalom of Heaven invade every area of your lives. May you sense more peace than you can remember. May the peace that passes understanding truly rule in your hearts and minds in Christ Jesus. Shalom and Selah to you in abundance. Amen and a thousand more amens.

Verse: John 14:27

> Peace I leave with you; my peace I give you. I do not give to you as the world gives. Do not let your hearts be troubled and do not be afraid.

Exercise: Meditation

Breathe in deeply and hold that breath for 3 seconds. Release it and repeat. Slow down. There is peace with Jesus. Remind yourself of that. He is with you. Breathe. Read John 14:27 slowly. Breathe again. Read this verse 10 times, pausing for 10 seconds in between each reading. Ask Jesus for His peace to fill your mind and chest so that all tension fades. Even if you have not been stressed lately, this will help you remain in His peace.

December 13

He Is Alive and Working (Ex)

May you know with absolute certainty that Jesus is alive and working in your life today. I am praying that you will see His activity in your life in a pronounced way. May you know that you are valuable, desirable, pivotal, strategic, and vital to His Kingdom efforts right there where you live. Blessings to you today my friends. Amen and a thousand more amens.

Verse: 1 Peter 2:9

> But you are a chosen people, a royal priesthood, a holy nation, God's special possession, that you may declare the praises of him who called you out of darkness into his wonderful light.

Exercise: Memorization and Meditation

Repeat 1 Peter 2:9 out loud to yourself. Say your name at the beginning of the verse: "_____, but you are a chosen. . .". If there is a mirror nearby, repeat the Scripture while looking into your eyes. Remind yourself of whose you are. Commit this verse to memory and repeat it when you get out of bed in the morning and when you go to sleep at night.

December 14

Inherent Value (Ex)

My prayer for you today is that you would realize your inherent value because you bear the image of God. In some form or fashion you resemble your Creator. May you not only resemble Him today, but go ahead and act like Him. Speak life or encouragement to someone. Bless someone, help someone, or do something for someone just for the sake of doing it. Blessings to you today as you act like the God you resemble. Amen and a thousand more amens.

Verse: 1 John 4:17

> This is how love is made complete among us so that we will have confidence on the day of judgment: In this world we are like Jesus.

Exercise: Service and Journaling

After reading the prayer and Scripture, ask God if there are any specific times today in which you can be like Jesus to those around you. If an opportunity comes to mind, write it down and pray for guidance in that moment, to share God's love. Also, ask for an awareness of those you come in contact with today. Challenge yourself to intentionally love someone in a way that interrupts your schedule, or is outside of your comfort zone. At the end of the day, write down the ways that you were able to be like Jesus and pray again for those with whom you interacted.

December 15

Fresh Anointing (Ex)

I AM PRAYING THAT the Holy Spirit would anoint you with fresh oil. By this I mean that you will feel refreshed and up to the task as it relates to your purpose for the Kingdom on this planet. "His Kingdom come and His will be done" will become personal for you as it becomes a reality in all that you do. You are an anointed and equipped vessel to actually see this happen. May you realize how valuable you are to God and live out of that relationship. Amen and a thousand more amens.

Verse: 1 John 2:20

> But you have an anointing from the Holy One, and all of you know the truth.

Exercise: Silence and Worship

Jesus is the Truth. If you have accepted Him, you know the Truth. You have been chosen and set apart by the Most High. Ask Him to remind you of this and fill you with His anointing power again. To be anointed meant to be chosen, recognized, and empowered by God to complete a certain task or lifestyle. Sit in silence for 5 minutes and think about How God has anointed you. End with a time of worship, singing to and adoring God for His holiness and power in your life.

December 16

Peace (Ex)

May the star of faith hover over the manger of your heart, the place where Christ dwells. And, like the Magi, may many be drawn to His life-giving, life-changing, peace-breathing presence in you. May His rest surround you and fill you today. Amen and a thousand more amens.

Verse: Luke 2:14

> Glory to God in the highest heaven, and on earth peace to those on whom his favor rests.

Exercise: Silence

Christ came so that we may have peace: peace with God, peace within ourselves, and peace in our world. Take 5 to 10 minutes to be quiet with God. As you sit or kneel or lay prostrate, close your eyes and picture just being with the Father. This scene can look however you want it to. As you breathe, imagine you are breathing in His presence and breathing out distractions. Simply be with Jesus and delight in this time with Him.

December 17

Covering and Wisdom (Ex)

I am asking God to cover you this day. Yes, may you feel Him keeping you safe, inspired, directed and if necessary, corrected. In the midst of deadlines, responsibilities, or stress in general, may you feel His hand on your life. Amen and a thousand more amens.

Verse: 2 Thessalonians 3:3

But the Lord is faithful, and he will strengthen you and protect you from the evil one.

Exercise: Prayer and Meditation

As the year is coming to a close, reflect upon all that God has brought you through since January. Think of the answered prayers, difficult challenges, and growth you have experienced. He has been with you through all of it, so sit with Him and ask Him to give you the strength and wisdom to finish this month strong. Pray over your schedule, your loved ones, your job, etc. You will thrive and reflect God's power these next several weeks.

December 18

Living out Christ's Redemption (Ex)

May you have a Merry Christmas season and experience Christ in some form or fashion in this time. The time when we celebrate Heaven coming down to redeem earth. Yes, may you too be redeemed, redeemed, and redeemed again and again and again times a thousand. Then, in the spirit of that gift, may you give it to someone you know. Or better yet, to someone you don't know. That's what Christmas is all about. Give, give, and then give some more, until you can't give and then give again. Today I give you thoughts and prayers of Redemption, Hope, Light, and Life to any and all who will receive and even to those who won't receive, in hope that they will. Amen and a thousand more amens.

Verse: James 1:17

> Every good and perfect gift is from above, coming down from the Father of the heavenly lights, who does not change like shifting shadows.

Exercise: Prayer and Evangelism

During your devotional time, reflect on the gift that we celebrate during this time of the year. Ask Jesus to make His birth, life, death, and resurrection all the more real to you. Ask Him to bring someone into your path today with whom you can share this Gospel.

December 19

Delivered from Shame (Ex)

I pray that you would be delivered from all of the shame that the enemy has tried to use to intimidate you. May you be free and filled with peace and joy like you haven't known for a long time. May you boast in the Lord who is your deliverer and the one who takes all shame from you and gives you a radiant and clean face (Psalm 34). Selah and Shalom to you all.

Verse: Psalm 34:4–6

> I sought the Lord, and he answered me; he delivered me from all my fears. Those who look to him are radiant; their faces are never covered with shame. This poor man called, and the Lord heard him; he saved him out of all his troubles.

Exercise: Reading and Prayer

Begin this time by asking God to speak to you through His Word. Read the entirety of Psalm 34 out loud. Pause for a minute to listen with the Psalm in front of you. Are any verses or words sticking out to you? If so, why do you think they are? Pray these words over yourself and others in your life. If no verses catch your attention, read the Psalm again, this time making the words into a prayer. (Ex for verse 4: "Thank you Jesus for seeing me and rescuing me. Those things in my past don't have a hold on me anymore because You have delivered me"). Pray through the entire Psalm, or a specific section, asking for clear direction.

December 20

God's Direction (Ex)

May God's direction be precise and obvious to you. May you have no doubt as to what it is that you are to do and which way you are to turn. I am praying that God would remove ALL doubt and indecision and hesitation, and that you would know that you know that you know that you are in His will and doing His work. Blessings and assurance and the Shalom of Heaven to you, my friends. Amen and a thousand more amens.

Verse: Psalm 119:105

Your word is a lamp for my feet, a light on my path.

Exercise: Prayer

Pray for clarity for another person today. Who in your life struggles with uncertainty and indecision? Pray that they would know the Word of God and the God of the Word, so that hesitation and fear disappear. Read today's prayer over their situation and expect God to bring freedom to that person soon.

December 21

A Reminder that God is Faithful (Ex)

My prayer for you today is that you would have a distinct sense that God is being faithful to you. May you sense His faithfulness as you are healed, encouraged, delivered, provided for, empowered, and set free. When He proves Himself as faithful, may you see and understand His working in your life and be in awe of His love. Amen and a thousand more amens.

Verse: Deuteronomy 7:9

> Know therefore that the LORD your God is God; he is the faithful God, keeping his covenant of love to a thousand generations of those who love him and keep his commandments.

Exercise: Prayer and Worship

Ask that God would reveal Himself clearly to you today. Pray over specific events on your schedule and relationships, both in your family and at work. Spend the last 5 to 10 minutes praising Him. This could be as you get ready, or as you drive. Focus on Him and honor Him for His faithfulness as you believe and expect to see Him work today.

December 22

A Fresh Move (P)

I AM PRAYING FOR a fresh move of God in my life, my church, my home, my car, my kids, and my work. Holy Spirit, open my eyes to the ways You are already working, so that I can join You. Show Your power in audacious fashion for Your glory. Amen and a thousand more amens.

Verse: Acts 4:31

> After they prayed, the place where they were meeting was shaken. And they were all filled with the Holy Spirit and spoke the word of God boldly.

Exercise: Prayer

Choose one area of your life to pray over today. Some examples include your church, your home, and your work. Pray that this area would be shaken by the Holy Spirit and would result in more people coming to know Christ and the power of God. Pray for freedom for those in bondage and healing for the broken. End by asking God how you might join Him in His work in that area.

December 23

A Revelation of Your Task (Ex)

I AM PRAYING TODAY that you get a revelation of what it is that God wants for you to do specifically for the Kingdom. He has a specific task for you and wants for you to dive in, and soon. May you be totally immersed in seeing His kingdom come and His will being done in your community. Amen and a thousand more amens.

Verse: John 15:16

> You did not choose me, but I chose you and appointed you so that you might go and bear fruit--fruit that will last--and so that whatever you ask in my name the Father will give you.

Exercise: Journaling

What is the task that the Lord has for you today? Ask Him. Is it to continue to be faithful with your current job and relationships, or to take a step of faith in some area? Is it time to start working on that dream that He gave you in the past? Or have you been called to encourage the dreams of others? Ask, listen, and write down what you hear, so you may take action soon.

December 24

Reason for the Season (Ex)

Jesus Christ, Son of God, please give us all a deep and abiding revelation of who You are over these next two days. May we be delivered from consumerism and greed and filled with the selfless glory of who You are. Help us to value others above ourselves, showing all with whom we come into contact that we embrace the power of what was done so humbly and powerfully in the manger on that first Christmas Eve. Thank you. Thank you. Thank you. We love and adore You, King of kings and Lord of lords. Amen and a thousand more amens.

Verse: Isaiah 9:6

> For to us a child is born, to us a son is given, and the government will be on his shoulders. And he will be called Wonderful Counselor, Mighty God, Everlasting Father, Prince of Peace.

Exercise: Worship and Community

Share today's prayer with friends or family. Talk about what this time of year means for you and listen to the thoughts of others, as well. Recount how God has delivered you and thank Him for everything He has done. Let the name of Jesus fill your interactions today.

December 25

Celebrate (Ex)

May you be swept up in the magnitude of this day and not the craziness of packages and tinsel and food. Jesus Christ was born. Hope came into a dying world. Light shone in the darkness. Healing was now available for humanity's terminal condition. God sought us out through the power of an innocent little baby boy who was born in a manger. Glory to His name!! Hallelujah forever!! Amen and a thousand more amens.

Verse: Luke 2:13–14

> Suddenly a great company of the heavenly host appeared with the angel, praising God and saying, "Glory to God in the highest heaven, and on earth peace to those on whom his favor rests."

Exercise: Meditation

We remember this day, the climax of God's redemptive plan: the incarnation of His Son. It tends to be a busy day for many, but intentionally slow down. Take 5 to 10 minutes to step away from the busyness and the gatherings. Take this time to imagine what it would have been like to stand in the fields with the Shepherds, to see countless angels appear, and to witness the divine outburst of joy. Reflect on what this means for you. Jesus is the reason. Do not get distracted and neglect spending time with the One whom you celebrate.

DECEMBER 26

Remain in the Rejoicing (Ex)

I PRAY TODAY THAT Christmas would not be over for you, but that you would live, breathe and function in the deepest sense that God is WITH you in Jesus. May the laughter, good food, singing, presents, much joy and the exhilaration of children swimming in wrapping paper stay with you, for a Savior was born and He is Christ the Lord. Sing and dance and party my friends, for God is with you and you are not, nor will you ever be alone again. You may feel alone at times, or have had difficult moments during this season, but the reality of Christ is even more real. If you are not in the Christmas spirit, may Immanuel get you there in fun, hilarious, and celebratory fashion. When you arrive, may He keep you at that place well into next December, just in time for the celebrating to start again. In Jesus' name, let it be so. Amen and a thousand more amens.

Verse: Luke 2:29–32

> Sovereign Lord, as you have promised, you may now dismiss your servant in peace. For my eyes have seen your salvation, which you have prepared in the sight of all nations: a light for revelation to the Gentiles, and the glory of your people Israel.

Exercise: Journaling

After the busyness of this season, which may still be continuing for some, take time to reflect upon what God has done. Write a prayer expressing how you are feeling during this season, how you perceive Jesus, and how you desire to know Him. A good format to use if you do not know what to pray, is to break up the prayer in five different sections: 1. Acknowledge: Recognize how God is with you and around you. Become more aware of His presence and your surroundings. 2. Gratitude: Identify the blessings in your life that God has given you. 3. Obedience: Record what things you have done well with and for Jesus recently. How have you been obedient? 4. Repentance: Record the things in which you could have done better recently. In what ways could you have been more obedient or missed the mark? 5. Hope for today: Give today to the Holy Spirit once more and bring before Him the responsibilities and concerns that you have. This can be as long or as short as you would like.

December 27

Identity in the Incarnation (Ex)

I am praying today that your levels of peace, joy, and happiness are not predicated upon others' perceptions of you. God's opinion of you is that you are an amazing creation, a possessor of His image. And yes, there is a fight to be had with the enemy, as he will try and tell you that you are less than what you are, but you win because of Jesus every time. Now, because God is WITH you, go out and live today like He is. Live like the amazing, Christ-like, image of God bearing, Kingdom building force in Him that you are. Go out and find a place where the enemy is moving, kick him in the teeth, and tell him "Merry Christmas, Immanuel is with me". Amen and a thousand more amens.

Verse: John 1:11–13

> He came to that which was his own, but his own did not receive him. Yet to all who did receive him, to those who believed in his name, he gave the right to become children of God— children born not of natural descent, nor of human decision or a husband's will, but born of God.

Exercise: Service

After reading today's prayer, pray and think about how you can bring God's Kingdom to earth. Is there someone you can intentionally reach out to in kindness? Can you show a family member love and vulnerability? Can you send an encouraging message to someone? Whatever you do, do something to live out your heavenly hope today!

December 28

God will Provide (Ex)

May you know today without a shadow of a doubt that God is your keeper and your provider. He is not intimidated by outside lack nor is He limited by it. His kingdom will come and His will shall be done regardless of economic indicators and markets. Jehovah Jireh is your provider so may you praise His glorious and mighty name. Amen and a thousand more amens.

Verse: Phillipians 4:12–13

> I know what it is to be in need, and I know what it is to have plenty. I have learned the secret of being content in any and every situation, whether well fed or hungry, whether living in plenty or in want. I can do all this through him who gives me strength.

Exercise: Prayer

Finances can be a point of stress, both personally and in your family; but it doesn't have to be so. The Apostle Paul shared in this letter how he learned to be content in all situations. Take this time to pray over your resources and finances. Ask that God would direct you in your stewardship of them and that you would live by faith, in peace, regardless of what is happening in the world. Ask Him to show you where to save money, when to be generous, and how to best honor Him with all that He has given you..

DECEMBER 29

An Awareness of His Mercy (P)

JESUS CHRIST, SON OF God, thank you for having mercy upon us! My prayer is that I would truly feel and sense Your mercy flowing towards me, around me, through me, and in me, so I can share it with the world. May mercy be palpable today. Amen and a thousand more amens.

Verse: Psalm 145:8

> The Lord is gracious and compassionate, slow to anger and rich in love.

Exercise: Prayer

After reading the prayer and verse for the day, ask the Father if there are any areas in which you have not experienced or believed His mercy. Do you have a mistake from your past that still brings you shame? Do you feel like you have to earn God's approval, or that He is disappointed in you? Spend 5 to 10 minutes walking through these questions with the Holy Spirit. Ask Him to reveal these areas, and then sit quietly for several minutes as you listen. Pray over these hurts and ask Jesus for His mercy to be real to you today. After this time, be on the lookout to share this mercy with others today, in the middle of their own mistakes and brokenness.

December 30

Sitting Still and Listening (Ex)

My prayer for you today is that you would sit still long enough to hear God speak to you. Be still and know that He is God. Stop, sit, listen, be quiet, wait, rest, and watch. May the Holy Spirit speak clearly to you in this time. Amen and a thousand more amens.

Verse: Psalm 46:10

> He says, "Be still, and know that I am God; I will be exalted among the nations, I will be exalted in the earth."

Exercise: Silence and Journaling

The Father wants to speak with you today. Have a Bible, a pen, and a piece of paper on hand. For 10 to 15 minutes, sit quietly and ask God what He wants to talk about today. This conversation could be about a current situation, an area He wants to change or heal in your life, or just time spent together. Quiet your mind, sit still, listen, and write down what you hear.

December 31

God is for You (Ex)

May God's grace be all over you today. I am praying that you get a deep sense that God is pleased with you and is on your side. God is for you, friends, and you need to know that. Grace to you. Peace to you. Life to you and hope to you, through our Blessed Hope, Jesus. Amen and a thousand more amens.

Verse: John 15:14–15

> You are my friends if you do what I command. I no longer call you servants, because a servant does not know his master's business. Instead, I have called you friends, for everything that I learned from my Father I have made known to you.

Exercise: Meditation and Silence

This passage was spoken to Christ's disciples. When we say "yes" to Christ and commit to follow Him, we are His friends. Read John 15:14–15 out loud. Afterwards, sit in silence for two to three minutes, asking God to speak to you. Do you grasp and believe what it says about you? How should it impact your mindset, and your outlook for the new year? Repeat this process two more times and meditate on this passage.

Bibliography

Psalm 119 Ministries, *The Hebrew root a amen*. https://www.youtube.com/watch?reload=9&v=3fk07gir6Hw, 2017

Lewis, C.S. *The Four Loves*. San Francisco: HarperOne, 2017.

CPSIA information can be obtained
at www.ICGtesting.com
Printed in the USA
FSHW020110241121
86197FS